Lecture Notes in Computer Sci

Commenced Publication in 1973
Founding and Former Series Editors:
Gerhard Goos, Juris Hartmanis, and Jan van Leeuwen

Panos Markopoulos   Boris de Ruyter
Wijnand IJsselsteijn   Duncan Rowland (Eds.)

Fun and Games

Second International Conference
Eindhoven, The Netherlands, October 20-21, 2008
Proceedings

 Springer

Volume Editors

Panos Markopoulos
Wijnand IJsselsteijn
Eindhoven University of Technology
Den Dolech 2, 5600MB, Eindhoven, The Netherlands
E-mail: {p.markopoulos, w.a.ijsselsteijn}@tue.nl

Boris de Ruyter
Philips Research, Media Interaction
Prof. Holstlaan 4, 5656 AE Eindhoven, The Netherlands
E-mail: boris.de.ruyter@philips.com

Duncan Rowland
The University of Nottingham, Mixed Reality Laboratory
Nottingham NG8 1BB, UK
E-mail: dar@cs.nott.ac.uk

Additional material to this book can be downloaded from http://extras.springer.com.

Library of Congress Control Number: Applied for

CR Subject Classification (1998): H.5, H.4, H.3, I.2.1, J.5, K.3, K.4.2

LNCS Sublibrary: SL 2 – Programming and Software Engineering

ISSN   0302-9743
ISBN-10   3-540-88321-5 Springer Berlin Heidelberg New York
ISBN-13   978-3-540-88321-0 Springer Berlin Heidelberg New York

Springer is a part of Springer Science+Business Media

springer.com

© Springer-Verlag Berlin Heidelberg 2008

Typesetting: Camera-ready by author, data conversion by Scientific Publishing Services, Chennai, India
Printed on acid-free paper   SPIN: 12536689   06/3180   5 4 3 2 1 0

Preface

The use of computing technology for entertainment purposes is not a recent phenomenon. Video game consoles, home computers and other entertainment media have been used widely for more than three decades, and people of all ages are spending an increasing amount of time and money on these technologies.

More recent is the rise of a vibrant research community focusing on gaming and entertainment applications. Driven by the growth and the coming of age of the gaming industry, and by its increasing recognition in the media and the minds of the broader public, the study of computer games, game development and experiences is attracting the interest of researchers from very diverse fields: social sciences, computing, electrical engineering, design, etc.

Research of this kind looks to extend the boundaries of gaming technologies. In a relentless drive for innovation, it looks to create and understand an ever increasing range of experiences, and examine how games can provide value for educational, therapeutic and other 'serious' purposes. These themes were reflected in the call for participation and eventually the papers accepted for presentation.

The Fun n' Games conference was the second event of a bi-annual series of conferences. The first event of the series was held in Preston in 2006 organized by the University of Central Lancashire. Following the success of this event it was decided to run a follow up.

The aim of this second event in the series was to bring together researchers creating innovations in games and technologies supporting games, researchers studying the experiences of playing games, and those exploring the emerging theme of serious games.

Fun n' Games was designed as a single-track conference for interaction between participants coming from different disciplines. It included a workshop program, a posters session and a demonstrations program. This volume contains the refereed technical papers presented at the conference and the invited papers by the keynote speakers. An adjunct proceedings volume distributed to the conference attendees includes the papers in the other categories (demos, posters, workshop abstracts).

Technical papers were selected after a rigorous review process. In all, 36 technical papers were submitted, of which 17 were selected for presentation. Each paper was reviewed by three to five reviewers and a meta-review was conducted separately by the Chairs. The selection criteria were designed to invite contributions from both scientific and design disciplines; they included soundness, originality, innovativeness, potential impact. We are confident that this process is reflected in the quality of the selected articles and we hope that the proceedings are a useful point of reference for designers and scientists working in this field.

The first section includes two invited papers contributed by keynote speakers. Roderick Murray-Smith presents his work on tightly coupled embodied control of movement-sensitive mobile devices. Matthias Rauterberg discusses the notions of hypercomputation and cultural computing and relates them to his design work in the project Alice.

The second section includes papers that all share a focus on innovation; emerging gaming paradigms, concepts and platforms to support gaming are described. The third section focuses on affective aspects of gaming: first the measurement of experiences relating to gaming is considered and second the use of psychophysiological measures is considered, either as an input to games or as a tool for evaluation.

The final section includes a collection of papers on seniors and on children, and addresses the notion of serious games; the aim here is to help provide cognitive or physiological training.

Fun n' Games 2008 was organized by the Eindhoven University of Technology, with the participation in the Organizing Committee of researchers from Philips Research, the University of Nottingham, and the University of Central Lancashire. The Program Chairs are grateful for the help of all members of the Organizing Committee and the reviewers for their voluntary work. We would also like to thank the department of Industrial Design, Philips, and Senter Novem, IOP Human-Machine Interaction (IOP-MMI) for sponsoring this event.

July 2007

Panos Markopoulos
Boris de Ruyter
Wijnand Ijsselsteijn
Duncan Rowland

Organization

Organizing Committee

General Chair

Panos Markopoulos   Eindhoven University of Technology

Program Co-chairs

Wijnand IJsselsteijn   Eindhoven University of Technology
Boris De Ruyter   Philips Research
Duncan Rowland   University of Nottingham

Demonstrations Chair

Jettie Hoonhout   Philips Research
Iris Soute   Eindhoven University of Technology

Workshops Chair

Jettie Hoonhout   Philips Research

Posters Chair

Janet C. Read   University of Central Lancashire

Communications Chairs

Iris Soute   Eindhoven University of Technology
Matthew Leslie Horton   University of Central Lancashire

Student Volunteer Chairs

Iris Soute   Eindhoven University of Technology
Janneke Verhaegh   Philips Research

Webmaster

Javed Vassilis Khan   Eindhoven University of Technology

Past Conference Chairs

Janet Read   University of Central Lancashire
Matthew Leslie Horton   University of Central Lancashire

Graphics Design

Atike Dicle Pekel   Eindhoven University of Technology

Organizational Support

Nora van den Berg   Eindhoven University of Technology

Sponsoring Organizations

Department of Industrial Design   Eindhoven University of Technology
Philips
Senter Novem   IOP Human-Machine Interaction (IOP-MMI)

Scientific Review Committee

Tilde Bekker   Eindhoven University of Technology,
                                     The Netherlands
Ed Huai-hsin Chi   Palo Alto Research Center, USA
Adrian Cheok   National University of Singapore, Singapore
Karin Coninkx   Hasselt University, Belgium
Nuno Correia   New University of Lisbon, Portugal
Jonathan Freeman   Goldsmiths, University of London, UK
Franca Garzotto   Politecnico di Milano, Italy
Matthieu Gielen   Delft University of Technology,
                                     The Netherlands
Ole Sejer Iversen   University of Aarhus, Denmark
Fusako Kusunoki   University of Tokyo, Japan
Jean-Baptiste LaBrune   INRIA Futurs / CNRS / Université Paris Sud,
                                     France
Bo Kampmann Walther   University of Southern Denmark, Denmark
Haruhiro Katayose   Kwansei Gakuin University, Japan
Hannu Korhonen   Nokia Research, Finland
Yvonne de Kort   Eindhoven University of Technology,
                                     The Netherlands
Irma Lindt   Fraunhofer, Germany
Daniel Livingstone   University of the West of Scotland, UK
Kris Luyten   Hasselt University, Belgium
Cornelius Malerczyk   ZGDV Computer Graphics Center, Germany
Ali Mazalek   Georgia Tech, USA
Laurence Nigay   Université Joseph Fourier Grenoble 1, France
Kazushi Nishimoto   Japan Advanced Institute of Science and
                                     Technology, Japan
Karolien Poels   Eindhoven University of Technology,
                                     The Netherlands
Narcis Pares   Universidad Pompeu Fabra, Spain

Celia Pearce	Georgia Tech, USA
Lyn Pemberton	University of Brighton, UK
Marianne Graves Petersen	University of Aarhus, Denmark
Judy Robertson	Heriot-Watt University, UK
Michael Rohs	TU Berlin, Germany
Marco Rozendaal	Eindhoven University of Technology, The Netherlands
Johannes Schoening	University of Muenster, Germany
Manfred Tscheligi	University of Salzburg, Austria
Dimitrios Tzovaras	Informatics and Telematics Institute Centre for Research and Technology, Greece
Albrecht Schmidt	University of Duisburg-Essen, Germany
Elise van den Hoven	Eindhoven University of Technology, The Netherlands
Wouter van den Hoogen	Eindhoven University of Technology, The Netherlands
Arnold P.O.S. Vermeeren	Delft University of Technology, The Netherlands
Annika Waern	SICS, Sweden
Daniel Wagner	Graz University of Technology, Austria
Stephen Wensveen	Eindhoven University of Technology, The Netherlands
Georgios N. Yannakakis	IT University of Copenhagen, Denmark
Panayiotis Zaphiris	City University London, UK

Table of Contents

Keynotes

Focus on Innovation

Affect and Gaming

Fun n'Games for Young and Old

Rotational Dynamics for Design of Bidirectional Feedback during Manual Interaction

Roderick Murray-Smith[1,2] and Steven Strachan[2]

[1] Department of Computing Science
University of Glasgow
Glasgow, Scotland
rod@dcs.gla.ac.uk
[2] Hamilton Institute
National University of Ireland, Maynooth
Maynooth, Ireland
steven.strachan@nuim.ie

Abstract. Rotational dynamic system models can be used to enrich tightly-coupled embodied control of movement-sensitive mobile devices, and support a more bidirectional, negotiated style of interaction. This can provide a constructive, as well as informative, approach to the design of engaging, playful elements in interaction mechanisms. A simulated rotational spring system is used for natural eyes-free feedback in both the audio and haptic channels, and in a Mobile Spatial Interaction application, using twisting and tilting motions to drag and drop content, where users perceived the effect of varying the parameters of the simulated dynamic system.

1 Introduction

Inertial sensing is now widely available in millions of mobile phones, music players and in computer games such as the Nintendo *Wii*. Samsung's SCH-S310 gesture recognition phone, released in 2005, was the first which could recognise simple motion gestures, and SonyEricsson's W580i, W910i mobile phones allow you to shake to shuffle your music, or change tracks. Designing and refining interaction with such techniques is a relatively new area, and the techniques used so far have leant heavily on classical interaction design, such that most gesture recognition systems classify certain conditions or motions as virtual buttons, and provide feedback based on discrete, abstract movements. Such classical approaches to gesture recognition can be difficult to learn, and break down when subject to disturbances which are common in mobile environments. This paper presents a contrasting, physical modelling approach which enables the provision of continuous interaction and rich feedback during gesture-like interaction, which has advantages when learning a new interaction, or using the system in adverse conditions. Physical modelling is increasingly used in game design[1] for the virtual environment the player interacts with, providing increased levels of realism, and reducing development time, as the designer does not need to pre-specify every possible interaction. This also means that users can sometimes complete tasks in ways designers had not anticipated.

---

[1] e.g. the *Havok* physics engine www.havok.com.

P. Markopoulos et al. (Eds.): Fun and Games 2008, LNCS 5294, pp. 1–10, 2008.

The interaction metaphor proposed in this paper uses the simulation of a rotational dynamic system driven by inertial sensor data, to facilitate and enrich interaction with a mobile device. Such tilt-based interaction is well-established (Rekimoto 1996, Hinckley 2002, Hinckley et al. 2000), but typically depended primarily on visual feedback, which in tilting interactions causes difficulty due to poor screen visibility. Our intention in using a tangible physical metaphor for interaction is that users instantly possess a natural intuition for the effects that their movements have on the system. Our earlier work looked at dynamic models linking the zoom level to speed of motion in tilt-based interaction (Eslambolchilar and Murray-Smith 2004). Feedback is provided via audio and haptic rendering of the internal states of the simulated system. Which aspects of the state vector you choose to feedback, be it torque, velocity, friction or a combination, depends on the metaphor presented to the user. Allowing users to perceive the changing physical characteristics of the modelled system in this way can thus be used to convey richer information about the current state of their device. Another significant advantage of this approach is that the user experience may be easily tuned in realtime by simply adjusting the parameters of the modeled system as a function of variables of interest to the user, allowing the interaction to provide a bi-directional coupling of the user and computer. Sheridan (2002) provides a concise discussion of ways in which humans couple with their environments.

This approach can be applied to any tilt-based system as a way to enrich the interaction experience but as an example we introduce the simulation of a rotational spring system for twisting-based interaction with a mobile device and we show how basic aspects of this kind of system can be associated with information, and can be manipulated by a user in an intuitive fashion. This allows its use in a range of settings from games input to mobile spatial interaction. The same models can be used for pitch tilting, lateral roll actions, and for yawing actions (where the yaw sensing usually requires a magnetometer and/or gyroscope sensors, as well as accelerometers).

2   Background

Eyes-free interfaces rely heavily on the provision of effective audio and vibrotactile sensations. Yao and Hayward (2006) investigated the simulation of physical systems with audio and vibrotactile feedback, recreating the sensation of a ball rolling down a hollow tube via the haptic and audio modalities. Using apparatus that simulated the physics and provided audio and haptic cues, they found that when subjects were asked to estimate the position of the ball rolling inside a tubular cavity, they used their natural intuition of objects falling under the influence of gravity to accurately estimate the position. Similarly, Rath and Rocchesso (2005) created a convincing sonification of the physical motion of a ball along a beam, finding that subjects were able to perceive the ball motion from the sonification alone.

Shoogle (Williamson et al. 2007) enables the sensing of the state of a mobile device via the simulation of a physical system which responds to gestural input. By modelling the relatively simple dynamics of some balls inside a box and the quite intuitive effects of a users shaking of this box, information can be conveyed to the user such as the battery life of the device or number of new text messages, via auditory impact sounds and haptic rendering, where each new text message is represented by one simulated ball sensed only by the shaking of the device. (Hummels et al. 2007) used stroking interactions with tactile objects, with capacitive and force sensing. Early work on tap-based interaction in mobile phones includes (Linjama and Kaaresoja 2004).

3 Rotational Spring Systems

There is a wide range of physical systems that could be used as metaphors for interaction and rotational spring systems are just one example. This kind of system has a number of features that make it appropriate for interaction design. Sensing the orientation state of the device via accelerometers allows us to use movement of the device to control interaction. Twisting the device, sensed via changes in roll angle, or tilting, sensed via changes in the pitch angle can be easily sensed and used to provide eyes-free feedback about the state of the device to the user. Some rotational metaphors that we can simulate using the dynamics of this kind of system include winding a clock, opening a door knob, turning a key or opening a box, all completely natural everyday metaphors for which people have a natural intuition and which can enhance and enrich the process of interaction.

There are a number of basic conventions that we must consider when describing this kind of system. Figure 1 defines some of the basic notation. θ is defined as the angular displacement of the rotating disk with respect to some reference and is expressed in radians, ω is defined as the angular velocity of the disk in radians per second, α is defined as the angular acceleration in radians per second^2 and τ is the torque, the rotational analogue of Force, in Newton-meters where $\tau = J\alpha$.

The four important characteristics of this kind of system from an interaction design perspective are *torque*, *friction*, *stiffness* and *mass*, which can be used to feedback device states to the user. *Torque* is important because it provides us with a measure for the amount of force present in the system. If this is fed back to the user in some way, via the audio or haptic channels, it can provide the user with a real sense of how the system is reacting to certain events or movements. *Friction* can significantly affect the

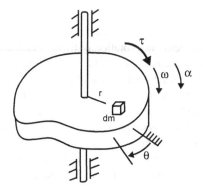

Fig. 1. Conventions for designating rotational variables. From (Close and Frederick 1995).

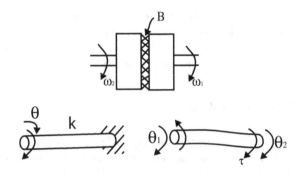

Fig. 2. a) Rotational stiffness element with one end fixed. b) Rotational stiffness element with $\Delta\theta = \theta_2 - \theta_1$. From (Close and Frederick 1995).

feel of a rotational system. A rotational friction element is one for which there is an algebraic relationship between the torque and the relative angular velocity between two surfaces. Figure 2a) shows rotational devices characterised by viscous friction, where the torque is defined as $\tau = B\omega$ (Close and Frederick 1995). So if we alter the friction between two surfaces the torque is altered and the state of the system can be fed back to and perceived by the user. *Rotational stiffness* is usually associated with a torsional spring, like that of a clock. An algebraic relationship between the torque τ and the angular displacement θ exists as illustrated in Figure 2b). For a linear torsional spring or flexible shaft $\tau = K\Delta\theta$ where K is the spring constant. Altering the value of K can then have an effect on the overall feel of the system. Higher K values result in a more stiff system.

There are other kinds of mechanical system that could prove useful for this kind interaction design. Translational mechanics is one such example. When an object is moved on a surface it is possible to take a lot of information about the object and the surface from the sensation of the interaction between the two and varying degrees of friction between the object and surface are easily perceived via audio or haptic feedback.

3.1   Two-Disk System

It is possible then for us to view the mobile device as being a minimal inertia element, coupled with a rotational system via a rotational stiffness element as illustrated in figure 3. Angle changes in the orientation of the phone, sensed from accelerometers, act as reference values which drive the rotational system of interest, with the states of that system fed back to the user via vibration or audio. The systems we have chosen to simulate, the 'Two-Disk' system and the 'Disk and Mass' system are illustrated in Figures 3 and 5 respectively. We represent these systems using a state-space model similar to that described in (Eslambolchilar and Murray-Smith 2006). For the two-disk system we treat the angular displacement θ_2 on disk 2 as an input to the system in order to observe the effects on θ_1 and ω_1 on disk 1. This system can be represented as follows:

$$\dot{x} = Ax + Bu \tag{1}$$

$$\begin{bmatrix} \dot{\theta}_1 \\ \dot{\omega}_1 \end{bmatrix} = \begin{bmatrix} 0 & 1 \\ -\frac{(k_2+k_1)}{J_1} & -\frac{B_1}{J_1} \end{bmatrix} \begin{bmatrix} \theta_1 \\ \omega_1 \end{bmatrix} + \begin{bmatrix} 0 \\ \frac{k_2}{J_1} \end{bmatrix} \theta_2 \qquad (2)$$

where k_1 and k_2 are the stiffness constants in shaft 1 and shaft 2 respectively, B is the friction element for disk 1 and J_1 is the moment of inertia for disk 1. If we imagine our mobile device to be represented by disk 2 and we exert some kind of roll-axis rotation on the device, this will induce a reaction in disk 1, the exact nature of which depends on the values chosen for k_1, k_2 and B. Figure 4a) shows a typical response in the displacement angle θ for disk 1 from the two-disk system for varying values of b_1, the friction between disk 1 and the surface, after disk 2 has been twisted through $90°$. As the friction parameter is increased, the simulated response of disk 1 to the input from disk 2 becomes increasingly damped. This more damped response, when fed back via the haptic and audio channels, can be clearly perceived by the user of the mobile device. Similar responses are observed for the varying of the k_1 and k_2 parameters of this model.

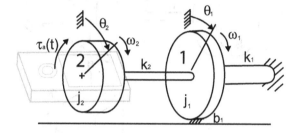

Fig. 3. Rotational system to illustrate the laws for reaction torques and angular displacements. Adapted from (Close and Frederick 1995).

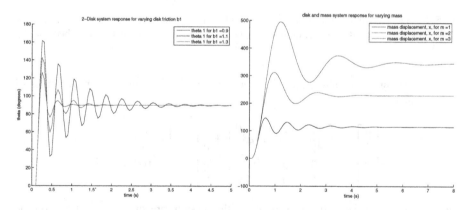

Fig. 4. a) System Response for a varying disk 1 friction (b_1) in the Two-Disk system. As the friction is increased the simulated response of disk 1 decreases and this is perceived by the user. b) System Response for a varying mass parameter. As a mass attached to the spring is increased the simulated response becomes more extreme.

3.2   Disk and Mass System

Figure 5 shows the same system but with a mass attached to the second disk via a spring, giving a sense of 'fishing' for content. There are a number of extra parameters for this system that can affect the way the system behaves. If the mobile device is rotated an effect is observed on disk 1 and hence on the movement of the mass, which also affects the torque experienced. Likewise, if we exert any force on the mass or change the value of the mass, this will also have an effect on the torque experienced in disk 1. The exact effect observed depends on the states x, v and θ_1, θ_2, measured from references corresponding to the position where the shafts k_1 and k_2 are not twisted and the spring k_3 is not stretched.

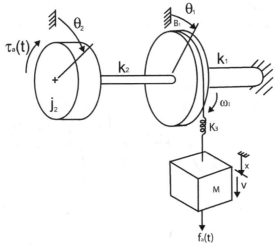

Fig. 5. System with translational and rotational elements. Adapted from (Close and Frederick 1995). This can be used to model drag-and-drop tasks, where the mass can be attached and detached.

Again, using a state-space approach we can represent the interaction dynamics of this system as follows:

$$
\begin{bmatrix} \dot{\theta} \\ \dot{\omega} \\ \dot{x} \\ \dot{v} \end{bmatrix} = \begin{bmatrix} 0 & 1 & 0 & 0 \\ \frac{AR^2}{J_1} & -\frac{B_1}{J_1} & \frac{k_3 R}{J_1} & 0 \\ 0 & 0 & 0 & 1 \\ \frac{k_3 R}{M} & 0 & -\frac{k_3}{M} & 0 \end{bmatrix} \begin{bmatrix} \theta \\ \omega \\ x \\ v \end{bmatrix} + \begin{bmatrix} 0 & 0 \\ 0 & \frac{k_2}{J_1} \\ 0 & 0 \\ 1 & 0 \end{bmatrix} \begin{bmatrix} mg \\ \theta_2 \end{bmatrix}
$$

where $A = -k_1 + k_2 + k_3$. The inputs to this system are the external force on the mass $f_a(t) = mg$ and the displacement angle of disk 2, θ_2. Varying the parameters of this model can significantly alter the feel of the interaction. For example, it is possible to convey the carrying of a varying mass by simply changing the mass parameter of the model, which then creates a different response. Figure 4b) shows how the system response changes as three different masses are added to the system. These varying responses, if converted to audio or vibrotactile feedback, are then perceived by the user. Similar responses are observed if we vary parameters k_1, k_2 and k_3.

4   Mobile Spatial Interaction

As an example use-case, we consider Mobile Spatial Interaction (MSI) – a form of interaction that enables users to interact in an eyes-free manner with a combined physical/virtual environment using their mobile device to scan the space around them using a virtual probe to discover information as illustrated in figure 6. For background on bearing-based MSI, see (Strachan and Murray-Smith 2008, Frohlich et al. 2008). An example of a mobile game is (Ballagas et al. 2007). The direction in which the user is pointing is taken from the magnetic compass heading, with accelerometers used to infer the orientation (pitch and roll) of the device. This orientation is used to control how far into the distance the user is pointing. To look ahead, the device is tilted forward, to bring the probe back to the current position the device is tilted back. The user obtains information about the space around them by listening and feeling for impact events, when their probe effectively collides with targets or information in the augmented content in the virtual environment. It is also possible for users to manipulate and arrange objects in the virtual environment, picking up and moving them around using the device.

The disk and mass dynamics described enhance this interaction by providing the user with a sense of the varying kinds of information that they are interacting with. By twisting the device to pick up an object, users can immediately perceive the increasing spring tension as an object of information becomes an attached mass. Users can constantly monitor the state of their system just by twisting the device and perceiving the response of the dynamics. Is the system currently 'stiff', indicating the presence of a lot of local information or 'loose', indicating an absence of local information? Is there a heavy mass, light mass or no mass attached to the system? Feedback is provided via audio and haptic cues. Simply providing discrete pulses and sounds to indicate different states lacks the intuitiveness, subtlety and richness of an oscillating dynamic system

Fig. 6. A user interacting with information in their combined virtual/physical environment

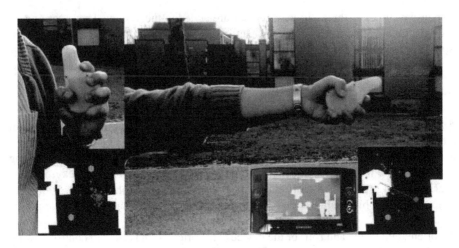

Fig. 7. A Samsung Q1 UMPC with a Bluetooth connection the WayStane inertial sensing device held in a users hand. Varying the orientation of the device alters the distance.

and can provide little information about the form or content of the object with which the user is interacting.

The current MSI system runs on a Samsung Q1 Ultra Mobile PC with a Bluetooth connection to the WayStane (Murray-Smith et al. 2008) inertial sensing device as shown in figure 7. This device, an adaptation of the SHAKE inertial sensing device (Williamson et al. 2007), contains the magnetometers, accelerometers and vibration devices required to produce this kind of interaction.

An initial user study was conducted where 5 participants were asked to comment on their perception of the system for varying parameters. First users were given a description of the Two-Disk system, with an illustrative figure (figure 3) and allowed to test it. The friction parameter b_1 was varied for five different values and users were asked to mark on a scale of 1-20 how they perceived the stiffness of the system as they applied 90° twists to the device.

Participants were then given a description of the second system using figure 5 and allowed to test it. The value of the mass parameter was then varied (for five different values) as the mass was attached and released from the system in order to generate a reaction and the participants were again asked to comment on the perceived change in the system.

In the first part participants had little problem distinguishing a 'stiff' system from a 'loose' system. All participants were able to distinguish the five levels, with the only confusion coming from the more stiff settings. Subjective comments from participants indicated that it was easy to differentiate a stiff system from a loosely coupled system. In the second part, the participants were able to differentiate a very high mass from a low mass but values in between appeared to be more uncertain. The two participants who performed best in this part had the greatest knowledge of dynamic systems. The others had more trouble in interpreting the slightly more complicated system, and their subjective comments reflected this. Other comments included the fact that the 'kick back' from the system when the mass was released was slightly easier to perceive than the attaching of the mass itself. We expect that a refinement of the audio and tactile cues which are linked to the dynamic model states will improve some of the trouble participants had in intuitively understanding the more complex model.

5 Outlook

This paper has sketched the potential use of rotational dynamic systems for the provision of rich feedback to the user of a mobile device or remote control. By taking advantage of user's natural familiarity with the dynamics of a rotational spring mechanical system, as would be found in a door-handle, we have shown that it is possible to produce an eyes-free multimodal display using a solid theoretical foundation as the basis for the interaction. Coupling such rich continuous-feedback models with real-time inference about the content and relevance of information sources on the mobile device allows designers to make the user aware of subtle variations in the nature of the content they are engaging with and manipulating. It is an important building block for enabling *negotiated interaction*, where there is a bi-directional flow of information during interaction with interface objects.

This introductory paper only considers linear friction and spring models, but it is straightforward to expand the idea to richer models. The most interesting immediate area is that of non-linear friction models. Friction characteristics allow us to make the angular velocity 'visible' in the torque the user can sense, and also with appropriate torque/relative velocity characteristic curves we can create dead-zones in which an applied torque has no effect. We can create patterns of varying friction coefficients at different angles, to achieve specific desired effects. It is also possible to include other mechanical features such as gears or levers in the interaction design metaphors. For example, if gearing ratios were made audible the user might be able to perceive motion through different menu sizes, for example. In general, there is broad scope for multimodal displays which could, e.g. display the velocity data in audio, and the torque in vibration, and which could have richly nuanced variations in audio and tactile patterns as a function of the friction characteristics.

The applicability of the rotational spring metaphor to a Mobile Spatial Interaction application was demonstrated but the potential exists for a wider range of applications, such as personal music players, where the content drives the dynamics of the rotational systems as the user navigates the tracks, desktop-based drag and drop applications and eyes-free interaction. Our initial exploration suggests that users can perceive the variation in this mechanism, but that tuning the cues and feedback are important to maintain the illusion of the chosen metaphor. We suggest that research which couples rich content inference mechanisms with realistic dynamic models, and high quality, low-latency haptic feedback devices will lead to systems which are engaging, fun and easier to use.

Acknowledgements. We are grateful for support from: SFI grants 00/RFP06/CMS052, 00/PI.1/C067, EPSRC project EP/E042740/1, European Commission OpenInterface Project. Nokia provided a donation of funds and equipment.

References

Ballagas, R.A., Kratz, S.G., Borchers, J., Yu, E., Walz, S.P., Fuhr, C.O., Hovestadt, L., Tann, M.: Rexplorer: a mobile, pervasive spell-casting game for tourists. In: CHI 2007: CHI 2007 extended abstracts on Human factors in computing systems, pp. 1929–1934. ACM, New York (2007)

Close, C., Frederick, D.: Modeling and Analysis of Dynamic Systems, 2nd edn. John Wiley and Sons, Chichester (1995)

Eslambolchilar, P., Murray-Smith, R.: Tilt-based automatic zooming and scaling in mobile devices – a state-space implementation. In: Brewster, S., Dunlop, M. (eds.) Mobile HCI 2004. LNCS, vol. 3160, pp. 120–131. Springer, Heidelberg (2004)

Eslambolchilar, P., Murray-Smith, R.: Model-based, multimodal interaction in document browsing. In: Renals, S., Bengio, S., Fiscus, J.G. (eds.) MLMI 2006. LNCS, vol. 4299, pp. 1–12. Springer, Heidelberg (2006)

Fröhlich, P., Baillie, L., Simon, R.: Realizing the vision of mobile spatial interaction. Interactions 15(1), 15–18 (2008)

Hinckley, K.: Input technologies and techniques. In: Handbook of Human-Computer Interaction, pp. 151–168. Lawerence Erlbaum Associates, Mahwah (2002)

Hinckley, K., Pierce, J., Sinclair, M., Horvitz, E.: Sensing techniques for mobile interaction. In: Proceedings User Interface Software and Technology (UIST 2000), pp. 91–100. ACM, New York (2000)

Hummels, C., Overbeeke, K.C., Klooster, S.: Move to get moved: a search for methods, tools and knowledge to design for expressive and rich movement-based interaction. Personal Ubiquitous Comput. 11(8), 677–690 (2007)

Linjama, J., Kaaresoja, T.: Novel, minimalist haptic gesture interaction for mobile devices. In: NordiCHI 2004: Proceedings of the third Nordic conference on Human-computer interaction, pp. 457–458. ACM Press, New York (2004)

Murray-Smith, R., Williamson, J., Quaade, T., Hughes, S.: Stane: synthesized surfaces for tactile input. In: CHI 2008: Proceeding of the twenty-sixth annual SIGCHI conference on Human factors in computing systems, pp. 1299–1302. ACM, New York (2008)

Rath, M., Rocchesso, D.: Continuous sonic feedback from a rolling ball. IEEE MultiMedia 12(2), 60–69 (2005)

Rekimoto, J.: Tilting operations for small screen interfaces. In: ACM Symposium on User Interface Software and Technology, pp. 167–168 (1996)

Sheridan, T.B.: Some musings on four ways humans couple: implications for systems design. IEEE Transactions on Systems, Man and Cybernetics, Part A 32(1), 5–10 (2002)

Strachan, S., Murray-Smith, R.: Bearing-based selection in mobile spatial interaction. Personal and Ubiquitous Computing (2008)

Williamson, J., Murray-Smith, R., Hughes, S.: Shoogle: excitatory multimodal interaction on mobile devices. In: CHI 2007: Proceedings of the SIGCHI conference on Human factors in computing systems, pp. 121–124. ACM, New York (2007)

Yao, H.-Y., Hayward, V.: An experiment on length perception with a virtual rolling stone. In: Eurohaptics 2006 (2006)

Hypercomputation, Unconsciousness and Entertainment Technology

Matthias Rauterberg

Industrial Design, Eindhoven University of Technology, The Netherlands

Abstract. Recent developments in computer science introduce and discuss new concepts for computation beyond universal Turing machines. Quantum computing relates to new insights in quantum physics as interference and entanglement based on nonlocality. Several ideas about a new kind of field are presented and discussed. Human unconscious can be interpreted as tapping in these fields for resonating and spreading information. Assuming that culture is based on collective unconscious I propose designing entertainment technology for a new kind of user experience that can influence the individual unconscious and therefore the collective unconscious as well. Our ALICE project can be seen as a first attempt in this direction.

Keywords: hypercomputation, quantum field, mind, unconscious, culture, entertainment.

1 Introduction

This paper discusses an interesting topic: how to use entertainment technology to enhance human life. Several years ago I met Naoko Tosa and got introduced in some of her work, in particular the ZENetic Computer (Tosa et al, 2005; Tosa & Matsuoka, 2006). Later I was invited by colleagues from Microsoft Research in Cambridge to propose something interesting for possible collaboration. Challenged by this invitation I started to think about a Western equivalent to the Asian ZENetic computer. Luckily the proposed project building an augmented reality system based on the narrative of 'Alice in Wonderland' (Carroll, 1865) got some start-up funding from Microsoft Research. Working hard for more than one year, we –the ALICE team[1]– achieved a first prototype ready for demonstration (Hu et al, 2008). Still this installation is not on the level of automation as originally planned, now we are at least able to give demos operated by several human 'stage operators'. We could already run a first experiment to test some of our research questions. During the whole project phase and till today a lot of colleagues are asking important questions: Why do you do so? What is the main purpose of this project? What can we gain from it? Although I tried to answer some of these questions already (Rauterberg 2006a, 2006b, 2006c, 2007), several issues still remain. In this paper I try to provide some post-rationalized and eclectic answers, although being aware of that some of these answers might be perceived

---

[1] For more information see http://www.alice.id.tue.nl/

P. Markopoulos et al. (Eds.): Fun and Games 2008, LNCS 5294, pp. 11–20, 2008.

as speculative, if not inconclusive or even just wrong. Don't worry, lean back, relax and enjoy reading; the 'quantum world' does not like linear causality anyway!

2 Hypercomputation and the Mind

The approach to mathematics, to formulate all the axioms needed to deduce all the truths in a particular branch of mathematics *mechanistically* by removing all unrecognized assumptions based on intuition, became known as the Hilbert Program. This search for axioms became something of a Holy Grail, although Hilbert, who had great respect for the role played by human intuition in the practice of mathematics, never recommended this program named after him (Devlin, 2002). This mechanistically approach to mathematics was complemented with the ideas of Turing (1937, 1938) in which the so called Turing machine was introduced: "A Turing machine is a finite-state machine associated with an external storage or memory medium" (Minsky, 1967, p. 117). The properties of Turing's 'universal machine' have long sustained functionalist intuitions about the nature of cognition. Eliasmith (2002) showed that there is a logical problem with standard functionalist arguments for multiple realizability. He further argued that functionalism is not a useful approach for understanding what it is to have a mind. In particular, it is shown that the difficulties involved in distinguishing implementation from function make multiple realizability claims untestable and un-informative. As a result, Eliasmith concluded that the role of Turing machines as a concept to conceptualize the *mind* needs to be reconsidered.

A Turing machine provides a mathematical definition of the natural process of calculating. It rests on trust that a procedure of reason can be reproduced mechanically. Turing's analysis of the concept of mechanical procedure in terms of a finite machine convinced Gödel of the validity of the Church thesis (Church, 1936). Gödel's (1951) later concern was if mental procedures cannot go beyond mechanical procedures as Turing recommended, it would imply the same kind of limitation on human mind. Therefore he decided to treat Turing's argument as inconclusive. The question then is: to which extent a computing machine operating by finite means could provide an adequate model of human intelligence. Lupacchini (2007) argued that a rigorous answer to this question can be given by developing Turing's considerations on the nature of mental processes. For Turing such processes are the consequence of physical processes and he seems to be led to the conclusion that quantum mechanics could help to find a more comprehensive explanation of them. The new view that Turing machines are not the most powerful computing mechanisms was already accepted by Turing himself, who showed in 1939 that his Turing machines with 'oracles' were more powerful than his Turing machines without oracles. This idea of an oracle leads us via *non-determinism* directly to the uncertainty principle in quantum mechanics of Heisenberg (1930). To go beyond the universal Turing machine, hypercomputation is introduced and discussed (Hanson, 2000; Mulhauser, 1998, 2001; Ord, 2006) and is also known as super-Turing, non-standard or non-recursive computation.

Nowadays hypercomputation is the computation of numbers or functions that cannot be computed in the sense of Turing i.e. cannot be computed with paper and pencil in a finite number of steps by a 'human mind' working effectively (Copeland, 2004). Hypercomputers are supposed to solve problems that lie beyond the scope of the standard universal Turing machine by having access to calculation processes with infinite time and to a 'supranatural' memory with infinite information (e.g., Bennett & DiVincenzo, 2000). Bringsjord and Arkoudas (2004, p167) asked, "one of the things that we don't know is whether the human mind hypercomputes, or merely computes – this despite informal arguments from Gödel, Lucas, Penrose and others – for the view that, in light of the incompleteness theorem, the human mind has powers exceeding those of Turing Machines and their equivalents". So far we know enough to assume that our mind is at least a hypercomputer.

3 Quantum Physics and Intuition

Turing used the concept 'machine' for describing mechanical processes and did not emphasize any distinction between a human 'worker-to-rule' and a physical system. If Turing was thinking about mental operations, it is unclear what he thought the brain was doing when it saw the truth in a manner that could not be modeled computably. Turing explained the principle that his universal machine could simulate any machine, if the behavior of these machines is in principle predictable by calculation, in contrast to the indeterminacy principle in quantum mechanics where such kind of predictions is even theoretically impossible. At the end of his life he came up with his 'Turing Paradox': that the standard principles of quantum mechanics imply that in the limit of continuous observation a quantum system cannot evolve. Turing's 'paradox (also know as the 'watched pot problem') in quantum measurement theory, is now called the *quantum Zeno effect* (Itano, Heinzen, Bollinger & Wineland, 1990). This effect is relevant to the new technology of quantum 'interaction free measurement' (Hodges, 2008). The quantum Zeno effect states that if we find a system in a particular quantum state, and repeatedly check whether it is still in that state, it will remain in that state. The watched quantum pot never boils (Vaidman, 2008). This looks as if human actions - although indirectly- can have an influence on quantum states (Nelson et al, 2002). Recent experimental evidence in physics suggests quantum non-locality occurring in [sub]conscious and unconscious brain function, and functional quantum processes in molecular biology are becoming more and more apparent. Moreover macroscopic quantum processes are being proposed as intrinsic features in cosmology, evolution and social interactions (Nelson, 2002a, 2002b, 2002c).

Quantum and vacuum physics shows that there is an *interconnecting layer* in nature, beyond the connectivity we are familiar with. Einstein claimed that no connection between particles can be achieved beyond light speed (the 'local' hypothesis); on the other side it seems to be possible to synchronize quantum states immediately (the 'non-local' hypothesis; see Aspect et al, 1982a, 1982b; Aspect, 2007). Bohm (1951) laid most of the theoretical foundations for the Einstein, Podolsky and Rosen (1935) experiments performed by Aspect et al (1982a, 1982b). These experiments demonstrated that if two quantum systems interact and then move apart, their behavior is correlated in a way that cannot be explained in terms of signals traveling between them at or slower than the light speed. This phenomenon is known as *non-locality*, and is open to two main interpretations: (1) it involves unmediated, instantaneous action at a distance, or (2) it involves faster-than-light signaling. For if nonlocal connections are propagated not at infinite speeds but at speeds greater than that of light through a 'quantum ether' (a sub-quantum domain where current quantum theory and relativity theory break down) then the correlations predicted by quantum theory would disappear if measurements were made in periods shorter than those required for the transmission of quantum connections between particles. The alternative position is that information always takes time to travel from its source to another location, that information is stored at some para-physical level, and that we can access this information, or exchange information with other minds, if the necessary conditions of 'sympathetic resonance' exist (see also the 'morphic resonance' concept of Sheldrake, 1981).

As for *precognition* one possible explanation is that it involves direct, 'nonlocal' access to the actual future. Alternatively, it may involve a new kind of perception (beyond the range of ordinary perception) of a probable future scenario that is beginning to take shape on the basis of current tendencies and intentions, in accordance with the traditional idea that coming events cast their shadows before them; such foreshadowing takes place deep in the implicate order which some mystical traditions would call the astral or Akashic realms (Laszlo, 2004). We can assume that there eventually exists an interconnecting cosmic field at the foundation of reality that conserves and conveys information. This cosmic field looks like a possible candidate for our required 'supranatural' memory. Recent discoveries in the field of vacuum physics show that this Akashic field is real and has its equivalent in the zero-point field that underlies space itself. This field consists of a subtle 'sea of fluctuating energies' from which all things arise: atoms and galaxies, stars and planets, living beings, and even [un]consciousness. This zero-point Akashic-field is not only the original source of all things that arise in time and space; it is also the constant and enduring memory of the universe. It holds the record of all that ever happened in life, on Earth, and in the cosmos and relates it to all that is yet to happen.

There are several phenomena like psycho kinesis, telepathy, out-of-body experiences, unidentified flying objects, near death experience, time travel, etc. that are waiting for some explanations (Talbot, 1991). Despite its apparent materiality, the universe looks like a kind of 4-D projection and is ultimately no more real than a hologram, a 4-D image projected in space and time. Using this holographic model Talbot (1991) has developed a new description of reality. It encompasses not only reality as we know it, including hitherto unexplained phenomena of physics, but is capable of explaining such occurrences as telepathy, paranormal and out-of-the-body experiences, 'lucid' dreaming and even mystical and religious traditions such as cosmic unity and miraculous healings.

Mitchell (1996) believes that all psychic phenomena involve nonlocal resonance between the brain and the quantum vacuum, and consequent access to holographic, nonlocal information. In his view, this hypothesis could explain not only psycho kinesis and extra sensorial perception, but also out-of-body and near-death experiences, visions and apparitions, and evidence usually cited in favor of a reincarnating soul. One has to admit that these theories are often seen as speculative and not yet part of main stream science.

4 What Is [Un]Consciousness?

When I think of being conscious, I think of being awake and aware of my surroundings. Being conscious also means being aware of myself as individual. Mostly, people tend to think of being conscious as being alive. If something is breathing and able to move, I think of it as being conscious. If a human being is breathing and able to move, but not able to talk to me, or give me some indication that s/he is aware of my presence, I might not be so sure whether the person is conscious. I tend to think that the person should be responsive to the surrounding environment to be conscious. Being in a coma is considered to be the opposite of conscious, so called *non-conscious*. There are at least three forms of consciousness for humans: (1) the conscious state; (2) the subconscious state; and (3) the unconscious state. In my understanding of 'unconsciousness' I do not really focus on patients which are anesthetized to the best of current ability, with no clinical, EEG, motor or post-operative indications of awareness, or any other similar situations (e.g. coma). The unconscious state I have in mind is full operational and functional for a normal human living as a parallel background process of our mind and body, we are just not aware of (e.g. activities of the cerebellum). The subconscious can be turned into conscious (i.e. by paying attention to subconscious activities); the unconscious normally is not available to the conscious (i.e. the first problem with the unconscious is that it is *unconscious*). That is, by definition the unconscious represents all that is unknown about us. So how can we talk about something unknown? One solution to the problem is to deny its existence or to not talk about it. To a perfectly logical and rational mind, therefore, the unconscious is just a lot of nonsense! But not for me; let me try to explain why not.

An *iceberg* can serve as a useful metaphor to understand the unconscious mind (Dijksterhuis, 2007). As an iceberg floats in the water, the huge mass of it remains below the surface. Only a small percentage of the whole iceberg is visible above the surface. In this way, the iceberg is like the mind. The conscious mind is what we notice above the surface while the sub- and unconscious mind, the largest and most powerful part, remains unseen below the surface. The unconscious mind holds all awareness that is not presently in the conscious mind. All activities, memories, feelings and thoughts that are out of conscious awareness are by definition sub- or even unconscious.

In addition to Freud's individual unconscious (Freud, 1933), Jung has introduced the *collective unconscious* (Jung, 1934). This is the area of mind where all humanity shares experience and from where we draw on the archetypal energies and symbols that are common to us all (e.g. past life, near death, etc. memories are drawn from this level of the collective unconscious). Another, even deeper level can be described as the *universal unconscious* where experiences beyond just humanity's can also be accessed with regression process. Jung (1952) coined the term *synchronicity*, a temporal relationship between causally not related events but experienced as a meaningful coincidence. For Peat (1987) is synchronicity a possible bridge between mind and matter, a way to transform ourselves into getting access to unlimited information. The unconscious connection 'under the iceberg' between people is definitively more powerful than the connection on the conscious level (Dijksterhuis et al., 2006). Although the conscious mind, steeped in cognition and thought, is able to deceive the unconscious mind, based in feeling and intuition, will often give us information from under the iceberg that contradicts what is being communicated consciously (Nakatsu, Rauterberg & Salem, 2006).

Libet (1994; 1999) proposed that the emergent conscious experience be represented in a field, the *conscious mental field*. The *conscious mental field* would unify the experience generated by the many neural units. It would also be able to affect certain neural activities and form a basis for conscious will. The *conscious mental field* would be a new 'supranatural' field. It would be a nonphysical field, in the sense that it could not be directly observed or measured by any external physical means. The *conscious mental field* theory is outrageously radical, in that it proposes a mode of intracerebral communication which can proceed without requiring neural pathways. The *conscious mental field* theory provides a 'mechanism' that fits the known properties of conscious experience, including that of conscious free will. It is not dualism, in the Cartesian sense; the *conscious mental field* does not exist without the living brain, and is an emergent property of that brain.

5 Discussion and Conclusions

Looking back, I started discussing the recent outcome to the question 'do humans hypercompute'. This resulted in the concept of hypercomputation beyond universal Turing machines. Hypercomputing seems to be timeless and accessing an infinite memory. A new type of field theory (i.e. Akashic, conscious mental, cosmic, hologram, planetary, quantum, morphic, noosphere, etc.) can provide this supranatural memory. But what has this all to do with entertainment? Nakatsu, Rauterberg and Salem (2006) introduced the concept of Kansei mediation as enabling entertainment technology for cultural transformations (Andrews, 1996). Here is my proposal: let us assume that the human is hypercomputing and this is done unconscious (Dijksterhuis & Nordgren, 2006; Dijksterhuis et al, 2006). The unconscious has access to a supranatural field and can communicate via resonance in a holistic manner. Let us further assume that the individual unconscious is part of the collective unconscious which is embedded in and forms culture.

Now I have to introduce my understanding of 'culture' (see also Rauterberg, 2007; Kooijmans & Rauterberg, 2007). Westerners and East Asians perceive the world and act in it in very different ways (Nisbett et al, 2001; Nisbett & Masuda, 2003). Westerners pay primarily attention to some focal object, analyzing its attributes and categorizing it in an effort to find out what determinate its behaviour. Determinates used mainly formal logic. Causal attributions tend to focus exclusively on the object and are therefore often mistaken. On the other side, East Asians pay primarily attention to a broad perceptual and conceptual field, noticing relationships and changes and grouping objects based on familiarities rather than categories. They relate causal attributions to the context instead of objects. Mainly social factors are directing the East Asians' attention. They live in complex social networks with determined role relations. Attention to the context is more important than to objects for effective functioning. Westerners live independently in less constraining social worlds and attend to the object and their goals with respect to it. Physical 'affordances' of the environment can also influence perception but is assumed less important. The built environments of the East are more complex and contain more objects than do those of the West. In addition, artistic products of the East emphasize the field and deemphasize objects. In contrast, Western art renders less of the field and emphasizes individual objects and people (Nisbett & Masuda, 2003).

Cultural theories can be discussed as falling into four focal areas (Keesing, 1974): (1) cultures as adaptive systems, (2) cultures as ideational systems, (3) cultures as socio-cultural systems, and (4) cultures as symbolic systems that are cumulative creations of mind. Conceiving culture as an ideational subsystem within a vastly complex system, biological, economical, social and symbolic, and grounding our abstract models and theories in the creation and usage of artefacts should make it possible to deepen the understanding of ourselves and our future. Whether the concept of culture has to be refined, radically reinterpreted, or progressively extinguished will probably not matter in the long run, unless we can not find a way to ask the right strategic questions, identifying connections that would otherwise be unseen, and therefore to enable us finding the best answers for our cultural development. Therefore ambient culture focuses nowadays on the development of open systems that understand and support the rituals of our living and adapt themselves to people through time and space (Marzano, 2006). Wegner (1997) can show that interactive systems (with a human in the loop) are more powerful than just rule-based machines.

I started the cultural computing project ALICE as an interactive, entertaining experience (see Nakatsu, Rauterberg & Vorderer, 2005) inspired from 'Alice in Wonderland' (Carroll, 1865). In the scope of this project interactive adventures are experiences provided by an augmented reality environment based on selected parts from Lewis Carroll's book 'Alice's Adventures in Wonderland'. The user assumes the role of Alice and explores this interactive narrative. ALICE is an exploration of interactive storytelling in augmented reality (Hu et al, 2008). By exploiting the unique characteristics of augmented reality compared to established media such as film and interactive media, the project uses augmented reality as a new medium for edutainment and entertainment as a particular carrier for cultural transformations. Innovations include the refashioning of conventions used in film and interactive tools for the development of an augmented reality narrative, and the use of simple artificial virtual and real characters (avatar and robot respectively) to create an immersive interactive experience.

In ALICE real and virtual agents (i.e. rabbit and caterpillar robot, Cheshire cat) act as characters who lead the user through virtual and real locations, moral choices and emotional states. The narrative is a surreal quest, sometimes funny, sometimes disturbing. The character White Rabbit (representing the concept of time) introduces him and joins with the user in a series of absurdist challenges. ALICE is an educational journey towards the user's heart's desire, designed to provoke self-reflection on a number of other issues: bullying and trusting others; selfish- and selfless-ness; enjoying the moment or sublimating pleasure. The user is given the opportunity to occupy and experience any of these mental and emotional positions. ALICE can be used to give interesting examples of many of the basic concepts of adolescent psychology. Alice's experiences can be seen as symbolic depictions of important aspects of adolescent development, such as initiation, identity formation, and physical, cognitive, moral, and social development (Lough, 1983). Alice's adventures are de- and reconstructive in nature and as such are directly challenging the strongly held belief of a linear, single track and sequential reality.

Acknowledgements. I am very grateful to my colleagues who made it possible: Sjriek Alers, Dimar Aliakseyeu, Chet Bangaru, Christoph Bartneck, Razvan Cristescu, Jun Hu, Elco Jacobs, Joran Jessurun, Tijn Kooijmans, Hao Liu, Jeroen Peerbolte,

Ben Salem, Christoph Seyferth, Vanessa Sawirjo, Joran van Aart, Dirk van de Mortel, Geert van den Boomen, Ton van der Graft, Arrens van Herwijnen, Tijn van Lierop, CheeFai Tan. I have also to thank Microsoft Research in Cambridge and my department of Industrial Design for the financial support.

References

Andrews, S.: Promoting a sense of connectedness among individuals by scientifically demonstrating the existence of a planetary consciousness? Alternative Therapies 2(3), 39–45 (1996)

Aspect, A.: Quantum mechanics: to be or not to be local. Nature 446, 866–867 (2007)

Aspect, A., Dalibard, J., Roger, G.: Experimental test of Bell's inequalities using time-varying analyzers. Physical Review Letters 49(25), 1804–1807 (1982a)

Aspect, A., Grangier, P., Roger, G.: Experimental realization of Einstein-Podolsky-Rosen-Bohm Gedankenexperiment: a new violation of Bell's inequalities. Physical Review Letters 49(2), 91–94 (1982b)

Bennett, C.H., DiVincenzo, D.P.: Quantum information and computation. Nature 404, 247–255 (2000)

Bohm, D.: Quantum theory. Prentice-Hall, Englewood Cliffs (1951)

Bringsjord, S., Arkoudas, K.: The modal argument for hypercomputing minds. Journal of Theoretical Computer Science 317(1-3), 167–190 (2004)

Carroll, L.: Alice's adventures in wonderland. Macmillan, London (1865)

Church, A.: An unsolvable problem of elementary number theory. American Journal of Mathematics 58, 345–363 (1936)

Copeland, B.: Hypercomputation: philosophical issues. Theoretical Computer Science 317, 251–267 (2004)

Devlin, K.: Kurt Gödel-separating truth from proof in mathematics. Science 298, 1899–1900 (2002)

Dijksterhuis, A.: Het slimme onbewuste, denken met gevoel. Bert Bakker, Amsterdam (2007)

Dijksterhuis, A., Nordgren, L.: A theory of unconscious thought. Perspectives on Psychology 1(2), 95–109 (2006)

Dijksterhuis, A., Bos, M.W., Nordgren, L.F., van Baaren, R.B.: On making the right choice: the deliberation-without-attention effect. Science 311, 1005–1007 (2006)

Einstein, A., Podolsky, B., Rosen, N.: Can quantum-mechanical description of physical reality be considered complete? Physical Review 47(10), 777–780 (1935)

Eliasmith, C.: The myth of the Turing machine: the failings of functionalism and related theses. Journal of Experimental & Theoretical Artificial Intelligence 14(1), 1–8 (2002)

Freud, S.: New introductory lectures on psychoanalysis, standard edn. vol. 22. Hogarth Press, London (1933)

Gödel, K.: Some basic theorems on the foundations of mathematics and their implications (Gibbs Lecture). In: Feferman, S., et al. (eds.) Collected works III. Unpublished essays and lectures, pp. 304–323. Oxford University Press, Oxford (1951)

Hanson, P.: Physics, logic and the phenomenal. Minds and Machines 10, 391–400 (2000)

Heisenberg, W.: Physikalische Prinzipien der Quantentheorie. Hirzel, Leipzig. English translation: The Physical Principles of Quantum Theory. University of Chicago Press, Chicago (1930)

Hodges, A.: Alan Turing, logical and physical. In: Cooper, S., Löwe, B., Sorbi, A. (eds.) New computational paradigms, pp. 3–15. Springer, Heidelberg (2008)

Hu, J., Bartneck, C., Salem, B., Rauterberg, M.: ALICE's adventures in cultural computing. International Journal of Arts and Technology (2008) (in press)

Itano, W., Heinzen, D., Bollinger, J., Wineland, D.: Quantum Zeno effect. Physical Review A 41(5), 2295–2300 (1990)

Jung, C.: Die Archetypen und das kollektive Unbewußte. Gesammelte Werke, vol. 9/I. Walter, Olten (1934)

Jung, C.: Synchronicity: an acausal connecting principle. Ark, London (1952)

Keesing, R.: Theories of culture. Annual Review of Anthropology 3, 73–97 (1974)

Kooijmans, T., Rauterberg, M.: Cultural computing and the self concept: towards unconscious metamorphosis. In: Ma, L., Rauterberg, M., Nakatsu, R. (eds.) ICEC 2007. LNCS, vol. 4740, pp. 171–181. Springer, Heidelberg (2007)

Laszlo, E.: Science and the Akashic field: an integral theory of everything. Inner Traditions (2004)

Libet, B.: A testable field theory of mind-brain interaction. Journal of Consciousness Studies 1(1), 119–126 (1994)

Libet, B.: Do we have free will? Journal of Consciousness Studies 6(8-9), 47–57 (1999)

Lough, G.C.: Alice in Wonderland and cognitive development: teaching with examples. Journal of Adolescence 6(4), 305–315 (1983)

Lupacchini, R.: Finite machines, mental procedures, and modern physics. Acta Biomedica. 78(1), 39–46 (2007)

Marzano, S.: Ambient culture. In: Aarts, E., Encarnação, J. (eds.) True visions- the emergence of ambient intelligence, pp. 35–52. Springer, Heidelberg (2006)

Minsky, M.: Computation: finite and infinite machines. Prentice-Hall, Inc., N.J (1967)

Mitchell, E.: The way of the explorer: an Apollo astronaut's journey through the material and mystical Worlds. Putnam, New York (1996)

Mulhauser, G.R.: Mind out of matter: Topics in the physical foundations of consciousness and cognition. Kluwer Academic Publishers, Dordrecht (1998)

Mulhauser, G.R.: Reply to Philip P. Hanson's review of 'Mind out of Matter'. Minds and Machines 11, 301–306 (2001)

Nakatsu, R., Rauterberg, M., Salem, B.: Forms and theories of communication: From multimedia to Kansei mediation. Multimedia Systems 11(3), 304–312 (2006)

Nakatsu, R., Rauterberg, M., Vorderer, P.: A new framework for entertainment computing: from passive to active experience. In: Kishino, F., Kitamura, Y., Kato, H., Nagata, N. (eds.) ICEC 2005. LNCS, vol. 3711, pp. 1–12. Springer, Heidelberg (2005)

Nelson, R.: EGGs in a global basket. The Golden Thread (5), 8–12 (2002a)

Nelson, R.: The global consciousness project-part 2. The Golden Thread (8), 6–10 (2002b)

Nelson, R.: The global consciousness project-part 3. The Golden Thread (11), 30–31 (2002c)

Nelson, R., Radin, D., Shoup, R., Bancel, P.: Correlations of continuous random data with major world events. Foundations of Physics Letters 15(6), 537–550 (2002)

Nisbett, R., Masuda, T.: Culture and point of view. Proceedings of the National Academy of Sciences 100(19), 11163–11170 (2003)

Nisbett, R., Peng, K., Choi, I., Norenzayan, A.: Culture and systems of thought: Holistic versus analytic cognition. Psychological Review 108(2), 291–310 (2001)

Ord, T.: The many forms of hypercomputation. Applied Mathematics and Computation 178, 143–153 (2006)

Peat, F.: Synchronicity: the bridge between matter and mind. Bantam, New York (1987)

Rauterberg, M.: From personal to cultural computing: how to assess a cultural experience. In: Kempter, G., von Hellberg, P. (eds.) uDayIV–Information nutzbar machen (pp, pp. 13–21. Pabst Science Publisher, Lengerich (2006a)

Rauterberg, M.: How to assess the user's experience in cultural computing. In: Bosenick, T., Hassenzahl, M., Müller-Prove, M., Peissner, M. (eds.) Usability Professionals 2006, pp. 12–17. Fraunhofer Informationszentrum Raum und Bau (2006b)

Rauterberg, M.: Usability in the future –explicit and implicit effects in cultural computing. In: Heinecke, A.M., Paul, H. (eds.) Mensch & Computer 2006: Mensch und Computer im StrukturWandel, pp. 29–36. Oldenbourg Verlag, München (2006c)

Rauterberg, M.: Ambient culture: a possible future for entertainment computing. In: Lugmayr, A., Golebiowski, P. (eds.) Interactive TV: a shared experience – Adjunct Proceedings of EuroITV-2007. Tampere International Center for Signal Processing, Tampere, Finland. TICSP series #35, pp. 37–39 (2007)

Sheldrake, R.: New science of life: the hypothesis of morphic resonance. Blond & Briggs, London (1981)

Talbot, M.: The holographic universe. HarperCollins, Canada (1991)

Tosa, N., Matsuoka, S., Ellis, B., Ueda, H., Nakatsu, R.: Cultural Computing with Context-Aware Application: ZENetic Computer. In: Kishino, F., Kitamura, Y., Kato, H., Nagata, N. (eds.) ICEC 2005. LNCS, vol. 3711, pp. 13–23. Springer, Heidelberg (2005)

Tosa, N., Matsuoka, S.: ZENetic Computer: Exploring Japanese Culture. Leonardo 39(3), 205–211 (2006)

Turing, A.: On computable numbers, with an application to the Entscheidungsproblem. Proceedings of the London Mathematical Society 2-42, 230–265 (1937)

Turing, A.M.: On computable numbers, with an application to the Entscheidungsproblem. A correction. Proceedings of the London Mathematical Society 2-43, 544–546 (1938)

Turing, A.M.: Systems of logic defined by ordinals. Proceedings of the London. Mathematical. Society 2, 45, 161–228 (1939)

Vaidman, L.: Quantum mechanics: evolution stopped in its tracks. Nature 451, 137–138 (2008)

Wegner, P.: Why interaction is more powerful than algorithms. Communications of the ACM 40(5), 80–91 (1997)

Pervasive Mobile Games – A New Mindset for Players and Developers

Hannu Korhonen[1], Hannamari Saarenpää[2], and Janne Paavilainen[2]

[1] Nokia Research, P.O. Box 1000, 00045 Nokia Group, Finland
hannu.j.korhonen@nokia.com
[2] University of Tampere, Kanslerinrinne 1, 33014 Tampereen Yliopisto, Finland
{hannamari.saarenpaa,janne.paavilainen}@uta.fi

Abstract. Pervasive games are an emerging new game genre, which includes context information as an integral part of the game. These games differ from traditional games in that they expand spatio-temporal and social aspects of gaming. Mobile devices support this by enabling players to choose when and where a game is played. Designing pervasive games can be a challenging task, since it is not only limited to the virtual game world, but designers must consider information flow from the real world into the game world and vice versa. In this paper, we describe a user study with an experimental pervasive multiplayer mobile game. The objective was to understand how the players perceive pervasiveness in the game and what the crucial factors are in the design. Based on the results, we propose initial design guidelines and compare them to other design guidelines for the pervasive games.

Keywords: Mobile Game, Pervasive Game, Game Design, Design Guidelines, Context, Asynchronous gameplay.

1 Introduction

Pervasive games introduce a new emerging game genre that pushes the boundaries of the traditional games and enables new kinds of gaming experiences for players. One of the most exciting aspects in these games is that the context information is utilized to modify a game world or it is converted to game elements. In addition, gaming can be blended into the daily life and normal social situations of the players.

Pervasive gaming is a wide domain, which can consist of the real world games augmented with computing functionality, or virtual computer entertainment is brought back into the real world [12, 13]. Magerkurth et al. introduce several pervasive game genres such as smart toys, affective gaming, augmented tabletop or real world games, and location-aware games [12]. Even though it is not a comprehensive list of pervasive game genres, it gives a good overview to the broadness of the domain.

Our research focuses on pervasive games that are played with mobile devices. The mobile device is a good platform for pervasive games, since it is pervasive by its nature. It is capable of acquiring information about the current context and it can send

P. Markoupoulos et al. (Eds.): Fun and Games 2008, LNCS 5294, pp. 21–32, 2008.

information (e.g. location) to a game system, which then defines the appropriate player context.

Designing pervasive mobile games is a challenging task as many new issues need to be taken into account in a design. As context information is a crucial element in these games, the designers should emphasize this aspect in the design as well. Moreover, the pervasive games are often played in environments inhabited by people who are not playing the game. The game design must ensure that the game does not disturb too much players' social interaction outside the gameworld or disrupt non-players' ongoing activities. Further, since the players may be distracted from their surroundings by focusing on the game at hand, they may become a hazard for themselves or others. Designing a game to avoid these problems is a key factor in acceptance of the pervasive games.

In this paper we describe a user study with an experimental pervasive mobile game. Our objective was to find out how players perceive pervasiveness and what issues are important in a pervasive mobile game design. The contribution of the paper is a list of initial design guidelines for pervasive mobile games.

2 Related Work

Pervasive games have been studied for several years, but there are only few design guidelines available for helping designers in their task. Eriksson et al. present design guidelines for socially adaptable games that are played in different social context than traditional games [5]. The guidelines are as follows: *support interruptability, allow multiple communication channels, consider ambiguity, design for external events, allow modes of play based on social roles, minimize social weight,* and *analyze intended player groups from several perspectives.* They highlight essential aspects in design and are focusing on how the game can be adapted to social environment in which the game takes place, but they are missing the role of context information.

Crossmedia games are one type of pervasive games that use multiple gaming devices in addition to media channels like TV and radio [14]. Ghellal et al. [6] discuss game design aspects that designers should take into account when designing pervasive crossmedia games. Many of the design challenges in crossmedia games are concentrated on using several devices at the same time, but pacing the game was also seen important. The initial design guidelines say that the game should support both active and passive participation as well as different temporal involvements. The problem with these guidelines is that they focus too much on the devices instead of players so they are not sufficient enough to be used for designing other pervasive games besides crossmedia games. For example these guidelines don't give any assistance on how one should design context sensitiveness.

Lankoski et al. describes a location-aware mixed reality game, *The Songs of North*, which was used to study design solutions for pervasive games [9]. One guideline they found was a support for communication since players can be present in the game at different times. They also discovered the importance of a player control which is related to the temporal gameplay; the player is not punished for not being present in the game or playing seldomly. Lankoski et al. did not present proper guidelines but rather observations on important design issues. That is probably one reason why they seem to have missed issues like communication between the player and the server.

3 The Game Concept

Mythical: The Mobile Awakening[1] is an asynchronous slow-update multiplayer game where players access a magical world through their mobile phone. The magical world is divided into four factions (Dawn, Sun, Dusk, and Moon). The players gain experience and learn spells by completing rituals either alone or together with other players. The spells are then used in encounters to battle against AI opponents or other players (Figure 1B). The game content is based on folklore mysteries and local history for creating an exciting atmosphere.

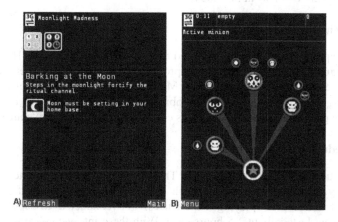

Fig. 1. Screenshots from the game. A) Context information sets conditions when the ritual component can be completed successfully. B) Slow update gameplay in the encounters.

The game features context-aware gameplay where the real world phenomena have an effect in the game world. Context information derived from the real world is used in the rituals where the reward of the ritual depends on how well the player has met the context conditions set initially (Figure 1A). There are three types of context information used: spatio-temporal, environmental and proximity. Spatio-temporal context is used in two ways: players select a home base from the predefined list and the game content and some environmental context information is then validated against information on that location. Time of the day is frequently used context information that defines when some rituals can be completed. Environmental context information is based on temperature, cloudiness and astronomy. Temperature is used in a breakpoint manner; some rituals require that the temperature is either above or below 0 degrees Celsius. Cloudiness has three possible options: clear, partly cloudy, and cloudy. Astronomy information is related to the Moon and Sun positions over the horizon and to the phases of the Moon. The proximity context is based on scanning Bluetooth devices. Rituals can require scanning either a specific or a given number of Bluetooth devices.

---

[1] http://www.mythicalmobile.com/

Asynchronous gameplay favors casual play style and Bogost has suggested that such feature could be the future of casual multiplayer gaming [3]. Slow update gameplay means that the game events are not continuous, but they happen in predefined intervals ranging from less than a minute to several hours.

The game was implemented upon MUPE[2] / Equip 2[3] platform and it is running on mobile phones supporting MIDP2.

4 User Study

To find out how pervasive features affect the gaming experience, we conducted a user study on the game on November 2007. Next we describe the procedure and the participants who took part in the study.

4.1 Participants

We had six participants, four females and two males, between 15 and 16 years. They were all regular video game players (approximately 10 to 25 hours per week). They played games mainly with a computer. Mobile games were not popular among the participants. Two participants played mobile games daily, but for others it was rare. None of the participants had any previous experience from pervasive games.

4.2 Procedure

The user study period lasted one week. The participants were instructed to play the game freely in their own time as much as they wanted to. Thereafter they were interviewed about their playing experiences. We conducted in-depth one-to-one interviews that lasted about 1.5 hours each. With these interviews we wanted to find out the overall opinion and attitudes towards the pervasive mobile game, and how the participants perceived context information that was embedded in the game design. The interviews revealed issues about how the implementation of these features had succeeded as well as opinions towards pervasive games in general. All interviews were audio recorded for later analysis. After the interview, the participants were also asked to fill in the background questionnaire, which revealed their gaming habits.

The interviews were processed in a way that all individual comments were written down to paper slips so each of them could be understood alone. After that we constructed an affinity diagram [2] from the approximately 700 comments we got from the interviews, combined related comments together, and gave a title for the group that described those comments (Figure 2). This method is well known in user-centered design projects for utility software, but in game evaluations it has not been used extensively as far as we know of.

We found this method to be time-consuming but useful; it forced us to think about each comment and what it actually meant. It also allowed us to see bigger entities as comments were not grouped based on the question, but according to their similarity of the topic. Results section describes some of the topics in more detail.

---

[2] http://www.mupe.org
[3] http://sourceforge.net/projects/equip/

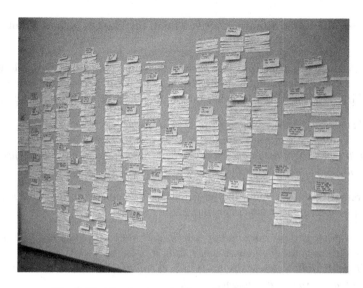

Fig. 2. First level categorization of interview comments

5 Results

In this section we describe some of the interview results, which revealed that pervasive mobile games will undoubtedly change many existing practices, but on the other hand they also provide new possibilities for gaming.

5.1 Rethink Game and Play Sessions

One of the first new things for the participants was the concept of a game session. In traditional video games the game session has a clear beginning and an ending and play sessions are mostly continuous. In pervasive mobile games this is not anymore straightforward as the game sessions might be fragmented and the whole game session can last hours or even days. The participants commented that this new style requires some learning and they had some troubles at the beginning to get used to it.

U2: *"I didn't leave the encounters unfinished before exiting the game."*
U4: *"I felt mostly like I could leave the game at any time. Still I wanted to finish started rituals and battles."*
U6: *"I had to get used to the playing style that you can leave the game in the background and it continues."*

For other participants this playing style was intuitive and they had accustomed to fragmented play sessions and slow update game mechanism that enabled flexibility.

U5: *"I felt like I could leave the game at any time."*
U3: *"I just started the encounter and let it play alone. I did not have to do any preparations, just to make sure that the game can roll on its own."*

5.2 Leaving the Game Situation Active Makes the Player Curious about It

Having the game active on the game server after log out caused an interesting dilemma for the participants. Do they just let the game play alone or should they log in again to see that everything is going alright? The participants stated that they were interested in and wondering what was going on in the game while they were away.

U6: *"I came back to the game if I was even a slightly curious about it."*
U3: *"I thought the game in some extend even though I was not playing it."*
U4: *"I thought about the game at times when I wasn't playing it if I had just left the game aside and thought that I would continue it later."*

After returning to the game the participants checked the current game state and reviewed previous game events in encounters.

U5: *"I usually read the texts that appeared after the battle I had just finished."*
U4: *" I have used the log feature and I think it is useful."*
U3: *"I could follow game events in the encounters and observe what kinds of minions or spells the opponent used."*

However, reviewing the current game state was not satisfactory, since the participants could have missed something interesting or important and it was too late to influence to the game events anymore at that point. Some participants tried to overcome this shortcoming by accessing the game several times a day to be on the safe side.

U3: *"Sometimes when I entered duels they seem to be almost finished."*
U2: *"If there would have been more actions happening at times when I wasn't playing the game, then it would be more interesting and it would irritate if I would have missed something important."*
U6: *"I checked the game quite frequently and I did not leave it alone for an hour or more."*
U2: *"I checked the game at least two to five times per day."*

5.3 The Game Should Notify about Important Events

Based on the participants' comments the game should have kept the players aware of the game events. Three participants mentioned that the game could send SMS messages to a player when something important has happened in the game and the player is not online. This would reduce frequent logins to the game.

U5: *"I think the SMS feature would be fun. Then you don't have to access the game all the time."*
U4: *"The SMS feature would have make things easier when you wouldn't have to go into the game just to check out if something interesting has happened."*

The notification feature was built in to the game, but none of the participants had activated it. There were UI design problems related to this feature, but since it is a novel feature in mobile games, the participants did not expect to find it in the game.

5.4   Finding Proper Intervals for Slow Update Mode

The important question for slow update gameplay is how to define event intervals that support this gaming mode. The participants stated that they had two approaches for this. They used short intervals (30-45 seconds), in which events occurred almost in real time or considerably longer intervals, which left room for other activities.

U6: *"Sometimes it was good that the encounters lasted longer, because then I had a chance to do something else."*

U4: *"I think that the encounters are sometimes really slow but then again it makes it possible to do something else at the same time."*

The game event intervals between one to five minutes were considered problematic. They are too short for leaving the game unattended, but at the same time it was boring to wait for the next game event to take place.

U2: *"You cannot choose the wave length in every battle so it leaves quite vulnerable feeling when you have like 2 min waves and you cannot leave the game. You have to be in the game and see what happens."*

5.5   Gaming Blends into Other Activities

One of the key features in pervasive games is that gaming is not anymore an isolated activity, but the players can share their time with a game and other tasks at the same time. The participants confirmed that they were listening to music, reading emails, eating and doing other tasks while playing the game. Concurrence of gaming and other tasks is pretty much dependent on concentration level and time that is required to perform actions in the game. If that time is long, it will disturb other activities.

U5: *"This game did not change my daily routines. It was just an addition."*

U6: *"It was really easy for me to concentrate on something else than playing the game even though it was running in the background".*

U3: *"I feel that it is not very distracting if I occasionally take a look what happens in the game world and it does not take very long time".*

5.6   Utilizing Context Information Was Appealing

Context information made the game appealing because setting conditions and defining the success rate of actions was different than what the participants were familiar with the traditional video games.

U5: *"I liked those rituals the best where there were different times of the day."*

U3: *"Rituals seem reasonable, especially when you have a multi-component ritual, which can be completed only in certain times of the day".*

The challenge was to find the right context where the ritual could be completed. As the players cannot rely anymore on information provided only in the game world, they must also exploit other sources.

U3: *"I would probably try to figure out the current time of day by checking the outdoor or using a calendar."*

5.7 Sometimes It Is Not Possible to Play the Game

Finding out the right circumstances to play the game can be a challenging task. Therefore, it is tempting to play when there is a possibility. However, the players' social context or more urgent tasks will limit this possibility. The participants commented that they were thinking about their influence on others while playing the game because they might unintentionally be impolite towards them.

U5: *"There are those rituals tied to a certain time of the day. So as I belong to the School of Dusk, it is quite short time when the rituals are open and we usually have a class at that time. It is quite hard for me to play then."*

U4: *"I think the playing would be quite much depended on my daily schedule."*

U5: *"The others became impatient when I was playing the game and they had to wait for me to finish."*

U2: *"It is quite rude to play this game in certain situations where you really have to be involved."*

6 Design Implications

The user study results indicate that pervasiveness sets some new requirements to the game design. In this section we present implications that the designers should take into account when designing asynchronous pervasive mobile games. Sections 6.1 and 6.2 discuss about utilization of context information in a game. Sections 6.3 and 6.4 deal with issues related to asynchronous gameplay.

6.1 Perception of the Current Context

Pervasive mobile games typically use context information to define some conditions in the game world or to convert context information to a game element. One part of the fun in the pervasive games comes from discovering the correct context and playing the game when conditions are favorable for the player.

The difficulty in using context information in a game design is that the game system and a player may not have a mutual understanding of the current context. The game design should not rely on context information blindly because it may be inaccurate or unavailable due to various reasons [7]. Inaccuracy can be a result of measurement variation due to different locations. For example, temperature can fluctuate several degrees even within a close range.

A player may also be uncertain how the game system interprets current context information even though it would be otherwise clearly recognizable. For example, the game can utilize environment context information such as cloudiness in the game. Even though cloudy and partly cloudy skies are different by definition, from the player point of view they are alike compared to the clear sky.

Using rigid thresholds with context information should be avoided because information from different sources may vary slightly and thus becomes ambiguous. Therefore, the designer should decide whether similar context information is considered as same or treated as different in the design. The best option is to utilize only context information that is clearly discernible and unambiguous for the players.

Furthermore, the game should notify the player what the game system considers as current context. The difficult issue for the designers is how the context information should be revealed to the player without contaminating the gaming experience. In addition, there can be several contexts that need be informed simultaneously.

6.2 Equal Chance to Play

Utilization of context information in the game should be carefully designed and the designers need to make sure that all players have an equal possibility to access relevant information. The player progression should not be depended on context that may be unreachable. Furthermore, most context information is also dynamic and the designers cannot control changes (e.g. weather information), which may place players to unequal position.

In addition to uncontrollable changes in context, there can be player-related reasons why the player cannot access certain information. For example specific time of the day may not be suitable for the player due to other activities or the player's current social context does not allow gaming at that point. The player may not be able to travel to retrieve location specific information or some resources are not available at the player's current location. Our results confirm the previous study, which state that the lack of time and unfavorable location were reported to be the major obstacles for playing the game successfully [1]. Peitz et al. also report results of a pervasive game in which players were frustrated because there were not necessary game resources available at the player's location [15].

However, if some context is available only for some players, the game design should enable and emphasize collaboration between the players. With this solution all players may access context information equally. This will also increase player-to-player interaction in the game. Other possibility is that context information is time-independent and the player can use it when it becomes available. If certain context is not available, the player should always be able to do some other things that will require some other information. Finally, the game should provide meaningful things to do that do not require any context conditions to be fulfilled. Other alternative is that the player can complete the task, but the reward is determined based on how well the context conditions were met.

6.3 Adjustable Play Sessions

Players play pervasive games as time permits it. Gaming can be very sporadic and the game design should take this into account. Moreover, as the play sessions are blended into other activities it is possible that the player needs to leave the game without prior notice or play sessions are short by default. Peitz et al. argue that short play sessions will promote social adaptability of the pervasive mobile game [15].

The game should be designed so that it is possible to leave the game at any time without reducing the player's chance to win the game. Disconnections are likely to happen in pervasive games and the game design should manage these properly [4]. In the multiplayer games the design should consider what kinds of effects the abandonment of the player has on other players.

In asynchronous gameplay the player should be able to adjust the pace of the game and match it to available playing time. Sometimes it is preferable to play the game almost in real time while some other time a slower game pace is preferred as it gives more possibilities to lie back, and time to do other things at the same time. In this case the game requires minimal attention, but the player can still keep track on game events. Our study results indicate that the length of the short play session should be less than five minutes. These short play sessions allow the players to play the game and have some other activities at the same time without disturbing each other. Longer play sessions are preferred when the players have time to be invested for gaming.

6.4 Communication Outside Gameworld

Communication is a very important factor in multiplayer games. Players quite often create their own tools or utilize existing tools if the game design lacks required features (e.g. for communication) [8]. Even though the support for communication between the online players is a common feature in many games, asynchronous communication is gaining attention as well. Linner et al. introduce a framework, which enables rapid development of pervasive games that also supports offline communication [11]. The system buffers received messages and the player can see them on the next login. Lindley et al. also describes a pervasive mobile game that allows the players to receive alerts, although they are not actually playing the game (the game character is in a dormant mode) [10].

The participants in our study highlighted very clearly that they want to be aware of the game events when they are offline. This observation expands the current design practice because currently the communication stays inside the game world and the players will receive messages when they log in to the game next time.

From the interaction design point of view communication to the offline players is interesting because the game user interface expands outside the game and the game events are communicated by using some alternative communication channel. The designers should decide both the communication and presentation methods when providing information from the game world.

The designer can use direct or indirect communication methods. The benefit of the direct communication is that messages will be delivered immediately and the player can act without delays. The drawback of this solution is that it will generate costs to the game master because one has to use a messaging service such as SMS, MMS, or email. Indirect communication means that important game data is accessible through a medium, which does not require the player to log into the game world. One viable option is to use a web page, which displays the game events to the players. This solution does not create extra costs as the game server and the web server can be in the same local network and information is transferred internally. Indirect communication assumes that the players are active and will check the web page spontaneously. However, it is possible that the players will not get information in time.

Instead of using messaging services or web services for communication it is possible to build automatic update functionality to the game itself. In this solution the client connects to the game server at certain intervals and retrieves the recent game events. Information is then displayed to the player. The player can view information without accessing the game, but if some actions are needed then the player has to log into the game. This solution creates frequent data traffic between the mobile device and the game server, and the player pays expenses of the traffic.

Presentation method depends on the communication method. SMS/MMS messages can have certain limits on how long messages can be, but for emails the length is not an issue. However, it should be noted that the emails are supposed to be read on a mobile device in order to achieve immediate information delivery. Textual information is in many cases sufficient, but images and graphics can make the messages more appealing.

Another important issue in a presentation method is to decide what game events are communicated to the player. In other words how many messages the player will receive when not logged in. The basic rule is that the player should be notified about anything that would cause actions when the player is actively playing the game. However, the number of the messages should not be overwhelming because it can easily lead to negligence and may disturb player's other activities. The player should be able to define the proper number of messages depending on the player's needs and interest in monitoring the game offline.

7 Conclusions

In this paper we have presented design challenges that game designers face when designing pervasive mobile games. We also present design implications how to overcome these challenges. These design implications were derived from a user study that was conducted with an experimental pervasive multiplayer mobile game. The game design utilized three types of context information in the game world: spatio-temporal, environmental, and proximity. Another important feature was an asynchronous slow update gameplay, which allowed the players to play the game whenever they wanted to and collaborate with other players without disturbing their gaming experience. The user study results indicated that when designing pervasive mobile games, the designer should pay attention to player's freedom to play the game. This means that the player should be able to adjust play sessions according to the available time they have. When the player is offline, communication outside the game world also becomes a crucial factor for convenient gameplay. Another important factor in pervasive games is the utilization of context information. The designers should ensure that both the players and the game system have mutual understanding of the current context. In addition, the game design should support that all players have equal chance to access relevant context information. By following these high level guidelines we believe that it is possible to design more enjoyable pervasive mobile games and introduce this new game genre to a wider player population.

Acknowledgements. IPerG (www.iperg.org) is an Integrated Project (FP6-004457) funded under the European Commission's IST Programme. We would like to thank all project members for their contribution to designing and implementing the game and the user study participants for their valuable comments.

References

1. Bell, M., Chalmers, M., Barkhuus, L., Hall, M., Sherwood, S., Tennent, P., Brown, B., Rowland, D., Benford, S., Capra, M., Hampshire, A.: Interweaving Mobile Games with Everyday Life. In: Proceedings of ACM SIGCHI, pp. 417–426 (2006)
2. Beyer, H., Holtzblatt, K.: Contextual Design: Defining Customer-Centered Systems, pp. 154–163. Morgan Kaufmann, San Francisco (1998)
3. Bogost, I.: Asynchronous Multiplay: Futures for Casual Multiplayer Experience. Other Players conference on Multiplayer Phenomena, The IT University of Copenhagen (2004), http://www.bogost.com/downloads/I.%20Bogost%20-%20Asynchronous%20Multiplay.pdf
4. Broll, W., Ohlenburg, J., Lindt, I., Herbst, I., Braun, A.: Meeting Technology Challenges of Pervasive Augmented Reality Games. In: Proceedings of 5th ACM SIGCOMM workshop on Network and system support for games (NetGames 2006) (2006)
5. Eriksson, D., Peitz, J., Björk, S.: Socially Adaptable Games. In: Proceedings of DIGRA 2005 Conference: Changing Views - Worlds in Play (2005)
6. Ghellal, S., Bullerdiek, S., Lindt, I., Pankoke-Babatz, U., Adams, M., Söderlund, T., Oppermann, L.: Design Guidelines for Crossmedia Game Production, Public IPerG Deliverable D8.1, http://www.pervasive-gaming.org/Deliverables/D8.1-Design-Guidelines-for-Crossmedia.pdf
7. Henricksen, K., Indulska, J.: Modelling and using imperfect context information. In: Proceedings of the Second IEEE Annual Conference on Pervasive Computing and Communications Workshops, pp. 33–37 (2004)
8. Koivisto, E.M.I.: Supporting Communities in Massively Multiplayer Online Role-Playing Games by Game Design. In: Proceedings of DIGRA Conference: Level Up (2003)
9. Lankoski, P., Heliö, S., Nummela, J., Lahti, J., Mäyrä, F., Ermi, L.: A case study in pervasive game design: the songs of north. In: Proceedings of the third Nordic conference on Human-Computer Interaction (NordiCHI 2004), pp. 413–416 (2004)
10. Lindley, C.A.: Game Space Design Foundations for Trans-Reality Games. In: Proceedings of the international conference on Advances in Computer Entertainment Technology (ACE 2005), pp. 397–404 (2005)
11. Linner, D., Kirsch, F., Radusch, I., Steglich, S.: Context-aware Multimedia Provisionning for Pervasive Games. In: Proceedings of the Seventh IEEE International Symposium on Multimedia (ISM 2005), pp. 60–68 (2005)
12. Magerkurth, C., Cheok, A.D., Mandryk, R.L., Nilsen, T.: Pervasive Games: Bringing Computer Entertainment Back to the Real World. ACM Computers in Entertainment 3(3) (2005)
13. Montola, M., Waern, A., Niewdorp, E.: Domain of Pervasive Gaming, Public IPerG Deliverable D5.3b (2006), http://iperg.sics.se/Deliverables/D5.3b-Domain-of-Pervasive-Gaming.pdf
14. Ohlenburg, J., Lindt, I., Pankoke-Babatz, U., Ghellal, S.: Report on the Crossmedia Game Epidemic Menace. ACM Computers in Entertainment 5(1) (2007)
15. Peitz, J., Saarenpää, H., Björk, S.: Insectopia – Exploring Pervasive Games through Technology already Pervasively Available. In: Proceedings of the international conference on Advances in Computer Entertainment Technology (ACE 2007), pp. 107–114 (2007)

EyeMote – Towards Context-Aware Gaming Using Eye Movements Recorded from Wearable Electrooculography

Andreas Bulling, Daniel Roggen, and Gerhard Tröster

ETH Zurich, Wearable Computing Laboratory
bulling@ife.ee.ethz.ch

Abstract. Physical activity has emerged as a novel input modality for so-called active video games. Input devices such as music instruments, dance mats or the Wii accessories allow for novel ways of interaction and a more immersive gaming experience. In this work we describe how eye movements recognised from electrooculographic (EOG) signals can be used for gaming purposes in three different scenarios. In contrast to common video-based systems, EOG can be implemented as a wearable and light-weight system which allows for long-term use with unconstrained simultaneous physical activity. In a stationary computer game we show that eye gestures of varying complexity can be recognised online with equal performance to a state-of-the-art video-based system. For pervasive gaming scenarios, we show how eye movements can be recognised in the presence of signal artefacts caused by physical activity such as walking. Finally, we describe possible future context-aware games which exploit unconscious eye movements and show which possibilities this new input modality may open up.

1   Introduction

The recognition of user activity has turned out to play an important role in the development of today's video games. Getting the player physically involved in the game provides a more immersive experience and a feeling of taking direct part rather than just playing as an external beholder. Motion sensors have already been implemented to recognise physical activity: Game controllers such as music instruments, guns, dance mats or the Wii accessories make use of different sensors to open up a whole new field of interactive game applications. However, in pervasive settings, the use of physical activity may not be sufficient or not always be desired. Furthermore, cognitive aspects like user attention and intentionality remain mainly unexplored despite having a lot of potential for gaming scenarios. Therefore, alternative input modalities need to be developed which enable new gaming scenarios, are unobtrusive and can be used in public without affecting privacy.

A lot of information about the state of the user can be found in the movement of the eyes. Conscious eye movement patterns provide information which

P. Markopoulos et al. (Eds.): Fun and Games 2008, LNCS 5294, pp. 33–45, 2008.

can be used to recognise user activity such as reading [1]. Explicit eye gestures performed by the player may be used for direct game input. Unconscious eye movements are related to cognitive processes such as attention [2], saliency determination [3], visual memory [4] and perceptual learning [5]. The analysis of these movements may eventually allow novel game interfaces to deduce information on user activity and context not available with current sensing modalities. In this paper we describe how Electrooculography (EOG) can be used for tracking eye movements in stationary and pervasive game scenarios. Additionally, we discuss which possibilities unconscious eye movements may eventually provide for future gaming applications.

2   Related Work

2.1   Eye-Based Human-Computer Interaction

Eye tracking using vision for human-computer interaction has been investigated by several researchers. Most of their work has focused on direct manipulation of user interfaces using gaze (e.g. [6,7]). Drewes et al. proposed to use eye gestures to implement new ways of human-computer interaction [8]. They showed that gestures are robust to different tracking accuracies and calibration shift and do not exhibit the "Midas touch" problem [9].

2.2   Eye Movements and Games

Smith et al. studied eye-based interaction for controlling video games across different genres, a first-person shooter, a role-playing game and an action/arcade game [10]. By comparing eye-based and mouse-based control they found that using an eye tracker can increase the immersion and leads to a stronger feeling of being part of the game. In a work by Charness et al., expert and intermediate chess players had to choose the best move in five different chess positions with their eyes [11]. Based on the analysis of eye motion they found that more experienced chess players showed eye movement patterns with a higher selectivity depending on chess piece saliency. Lin et al. developed a game interface using eye movements for rehabilitation [12]. They reported that the subjects' eyes became more agile which may allow for specific applications to help people with visual disabilities.

2.3   EOG-Based Interfaces

Several studies show that EOG can be implemented as an easy to operate and reliable interface. Eye movement events detected in EOG signals such as saccades, fixations and blinks have been used to control robots [13] or a wearable system for medical caregivers [14]. Patmore et al. described a system that provides a pointing device for people with physical disabilities [15]. All of these systems use basic eye movements or eye-gaze direction but they do not implement movement sequences which provide a more versatile input modality for gaming applications.

3   Wearable Electrooculography

3.1   Eye Movement Characteristics

The eyes are the origin of an electric potential field which is usually described as a dipole with its positive pole at the cornea and its negative pole at the retina. This so-called corneoretinal potential (CRP) is the basis for a signal measured between two pairs of electrodes commonly placed above and below, and on the left and right side of the eye, the so-called Electrooculogram (EOG).

If the eyes move from the centre position towards the periphery, the retina approaches one of the electrodes while the cornea approaches the opposing one. This results in a change in the electric potential. Inversely, eye movements can be tracked by analysing these changes in the EOG signal.

In the human eye, only a small central region of the retina, the fovea, is sensitive enough for most visual tasks. This requires the eyes to move constantly as only small parts of a scene can be perceived with high resolution. Simultaneous movements of both eyes in the same direction are called *saccades*. *Fixations* are static states of the eyes during which gaze is held at a specific location.

3.2   EOG Data Recording

EOG, in contrast to well established vision-based eye tracking[1], is measured with body-worn sensors, and can therefore be implemented as a wearable system. In earlier work we described how unobtrusive EOG recordings can be implemented with a light-weight and potentially cheap device, the *wearable eye tracker* [16]. The device consists of *Goggles* with integrated dry electrodes and a signal processing unit called *Pocket* with a Bluetooth and a MMC module. This unit can also be worn on the body, e.g. in a cloth bag fixed to one of the upper arms. Four EOG electrodes are arranged around the left eye and mounted in such a way as to achieve permanent skin contact. Finally, a 3-axis accelerometer and a light sensor are attached to the processing unit with the latter pointing forward in line of incident light (see Figure 1). The system weights 208g and allows for more than 7 hours of mobile eye movement recording.

3.3   EOG Signal Processing

To detect complex eye gestures consisting of several distinct movements from EOG signals the stream of saccades needs to be processed and analysed in a defined sequence [16]. This detection has several challenges with the most important one being to reliably detect the saccade events in the continuous vertical and horizontal EOG signal streams. Another challenge are the various types of signal artefacts which hamper the signal and can affect eye gesture recognition. This involves common signal noise, but also signal artefacts caused by physical activity which need to be removed from the signal. The characteristics of blinks

---

[1] With "eye tracking" we understand the recording and analysis of eye motion in contrast to "gaze tracking" which deals with tracking eye-gaze direction.

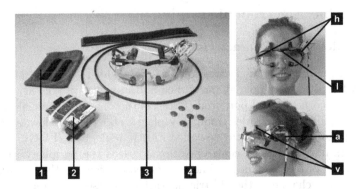

Fig. 1. Components of the EOG-based *wearable eye tracker*: armlet with cloth bag (1), the *Pocket* (2), the *Goggles* (3) and dry electrodes (4). The pictures to the right show the *Goggles* worn by a person with the positions of the two horizontal (h) and vertical (v) electrodes, the light sensor (l) and the accelerometer (a).

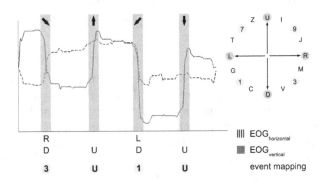

Fig. 2. Eye movement event encoding from horizontal and vertical EOG signals for gesture 3U1U: Windows marked in grey with distinct eye movement events detected in the horizontal and vertical signal component and final mapping to basic (U) and diagonal (3, 1) movements. The top right corner shows the symbols representing the possible directions for eye movement encoding.

are very similar to those of vertical eye movements, therefore they may need to be removed from the signal. However, for certain applications, blinks may also provide a useful input control, thus only reliable detection is required.

The output of the *wearable eye tracker* consists of the primitive controls *left*, *right*, *up*, *down* and *diagonal* movements (see Figure 2), blinks (conscious and unconscious), saccades and fixations. In addition, the system provides the following low-level signal characteristics and additional sensor inputs: EOG signal amplitudes (horizontal, vertical), timing of eye movement events, relative gaze angle, head movement (3-axis acceleration signal) and level of ambient light. Finally, the device can provide high-level contextual information, e.g. on user activity [1] or eventually the user's cognitive load or attention.

4 Application Scenarios

In this section we describe how eye movements recorded from wearable EOG can be used for different game scenarios. We first focus on stationary and pervasive settings involving direct game control. Afterwards, we give an outlook to future work and discuss which possibilities the analysis of unconscious eye movements may eventually provide and which novel gaming applications this may enable.

4.1 Stationary Games

The first scenario considers interactive games which are played in stationary settings with constrained body movements. These types of gaming applications are typically found at home, e.g. while sitting in front of a console in the living room or at the computer in the workroom. As the player does not perform major body movements, the weight and size of a game controller is not a critical issue. Instead, aspects such as natural and fast interaction are of greater importance.

To assess the feasibility of using the *wearable eye tracker* as an input device in stationary settings we investigated a simplified game consisting of eight different levels. In each game level, subjects had to perform a defined eye gesture consisting of a changing number of consecutive eye movements (see Table 1). The gestures in the experiment were selected to be of increasing complexity. For future stationary games, eye gestures may for example be used for direct user feedback or ingame task control.

Each eye gesture was to be repeatedly performed as fast as possible until the first successful try. If a wrong eye movement was recognised, i.e. one which was not part of the expected gesture, the level was restarted and a penalty was rewarded on the game score. Once the whole eye gesture was successfully completed the next game level showing the next gesture was started. For each level, the number of wrong and correct eye movements as well as the required time were recorded.

The subjects had to perform three runs with all game levels being played in each run. The first was a test run to introduce the game and calibrate the system for robust gesture recognition. In two subsequent runs the subjects played all levels of the game once again. At the end of the experiment, the subjects were asked on their experiences on the procedure in a questionnaire.

Table 1. Eye gestures of increasing complexity and their string representations used in the eight levels of the computer game (cf. Figure 2). The grey dot denotes the start and the arrows the order and direction of each eye movement.

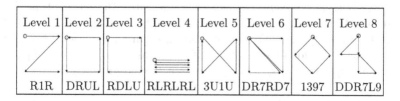

Level 1	Level 2	Level 3	Level 4	Level 5	Level 6	Level 7	Level 8
R1R	DRUL	RDLU	RLRLRL	3U1U	DR7RD7	1397	DDR7L9

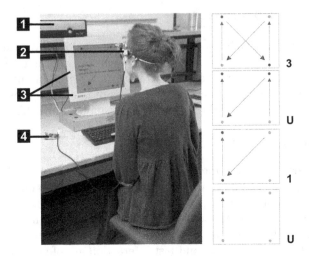

Fig. 3. Experimental setup consisting of a desktop computer running the game (1), the *Goggles* (2), a flat screen with red dots used for calibration (3) and the *Pocket* (4). The screenshots on the right show the sequence of eye movements and the generated event symbols for gesture 3U1U (from top to bottom). The red dot denotes the start of the gesture and the blue dot its end point. Blue arrows indicate the order and the direction of each expected eye movement.

The experiment was conducted using the *wearable eye tracker*, a standard desktop computer and a 17" flat screen with a resolution of 1024x768 pixels. The subjects were sitting in front of the screen facing its centre with movements of the head and the upper body allowed at any time. The expected eye movement order and their directions were shown as blue arrows with grey dots denoting the start and end point of a movement (see Figure 3).

Results. We collected data from 11 subjects - 2 female and 9 male - aged 24 to 64. The results for each individual subject only show a small range of different accuracies (see Table 2). The results were calculated using data from the second and the third run as the first one was for testing. The accuracy was calculated as the ratio of eye movements resulting in a correct gesture to the total number of eye movements performed in the level. The highest result is 95% (subject 3) while the worst result is for subject 8, with an accuracy of 86%. It can be seen from the table that performance does not correlate to the gender of the subject.

Table 3 shows the average performance over all subjects, i.e. the time and the accuracy to perform each of the eight gestures. T_T denotes the total time the subjects spent trying to complete each of the gestures; the success time T_S only measures the time spent on all successful attempts.

Table 4 shows the average response time T_R required to perform five gestures in comparison to a video-based system [8]. T_R was calculated from T_T to take the different experimental setups into account (see [16] for details).

Table 2. Accuracy for the different gestures for each individual subject without test run. The accuracy gives the ratio of eye movements resulting in a correct gesture to the total number of eye movements performed. The table also shows the subjects' gender (f: female, m: male).

Gesture	Accuracy [%]										
	S1(m)	S2(f)	S3(f)	S4(m)	S5(m)	S6(m)	S7(m)	S8(m)	S9(m)	S10(m)	S11(m)
R1R	88	69	100	100	69	100	100	100	100	90	66
DRUL	100	71	100	100	86	100	100	90	100	100	90
RDLU	100	100	100	100	100	88	100	90	100	100	100
RLRLRL	100	100	95	93	100	100	92	82	100	89	88
3U1U	79	100	90	100	100	100	75	100	90	90	92
DR7RD7	90	95	78	71	90	93	88	75	96	80	100
1379	73	90	100	83	88	81	100	76	85	89	100
DDR7L9	95	91	93	71	89	77	100	73	76	76	100
Average	91	89	95	90	90	92	94	86	93	89	92

Table 3. Average performance and accuracy for the different gestures over all subjects without test run. The accuracy is the ratio of eye movements resulting in a correct gesture to the total number of eye movements performed until success. T_T is the total time spent to complete the gesture and T_S the success time spent only on successful attempts.

Gesture	$T_T [ms]$	$T_S [ms]$	Accuracy [%]
R1R	3370	2890	85
DRUL	4130	3490	90
RDLU	3740	3600	93
RLRLRL	6680	5390	90
3U1U	4300	3880	89
DR7RD7	12960	5650	83
1379	6360	3720	84
DDR7L9	25400	5820	83

Table 4. Average response time T_R required to perform five different eye gestures over all subjects without initial test run in comparison to a video-based system

Gesture	$T_R [ms]$	
	EOG	Video
DRUL	1520	1818
RDLU	1630	1905
RLRLRL	2860	3113
3U1U	1940	2222
DR7RD7	5890	3163

Figure 4 shows the average accuracy for different eye movements and its increase during the three experimental runs.

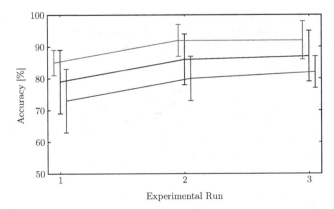

Fig. 4. Plot of distinct eye movement performance with standard deviation over all subjects for each experimental run. The topmost line shows the accuracy for movements in the basic directions (U,D,R,L), the middle one for diagonal movements (1,3,7,8) and the one at the bottom plot the average over all movements.

4.2 Pervasive Games

The second scenario considers pervasive games which are not constrained in terms of the players' body movements and/or not restricted to a certain location [17]. These games may therefore either be played indoors in front of a console, in combined virtual and physical environments or in daily life settings (e.g. role plays in natural environments). They require wearable equipment which needs to be light-weight and low-power to allow for unobtrusive and autonomous (long-term) use. Furthermore, pervasive games allow potentially more complex multimodal and ubiquitous interaction with(in) the environment, for example with combined hand and eye gestures. Eye gestures in pervasive games may provide two functions: (1) they allow the player to be immersed in the environment, especially when/if combined with head up displays and (2) at the same time allow for privacy, since eye gestures are not likely to be noticed as it is the case for body gestures.

As EOG is measured with body-worn sensors, body motion causes artefacts in the signals and affects eye movement detection. However, EOG can still be used in mobile settings. To show the feasibility of using the *wearable eye tracker* with simultaneous physical activity we carried out an experiment which involved subjects to perform different eye movements on a head-up display (HUD) while standing and walking down a corridor. Walking is a common activity, thus serves well as a test bench for investigating how artefacts induced by body motion can be automatically compensated in EOG signals. We evaluated an adaptive median filter which first detects walking activity using the data from the acceleration sensor attached to the *Goggles*. If walking is detected, the filter then continuously optimises its parameters to the walking pace to reduce signal artefacts.

The experiment was done using the *wearable eye tracker*, a standard laptop, a SV-6 head-up display from MicroOptical with a resolution of 640x480 pixels

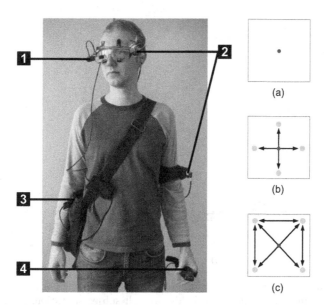

Fig. 5. Experimental setup consisting of a head-up display (1), the *wearable eye tracker* (2), a laptop (3) and a Twiddler2 (4). The screenshots on the right show the different eye movements performed in the three runs: Fixations on the centre of the screen (a), simple movements in vertical and horizontal direction (b) and additional movements along the diagonals (c) (cf. Figure 2). The red dots in the centre denote the start; arrows indicate the directions of the movements.

mounted to the *Goggles* frame and a wearable keyboard Twiddler2 (see Figure 5). The laptop was used to run the experiment software. During the experiments, the laptop was worn in a backpack in order not to constrain the subjects during walking. As the experimental assistant did not have control over the system, once the experiment was started, the Twiddler2 was needed to allow the subjects to control the software and start the different recordings.

The subjects were first trained on the game from the first experiment using the laptop screen. Once the game was finished, the HUD was attached to start the second experiment. The subjects performed three runs each consisting of different visual tasks while standing and walking down a corridor. Similar to the first experiment, for each of these tasks, the sequence and direction of the expected eye movements were indicated on the HUD as arrows and a moving red dot. The subjects were asked to concentrate on their movements and fixate this dot permanently.

The first run was carried out as a baseline case with fixations on the centre of the screen and large saccades without using the HUD. In two subsequent runs the subjects were asked to perform different sequences of eye movements on the HUD while standing and walking: The second run only contained simple movements in vertical and horizontal direction. The third run also included additional movements along the diagonals (cf. Figure 2).

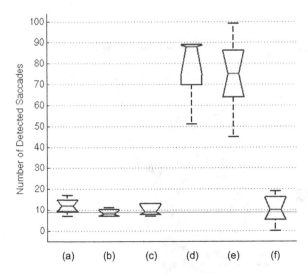

Fig. 6. Boxplot for the total number of detected saccades in the horizontal EOG signal component of run 3 with fixed thresholds over all subjects: stationary/raw (a), stationary/fixed median filter (b), stationary/adaptive filter (c), walking/raw (d), walking/fixed median filter (e), walking/adaptive filter (f). Horizontal red lines in each box indicate the lower quartile, median and upper quartile; dashed vertical lines show the data range; outliers are given as red crosses; the single solid horizontal line indicates the expected number of saccades.

Results. We recorded 5 male subjects between the age of 21 and 27 totalling roughly 35 minutes of recording with walking activity accounting for about 22 minutes. To assess a relative performance measure, we did a comparison to a standard median filter with fixed window size.

Figure 6 shows a boxplot for the total number of detected saccades in the horizontal EOG signal component of run 3. Each box summarises the statistical properties of the data of the 5 subjects: The horizontal red lines in each box indicates the median and the upper and lower quartiles. The vertical dashed lines indicate the data range, points outside their ends are outliers. Boxes are plotted for the following cases: stationary and raw signal, stationary and fixed median filter, stationary and adaptive filter, walking and raw signal, walking and fixed median filter, walking and adaptive filter. The single solid horizontal line indicates the expected number of saccades defined by the experimental procedure.

What can be seen from the figure is that in the stationary case, both filters perform equally well. During walking, however, significant differences can be recognised: The raw recordings show about eight times more detected saccades than in the stationary case. As the number of expected eye movements was constrained by the software these additionally detected saccades can be considered signal artefacts caused by walking. While the median filter with a fixed window size fails in removing these artefacts, the adaptive filter still performs well. This shows that signal artefacts caused by motion can be cancelled, thereby enabling the use of EOG-based game interfaces in pervasive gaming scenarios.

4.3 Future Context-Aware Games

Given the success of the new input controllers of today's active video games, future games will probably see more natural and more sophisticated interaction. These may increasingly take place in everyday scenarios with multi-modal input, several people being involved in the same game and a high level of collaboration. In terms of eye movements as an input modality, game interfaces based on direct input will probably remain an important focus of research [18]. However, additional information related to the underlying cognitive processes and the user's context may open up new possibilities for game developers and players.

Inducing Flow and Optimal Game Experience. Based on eye movement analysis, future games may be aware of the user's cognitive load, and adapt the individual gaming experience accordingly [19]. In particular, such games may increase the demand on the user when his cognitive load is assessed as being too weak, whereas demand may be decreased if cognitive load is recognised as being too high. This may enable the player to keep experiencing the feeling of full involvement and energised focus characteristic of the optimal experience, also known as *flow* [20]. In a collaborative game scenario this would allow to distinguish players with different game experience and adapt the game difficulty for a more balanced game experience.

Rehabilitation and Therapy Games. Designers may also develop special games which require eye movements to be performed as exercises for medical purposes in rehabilitation or visual training. By using wearable EOG, these games could be brought to daily-life settings which would allow for permanent training independently from a special therapy at the doctor. The game exercises may be automatically adapted to the visual learning process derived from eye movement characteristics to optimise the training [5]. These games could be specifically optimised to fit the special requirements of children, elderly or even disabled people who still retain control of eye motion.

Context-Aware Gaming. In a more general sense, future games may also provide new levels of context-awareness by taking into account different contextual aspects of the player. This context may comprise the player's physical activity, his location or mental state. Specific activities expressed by the eyes such as reading [1] could for example be used in games to adaptively scroll or zoom textual information. Context-aware games may also incorporate additional information derived from eye movements such as attention [21], task engagement [22] or drowsiness [23] to adapt to individual players. Other aspects of visual perception such as attention [2], saliency determination [3] and visual memory [4] may also enable new types of context-aware game interfaces not possible today. For collaborative games, this knowledge could be exchanged and combined into a common game context to integrate several players over potentially large geographical distances.

5 Discussion and Conclusion

In this work we have shown how a wearable electrooculographic system can be used for tracking eye movements in stationary and pervasive gaming scenarios. In the experiments, several subjects reported that the electrode placed below the eye was rather uncomfortable. In general, however, they did not feel constrained or distracted by wearing the goggles while gaming. To solve this issue, we are currently developing a new prototype of the system with improved electrode mounting. From the questionnaire we found that all subjects easily learned to use their eyes for direct game control. However, using explicit eye gestures was tiring and about 30% of the subjects had problems to stay concentrated during the game. Fatigue is an inherent problem also for input modalities such as hand gestures or speech. In pervasive settings, eye gestures outperform these modalities if the hands can not be used or if speech input is not possible.

Therefore, we believe EOG has a lot of potential for interactive gaming applications, in particular for those with unconstrained body movements. In contrast to video-based systems, EOG only requires light-weight equipment and allows for long-term use due to low power implementation. Unlike body movements, eye-based input allows for privacy which may prove extremely relevant in pervasive scenarios. Combined with a head-up display, EOG-based wearable eye tracking may eventually allow a more immersive game experience in outdoor environments. Information derived from unconscious eye movements may provide a more natural input modality for game control and future context-aware games. Thus, wearable EOG may become a powerful measurement technique for game designers and may pave the way for novel video games not possible so far.

References

1. Bulling, A., Ward, J.A., Gellersen, H., Tröster, G.: Robust Recognition of Reading Activity in Transit Using Wearable Electrooculography. In: Proc. of the 6th International Conference on Pervasive Computing (Pervasive 2008), pp. 19–37 (2008)
2. Selker, T.: Visual attentive interfaces. BT Technology Journal 22(4), 146–150 (2004)
3. Henderson, J.M.: Human gaze control during real-world scene perception. Trends in Cognitive Sciences 7(11), 498–504 (2003)
4. Melcher, D., Kowler, E.: Visual scene memory and the guidance of saccadic eye movements. Vision Research 41(25-26), 3597–3611 (2001)
5. Chun, M.M.: Contextual cueing of visual attention. Trends in Cognitive Sciences 4(5), 170–178 (2000)
6. Zhai, S., Morimoto, C., Ihde, S.: Manual and gaze input cascaded (MAGIC) pointing. In: Proc. of the SIGCHI Conference on Human Factors in Computing Systems (CHI 1999), pp. 246–253 (1999)
7. Qvarfordt, P., Zhai, S.: Conversing with the user based on eye-gaze patterns. In: Proc. of the SIGCHI Conference on Human Factors in Computing Systems (CHI 2005), pp. 221–230 (2005)
8. Drewes, H., Schmidt, A.: Interacting with the Computer Using Gaze Gestures. In: Baranauskas, C., Palanque, P., Abascal, J., Barbosa, S.D.J. (eds.) INTERACT 2007. LNCS, vol. 4663, pp. 475–488. Springer, Heidelberg (2007)

9. Jacob, R.J.K.: What you look at is what you get: eye movement-based interaction techniques. In: Proc. of the SIGCHI Conference on Human Factors in Computing Systems (CHI 1990), pp. 11–18 (1990)

10. Smith, J.D., Graham, T.C.N.: Use of eye movements for video game control. In: Proc. of the International Conference on Advances in Computer Entertainment Technology (ACE 2006), pp. 20–27 (2006)

11. Charness, N., Reingold, E.M., Pomplun, M., Stampe, D.M.: The perceptual aspect of skilled performance in chess: Evidence from eye movements. Memory and Cognition 29(7), 1146–1152 (2001)

12. Lin, C.-S., Huan, C.-C., Chan, C.-N., Yeh, M.-S., Chiu, C.-C.: Design of a computer game using an eye-tracking device for eye's activity rehabilitation. Optics and Lasers in Engineering 42(1), 91–108 (2004)

13. Wijesoma, W.S., Kang, S.W., Ong, C.W., Balasuriya, A.P., Koh, T.S., Kow, K.S.: EOG based control of mobile assistive platforms for the severely disabled. In: Proc. of the International Conference on Robotics and Biomimetics (ROBIO 2005), pp. 490–494 (2005)

14. Mizuno, F., Hayasaka, T., Tsubota, K., Wada, S., Yamaguchi, T.: Development of hands-free operation interface for wearable computer-hyper hospital at home. In: Proc. of the 25th Annual International Conference of the Engineering in Medicine and Biology Society (EMBS 2003), pp. 3740–3743 (2003)

15. Patmore, D.W., Knapp, R.B.: Towards an EOG-based eye tracker for computer control. In: Proc. of the 3rd International ACM Conference on Assistive Technologies (Assets 1998), pp. 197–203 (1998)

16. Bulling, A., Roggen, D., Tröster, G.: It's in Your Eyes - Towards Context-Awareness and Mobile HCI Using Wearable EOG Goggles. In: Proc. of the 10th International Conference on Ubiquitous Computing (UbiComp 2008), pp. 84–93 (2008)

17. Magerkurth, C., Cheok, A.D., Mandryk, R.L., Nilsen, T.: Pervasive games: bringing computer entertainment back to the real world. Computers in Entertainment (CIE 2005) 3(3), 4 (2005)

18. Isokoski, P., Hyrskykari, A., Kotkaluoto, S., Martin, B.: Gamepad and Eye Tracker Input in FPS Games: Data for the First 50 Minutes. In: Proc. of the 3rd Conference on Communication by Gaze Interaction (COGAIN 2007), pp. 78–81 (2007)

19. Hayhoe, M., Ballard, D.: Eye movements in natural behavior. Trends in Cognitive Sciences 9, 188–194 (2005)

20. Csíkszentmihályi, M.: Flow: The Psychology of Optimal Experience. Harper Collins, New York (1991)

21. Liversedge, S.P., Findlay, J.M.: Saccadic eye movements and cognition. Trends in Cognitive Sciences 4(1), 6–14 (2000)

22. Skotte, J., Nøjgaard, J., Jørgensen, L., Christensen, K., Sjøgaard, G.: Eye blink frequency during different computer tasks quantified by electrooculography. European Journal of Applied Physiology 99(2), 113–119 (2007)

23. Caffier, P.P., Erdmann, U., Ullsperger, P.: Experimental evaluation of eye-blink parameters as a drowsiness measure. European Journal of Applied Physiology 89(3), 319–325 (2003)

The Audio Adventurer: Design of a Portable Audio Adventure Game

Philip Mendels and Joep Frens

Designing Quality in Interaction group,
Department of Industrial Design
Eindhoven University of Technology
Den Dolech 2, 5612 AZ Eindhoven, The Netherlands
+31 40 247 91 11
{p.mendels,j.w.frens}@tue.nl

Abstract. In this paper we describe the design of a portable device for playing audio adventure games. This device enables the player to explore an audio world, interact with it, and solve challenges while a narrative evolves. To avoid the difficulties that can arise when freely navigating open spaces in audio-only worlds, we structured our audio world as a network of paths. Different ways of panning the audio to fit this model are proposed. Two initial rotational devices for navigating the audio world were created and evaluated: a relative and an absolute one. The relative one was worked out to a final prototype. Inventory functionality was added to increase the interactive possibilities and to make the device more expressive. Initial reactions were positive, but additional content and experiments are needed to investigate whether the Audio Adventurer can offer a long-lasting immersive and engaging experience.

Keywords: audio game, adventure game, interactive narrative, interactive audiobook, auditory environment.

1 Introduction

The possibilities of sound for computer games are largely under-investigated as most games and game research focus on visuals. However, audio is an important interactive element of games, and frameworks about game audio are gradually emerging [1, 2, 3]. Although audio is commonly used to complement visuals in games, we feel that the unique aspects of audio are best experienced when visuals are omitted. One reason for this is that the lack of visual information enables the player to use his imagination to visualize the audio world, like a book requires the reader to imagine the textual world. Imagination plays an important role in the feeling of presence of the user [4].

We are interested in audiogames, computer games that only use audio. They come in all genres, ranging from puzzle games to first-person shooters. A description of audiogames is given by Friberg an Gärdenfors [5] and the interested reader can find an overview of audiogames on the audiogames.net website [6]. The majority of the

P. Markopoulos et al. (Eds.): Fun and Games 2008, LNCS 5294, pp. 46–58, 2008.
© Springer-Verlag Berlin Heidelberg 2008

audio games is made for visually impaired players and are adaptations of visual games that do not exploit the full potential of audio only gaming. In line with Röber and Masuch [7] we think that new opportunities will arise when audio games leave the realm of the pc and if they are not developed for visually impaired players exclusively. To maximally exploit these new opportunities, interfaces need to be designed specifically for audio games. Additionally, audio games can be enjoyed in different settings if the interfaces are made portable.

In this project we envisioned a relaxed and casual setting, a setting similar to reading a book or listening to an audio book in bed, on the beach or in the train. We focus on audio adventure games because we think their emphasis on narrative is especially appropriate for this setting. Adventure games are games in which a narrative gradually evolves while the player solves challenges that are intellectual rather than based on dexterity [8]. We set out to construct a portable device dedicated for audio adventure games, which enables the player to explore an immersive audio world and the embedded narrative. This device and the associated software and content were developed during the Msc graduation project of the first author [9].

In what follows we first discuss the Audio Adventurer by comparing it with related work. Then we describe the spatial structure that we used for creating our audio adventure game worlds, and two initial controller prototypes that were created and evaluated. Finally we describe our final prototype, followed by suggestions for future work, and draw our conclusions.

Fig. 1. A player interacting with the final prototype, as illustration of the relaxed and casual setting that we aimed for

2 Related Work

When designing an audio adventure game experience for a relaxed and casual setting three aspects play an important role: an interactive audio world, an interactive narrative and a physical interface. In this chapter we will discuss these by examining related work.

Audiogames were already introduced in section one. A problem with many existing audio games is that navigating the audio-only world is not a trivial task. The first-person shooter Terraformers [10] offers a three-dimensional world in which the player can move around freely. Several in-game navigation interfaces (spoken GPS, sonar beep, compass beep) are available, but even with these interfaces navigation remains rather difficult. Although they fit in the narrative setting of this particular game, we think that they are not suitable for all narratives. We also think that these audio interfaces can conflict with the sounds of the audio world and possibly annoy the player. Chillingham [11] is an audio adventure game that requires the player to use the arrow keys to make combinations of verbs, world elements and inventory items. (e.g. *look at – statue*) The advantage of this interface is that it is impossible for the player to get lost. A disadvantage is that the interface is very present: Looping through narrated verbs, hotspots and items can become tedious and the feeling of traveling the audio world in an analogue way is missing. Moreover, the element of exploration (searching for places and items) is lost. These examples show that a balance is needed between freedom of exploration and ease of navigation. Especially for games that draw heavily on narrative, navigation should not demand all the player's attention. In this paper we show how the structure of the audio world can be changed to achieve such a balance.

Examples of portable interactive audio devices that suit a relaxed and casual setting are *interactive audiobooks*, or interactive audio theatre, depending on how much is narrated in relation to how much is directly represented through sound. Furini uses this term for describing a system that enables the listener to make choices at certain points in the narrative [12]. This system requires simple interaction and no advanced hardware for mixing and rendering audio, so it can run on relatively simple portable music players. Huber et al. describe a system with more interactivity, which is realized on a PocketPC [13]. Apart from a branching narrative, they add interactive scenes in which the user can play part of the story as a small audio game. A danger of branching narratives is that immersion can be broken when the choices are presented too literally. Ryan illustrates this with the example of clicking on a link in a hypertext narrative: When the user has to decide on which link to click, his attention is redirected from the textual world to the real world [14]. We are therefore much more interested in situating the entire narrative in an interactive audio world. In an interactive virtual (audio) world the choices can be embedded in a seamless way: The user makes choices (perhaps unconsciously) with actions that are meaningful in that world. Moreover, this project differs from the previously mentioned interactive audiobooks because we set out to design a *new* portable device dedicated for audio adventure games.

The physical interface can help the player to navigate and interact with the audio world. Natural, immersive interaction techniques are considered to improve these aspects. The audio game Demor is a good example of this [15]. In this game the player is placed almost literally in the audio world. Players are tracked via GPS in an open field in the real world and a head-tracker is used to make the 3d audio experience complete. A disadvantage of these forms of interaction is that they are not very suitable for the relaxed and casual setting that we aimed for. We set out to design a portable interface that assists in navigation and interaction, but that requires less intense actions from the player. Inspiration for such actions can be drawn from research frameworks such as tangible interaction [16], which concerns physicalization of digital information and functionality, and rich interaction [17], which states that functionality should be directly accessible through expressive form. We think that a device that requires mainly subtle hand movements can still make the player feel present in the audio world and the narrative. A discussion on the relation between immersion, presence, interaction and narrative is beyond the scope of this paper. For a more elaborate view we refer the reader to the thesis [9].

3 The Audio World

Before describing prototypes of the portable device in the next chapter, we will first discuss the structure of the audio world and different models for stereo-panning the audio. Although software and hardware prototyping happened more or less concurrently, we present them separately for the sake of clarity.

3.1 World Structure and Navigation

To make navigation easier, we restricted the audio world to a network of paths, rather than a collection of open spaces that can be explored freely. A network of paths can still become quite complex: The player needs to know when he is at an intersection, and how to move the player-character into a side-path (fig. 2a). To give the audio world a clear structure, we constructed it out of scenes with each a matching ambient sound and/or music, and assigned a single path to each scene (fig. 2b and 2c). When

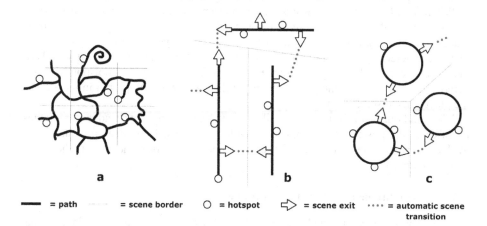

Fig. 2. Different models for connecting paths. A: Complex network of paths without automatic scene transitions. B: Network of discontinuous paths. C: Network of continuous paths.

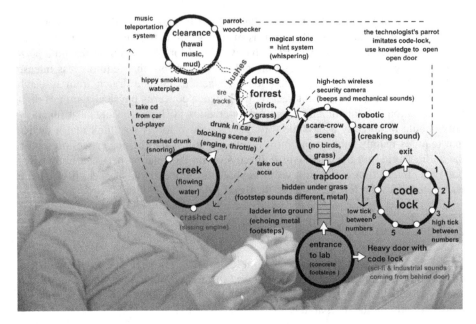

Fig. 3. A schematic representation of a part of one of the constructed audio worlds

the sound of an adjacent scene is heard, the player can select to exit the current scene and automatically move the player-character to the adjacent scene. A path can be discontinuous (open-ended) (fig. 2b) or continuous (closed) (fig. 2c). We initially chose for continuous paths because of their inherent spatiality (the path encloses the space of a scene), and because they can be mapped easily to a rotational controller, which is discussed in the next chapter. A continuous path can be abstractly modeled as a circle, although it can have any closed shape in the imagination of the player.

When the player-character walks audio footsteps are played, matching the terrain of the scene and the speed of movement. Each path contains hotspots that can be places, objects, characters or scene-exits. When the player selects a scene-exit the player-character automatically moves to the adjacent scene and the ambient sounds of the current scene and the adjacent scene are cross-faded. Sometimes hotspots are triggered automatically (e.g. the player-character slips over something), but in most cases the player has to select them.

We found out that it is already possible to create engaging simple adventure games by offering the possibility to explore and select hotspots. New ideas for interaction evolved, for example that the controller can represent an in-game object (the code-lock in figure 3).

3.2 Stereo-Panning and Player Perspective

Some hotspots are event-sounds that are played back once each time the player walks by. An example is a footstep that sounds different because there is something hidden under the grass. Most hotspots are continuous sounds, for example a bartender humming and washing glasses, or the ambient sound of an adjacent scene (a scene-exit).

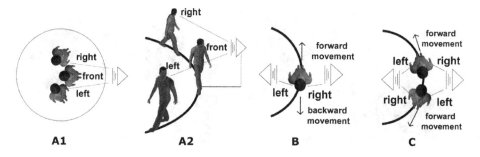

Fig. 4. Different ways of panning the audio of a hotspot

These continuous sounds are stereo-panned and attenuated when the player walks by. The angular range and the maximum volume of each hotspot varies, depending on how big the scene is, how loud the sound is, or how hard it should be to find the hotspot.

The movement of a rotational controller can be interpreted as a rotation of the player-character (fig. 4A1), or as a movement over a path (fig. 4 A2, B, C). Apart from the axis of rotation of the controller, this is influenced by the (amount of) footsteps played back during a rotation and by the way the audio is panned.

If the sound of a hotspot passes from left to right (or vice versa) when passing by, a line of sight perpendicular to the path can be assumed. We used this way of panning the audio because it offers a certain freedom: It can either mean that the player-character rotates in the centre of the scene (fig. 4A1), or that he moves over the path with his head turned towards the hotspots (fig. 4A2), depending on the amount of footsteps played back.

If the sound of a hotspot stays at the same side of the player when passing by, movement over a path with a line of sight along the path can be assumed (fig. 4 B,C). This model might be more realistic when compared with that of figure 4A2, but raises additional questions. Is it desirable to enable the player-character to turn around (rather than simply walking backward)? If so, how can the difference between walking backward and turning around be communicated by the controller? We have not explored these issues yet.

4 Exploring Hardware Possibilities

One reason why we chose for continuous (closed) paths is that they enabled us to explore the possible benefits of an absolute rotational controller (fig. 5A). Such a controller with a tangible rotational reference point can help the player to understand his position or orientation in the scene and the configuration of the scenes in relation to each other. One rotation of the controller is mapped 1:1 to the continuous path of a scene. The controller represents an abstract top view of the scene. We also constructed a relative rotational controller with a different axis of rotation (fig. 5B), which is more likely to evoke a feeling of forward and backward movement. One rotation of the relative controller can also be mapped 1:1 to the path of a scene.

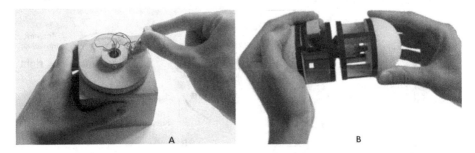

Fig. 5. The two initial controller prototypes. A: Absolute rotational controller with a tangible moveable reference point (the handle). The top part rotates around the z-axis. The handle can be moved outwards to select a hotspot and moves back automatically when released. B: The relative rotational controller. The right part can rotate around the y-axis. On the left part is a button that can be pressed/grabbed to select hotspots.

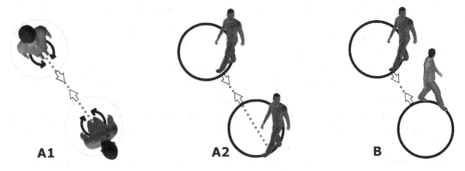

Fig. 6. Different implementations of scene transitions. A2: Automatic scene crossing needed for the absolute controller.

A problem associated with the absolute prototype is that when entering a new scene, the handle (tangible reference point) is opposite to the point of entering the scene. This problem is not so severe when the player assumes that he is turning in the centre of the scene (fig. 6A1), but it is when the player assumes that he is walking at the border of the scene (fig. 6A2). In the latter case the player has to assume that he automatically crosses the new scene after a scene transition. For the relative prototype the much more natural situation of figure 6B can be used.

4.1   Evaluation of Prototypes

Before going into the process of designing a final prototype, the two rotational prototypes and a keyboard were compared by nine participants. Three small audio adventure games with the same world structure, the same general narrative setting (Wild West) but with different stories, scenes and hotspots were created. Each participant evaluated all three controllers, each controller with a different audio world (combinations and order balanced out). In all cases a perspective perpendicular to the path (fig. 4A) and automatic scene crossings (fig. 6A2) were used. In each audio world the participant was first guided through the world in a structured way (the protagonist reading aloud from a tourist guide), and when the whole world was explored the narrative started. During the narrative a sequence of hotspots needed to be visited in a certain order. The complexity of the exploration route and narrative route were the same for all three worlds. The experimenter was sitting in the same room, observing the participant as well as a visual representation on a laptop of the participant's position in the audio world. At the end of each narrative the participant was provided with the scene and hotspot names and asked to draw a map of the world. Each controller session took 30 minutes on average. At the end of all three sessions the audio world structure, the controllers and the maps were discussed with the participant.

Eight participants were positive about the overall experience and well able to complete the narratives without help. One participant became frustrated and gave up. This participant did not understand that scene-exits needed to be selected (rather than just walking from one scene to the other). The difference between standing in front of the path to an adjacent scene and actually being in that scene was not clear enough, because the same sound was used for both. This problem might not occur when a perspective along the path is used (fig. 4 B,C), because the sound of a scene-exit will then be heard to the right or to the left and will less likely be mistaken for being ambient.

Following is a summary of conclusions obtained from observations of and discussions with the eight participants that completed the test. For a more elaborate discussion we refer the reader to the thesis [9].

1. No participant preferred the keyboard. Six participants preferred both rotational controllers to the keyboard. The fact that the keyboard gave no analogue control over the speed of moving through the audio world played an important role in this.
2. There are aspects of the absolute rotational prototype that were mentioned as very confusing by most of the participants: It requires automatic scene crossings (fig. 6A2), and inconsistencies can occur when the reference point is moved during narrative segments in which the player-character should stay at the same angle (e.g. during a scene transition or a conversation).
3. Three participants preferred the absolute prototype. They mentioned that it made them actively think about the spatial configuration of the audio world, in contrast to the relative prototype that they sometimes experienced as a more generic interface for browsing linear sequences of hotspot sounds. The latter especially happened while revisiting locations and searching for previously discovered hotspots.
4. Five users preferred the relative prototype, using as arguments that it made them focus on the audio and left enough space for their imagination, in contrast to the absolute prototype that redirected their attention from the audio world to the controller. Figure 7 shows the maps drawn by one of these participants. The map associated with the absolute controller (fig. 7a) matches the spatial configuration of the audio world much better but the other maps are less schematic and more vivid.
5. It was difficult to tell what the effect was of the differences in rotation axis on the perspective of the users and the perceived way of moving, because of the absolute/relative difference and because we used a panning model that imposes a line of sight perpendicular to the path (fig. 4A). Most users did mention that the way of holding and turning the relative prototype was more comfortable.

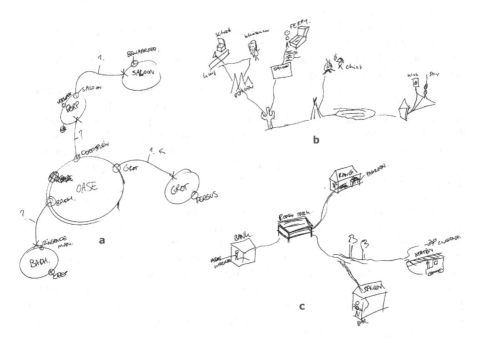

Fig. 7. Maps drawn by one participant. A: absolute rotational controller. B: keyboard. C: relative rotational controller.

5 Final Prototype

We chose to work out the relative prototype because we think that it provokes a stronger focus on the audio and because of the previously mentioned problems that are associated with the absolute prototype. Blocking the rotation of the absolute prototype at appropriate points in the narrative can help to avoid inconsistencies, but solutions for avoiding the automatic scene crossings (e.g. repositioning the reference point using a motor) seem to be rather obtrusive. Moreover, the continuous-path scenes that are needed for the absolute controller severely limit the freedom of the author of the adventure game: For a relative controller more complex networks of paths can be designed, using scenes with discontinuous (open-ended) paths, for example for a mountain path. Continuous paths can then still be used when desired, for example for open spaces such as a village square.

A drawback of the initial relative controller was that some users at moments, especially when revisiting locations, perceived its interaction as rather generic. A player should get the feeling that he is really exploring and interacting with an audio world, not that he is using a generic device to browse through a sequence of hotspot sounds.

Offering additional actions beside exploration and navigation can enrich the interaction with the controller. We chose to explore how the inventory (the virtual backpack of the player-character) can be represented by the controller. We considered this a good starting point because it is a relatively simple construct for adding a lot of new challenges to the audio game.

Fig. 8. Side view of the final prototype

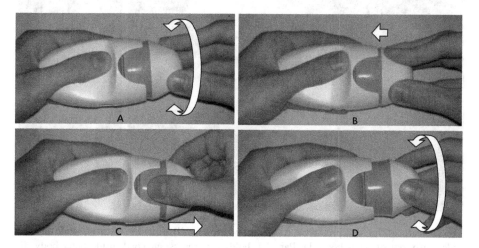

Fig. 9. Interaction with final prototype. A: Rotate right part to navigate audio world. B: Press together to select a hotspot in the audio world. C: Pull out right part to open the inventory. D: Rotate right part to browse inventory.

The main interaction with the final prototype is shown in figure 9. When an inventory item is selected a short sound that represents the item is played, and if the player waits for a short amount of time, the player-character tells what the item is. The latter is interrupted when the next item is selected. When the player closes the inventory while an object is selected, the player-character tries to use that object at the current position in the audio world. While opening/closing the inventory the sound of a zipper is played back and the sounds of the audio world are partly faded out/in.

The challenge was to express the actions and state of the inventory in a rich way, without directing the attention of the player from the audio world to the device. We therefore chose for a design that does not add an additional distinctive action for browsing the inventory (the same rotational movement is used). We however do not imply that it is impossible to add such a distinctive action in a way that does not harm the immersion in the audio world. We think that there are still many design explorations possible for making the controller more expressive.

5.1 Technical Implementation

The final prototype is 3d-printed. A stopless potentiometer (fig. 10H) is used to measure the angle of rotation, and a single slider potentiometer (fig. 10E) is used to measure if the inventory is opened/closed and if the rotational part is pressed to select a hotspot. Inside the controller is an Arduino mini microcontroller (fig. 10F) that is connected to a laptop via USB. The audio world is created in Adobe Flash using Actionscript 2. The audio is streamed from the laptop to wireless headphones.

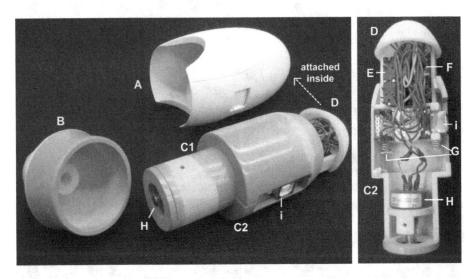

Fig. 10. Parts of the final prototype. A: Outer body to hold. B: Rotational part. C: Part that can slide partly out of outer body. D: Part that holds electronics, attached inside outer body. E: Slider potentiometer measures how far C is out. F: Arduino mini microcontroller. G: Springs. H: Stopless potentiometer. I: USB-interface.

6   Future Work

There is still much room for improvement considering the spatial representation of the audio. Two possible improvements are to use 3d audio and to adapt the audio to individual players by using head related transfer functions. But more important improvements can be made using only stereo panning. It will be essential to experiment with an audio model in which the line of sight of the player-character is along the path (fig. 4B,C). The additional questions that this model brings along regarding the difference between walking backward and turning around need to be answered.

Additionally, the freedom of exploring the audio world might be increased. A more complex network of paths should be explored, rather than our model that is structured out of scenes that are each a single continuous path. Eventually, it would also be interesting to investigate how a controller can aid in navigating open spaces in an audio world, as opposed to paths. An absolute controller, offering for example a tangible representation of the position and/or orientation of the character might help, but might also break immersion because it can direct the attention of the player from the audio world to the controller in the real world.

Finally, the controller itself can be improved. A practical next step is to make the communication between computer and controller wireless. We however think that the most interesting opportunities lay in exploring new functionality of the controller. The controller might represent more actions, in-game objects and locations in an expressive way. Changes in shape, resistance, rotation mode (absolute/relative) and rotation axis of the controller can change when the controller represents these elements.

7 Conclusion

First reactions showed that it is possible to create an engaging audio adventure game experience that offers enough freedom for exploration and interaction on the one hand, and focus on narrative and ease of navigation on the other hand. We found out that creating your own adventure game content can be very inspirational for new interaction ideas, and consider this an important part of the design process. Constraining the freedom of exploration in the audio world to a network of paths was an important decision. Also, a dedicated interface can improve the experience, by aiding in navigation and by enabling expressive actions. It showed that these aspects can be integrated in a subtle interface that fits a relaxed and casual setting, as an alternative to technologies like GPS, head trackers or free moving controllers (like the WII-mote) that track more intense body movements. We assume that the Audio Adventurer can offer a long lasting immersive and engaging portable audio adventure game experience, but additional content and experiments are needed to prove this.

Acknowledgements. The authors would like to thank Berry Eggen and Richard Appleby for their advice during the project, Chet Bangaru for his support with the final prototype, the /d.search -labs, and the participants of the evaluation for their time and enthusiasm.

References

1. Grimshaw, M., Schott, G.: Situating Gaming as a Sonic Experience: The Acoustic Ecology of First-Person Shooters. In: Situated Play, Proceedings of DIGRA, Digital Games Research Association, University of Tokyo, Tokyo, Japan (2007)
2. Huiberts, S., van Tol, R.: IEZA: A framework for Game Audio (2008), http://www.gamasutra.com/view/feature/3509/ieza_a_framework_for_game_audio.php

3. Stockburger, A.: The game environment from an auditive perspective. In: Level Up, Proceedings of DIGRA, Digital Games Research Association, Utrecht University, Utrecht, The Netherlands (2003)
4. Jacobson, D.: Presence revisited: imagination, competence, and activity in text-based virtual worlds. CyberPsychology & Behavior 4, 653–673 (2001)
5. Friberg, J., Gärdenfors, D.: Audio games: New perspectives on game audio. In: Advances in Computer Entertainment Technology 2004, Singapore (2004)
6. van Tol, R., Huiberts, S.: Audiogames Website, http://www.audiogames.net
7. Rober, N., Masuch, M.: Leaving the Screen: New Perspectives in Audio-Only Gaming. In: 11th International Conference on Auditory Display (ICAD), Limerick, Ireland (2005)
8. Tanguay, D.: A guide to create the ideal adventure game (1999), http://www.adventureclassicgaming.com/index.php/site/features/105/
9. Mendels, P.: The Audio Adventurer. Unpublished Master Thesis, Eindhoven University of Technology, Eindhoven, The Netherlands (2007),
http://www.relmuis.nl/AudioAdventurer
10. Pin Interactive: Terraformers. PC-game (2003), http://www.terraformers.nu/
11. Bavisoft: Chillingham. PC-game,
http://www.bavisoft.com/chillingham.htm
12. Furini, M.: Beyond passive audiobook: How digital audiobooks get interactive. In: Proceedings of the IEEE Consumer Communication & Networking 2007 (CCNC 2007), Las Vegas, NV (2007)
13. Röber, N., Huber, C., Masuch, M.: Interactive audiobooks: combining narratives with game elements. In: Göbel, S., Malkewitz, R., Iurgel, I. (eds.) TIDSE 2006. LNCS, vol. 4326, pp. 358–369. Springer, Heidelberg (2006)
14. Ryan, M.: Narrative as Virtual Reality. John Hopkins University Press, Baltimore (2001)
15. Cohen, Y., Dekker, J., Hulskamp, A., Kousemaker, D., Olden, T., Taal, C., Verspaget, W.: Demor - Location based 3D Audiogame (2004), http://www.demor.nl
16. Ullmer, B., Ishii, H.: Emerging frameworks for tangible user interfaces. IBM System Journal 39(3-4), 915–931 (2000)
17. Frens, J.W.: Designing for Rich Interaction: Integrating Form, Interaction, and Function. Unpublished Doctoral Dissertation, Eindhoven University of Technology, Eindhoven, The Netherlands (2006), http://www.richinteraction.nl

Building RFID-Based Augmented Dice with Perfect Recognition Rates

Steve Hinske[1], Marc Langheinrich[2], and Yves Alter[1]

[1] Inst. for Pervasive Computing,
ETH Zurich,
8092 Zurich, Switzerland
steve.hinske@inf.ethz.ch
[2] Faculty of Informatics,
University of Lugano (USI),
6904 Lugano, Switzerland
langheinrich@acm.org

Abstract. We report on the construction of real-world dice equipped with radio frequency identification (RFID) technology that support the automated readout and processing of rolled results. Such augmented dice help to build "smart" tabletop games that are able to unobtrusively detect the players' actions, allowing them to better focus on the gameplay and the social interaction with other players. Since the technology is completely integrated into the play environment, the look and feel of the dice is unaltered. This article provides an overview of the challenges in building augmented dice and describes the various prototypes that we built. Our latest model resembles a regular die of about 16mm side length and achieves a perfect recognition rate of 100%.

Keywords: Augmented dice, radio frequency identification (RFID) technology.

1 Introduction

For millennia people have enjoyed playing games and the social integration provided by such gatherings. Be it for a nice chat, the inner urge for competition, or simply for the feeling of belonging to a group – playing games can be regarded as one of the main recreational activities of mankind. Hitherto, a countless number of games have been invented: some focus on the players' physical skills, others on their mental abilities, some simply test the players' luck. Given the latter category, dice have become the standard game piece whenever an element of randomness is required – either as a part of the game (e.g., Monopoly) or as its core element (e.g., Yathzee).

Depending on the game and the random component required for advancing the game, there are several die types in use with the "D6" being the most prominent one. Many games use one or two six sided dice to simply advance game figures on a board, yet more complicated uses of dice rolls are also common, e.g., looking for a particular combination of eyes, requiring the sum to exceed or undercut a certain value, or comparing several dice with each other. Some games require the usage of many dice which can result in spending quite some time on "eye counting". While modern electronics might allow for other approaches to provide this random

P. Markopoulos et al. (Eds.): Fun and Games 2008, LNCS 5294, pp. 59–64, 2008.

component (e.g., an electronic random number generator that simply displays the results of the above mentioned calculation at the push of a button), people might prefer the use of traditional dice for three reasons: the haptic and spatial experience; the transparency of the process (one can see the numbers being "generated"); and the feeling that one can influence the result (i.e., the idea of having a "lucky hand").

So-called "augmented dice" aim at combining both aspects, that is, to allow players to continue using typical dice in the traditional sense, while the results can be automatically retrieved and forwarded to the gaming application. The idea is to embed computers and sensors into both the gaming environment and, due to the continuous miniaturization of these technological components, even into individual game pieces. This allows us to map the users' real-world activities onto a virtual game model that in turn can drive displays or other game elements.

This paper describes our continuing work on RFIDice [4], our initial prototype of an RFID-enhanced traditional D6. Compared to our earlier models, we were able to significantly increase the recognition rate while reducing the form factor, making our augmented die no bigger than a standard, off-the-shelf D6. To the best of our knowledge, we are the first to present RFID-enhanced augmented dice that could actually be used in real world gaming applications.

2 Using RFID Technology for Realizing Augmented Dice

There are basically three approaches to build an augmented die:

- A *visual approach* using, for example, a scanner or video camera to capture and analyze the results shown on the die sides.
- An *internal sensors* approach that employs some kind of integrated sensor (e.g., an accelerometer, or force pressure sensors) that internally detects the position and sends it to an application.
- An *external sensors* approach that detects some (non-visual) quality of the rolled die using, e.g., sensors embedded in the tabletop surface.

We have discussed the advantages and disadvantages of the three approaches previously [4] and thus only summarize them briefly in Tab. 1. The use of external sensors offers high robustness, a small die size, and low costs, at the expense of a limited rolling area, however. We believe that these advantages outweigh this limitation and thus decided to explore the use of external sensors in our system.

Table 1. Advantages and disadvantages of different approaches for building augmented dice

Criterion	Visual approach	Internal sensors	External sensors
Size of rolling area	limited	unlimited	limited
Maintenance of die	n/a	batteries, damaged h/w	n/a
Configuration / calibration	yes	possibly	n/a
Robustness of die	very high	low	high
Size of die	small	large	small
Costs of one die	very low	high	low

RFID technology is a representative of this category inasmuch that the actual reading is done by an antenna integrated into the environment which reads identification strings from small, battery-less transponders that can be unobtrusively embedded into everyday objects, allowing us in effect to bridge the gap between the real and the virtual world [1]. Several projects have demonstrated how well-integrated RFID technology in toy and game environments can yield better player support and even enable a range of novel gaming applications [2,3,5]. In the case of an augmented die, the die itself is equipped with passive RFID tags (one tag for each face of the die), which do not require any internal power supply but receive energy through the radio field induced by the reader. The availability of very small tags makes it possible to equip a die with multiple tags that do not require any further maintenance.

Using RFID technology for realizing an augmented die has a number of advantages compared to other technologies, which become apparent when examining the requirements of an augmented die: first, rolling an augmented die must feel the same as rolling a traditional die; second, an augmented die should still be usable in the "old-fashioned" way if the technology is switched off or inoperable; third, the detection system that automatically reads the rolled result must be hidden and unobtrusive; fourth, the system should moreover be inexpensive and easy to use, i.e., the user should not be burdened with configuration, calibration, or maintenance tasks.

The problem, though, is that RFID technology was not designed for precise localization: the main purpose is to detect and identify items in read range of an antenna, e.g., at a loading dock or on a smart shelf. In our case, however, we do not want to read any tags except for one – the one at the bottom of the die – in order to infer which side of the die lies on top. One option would be to dynamically lower the reader field strength until a single tag remains (hopefully the one at the bottom), another to measure the individual field strength reflected from each tag and inferring that the strongest measurement comes from the bottom tag. Unfortunately, RFID readers that support these options are rather bulky and very expensive, rendering their usage suboptimal for entertainment appliances.

To ensure that only a single tag would be read, we initially investigated the use of metallic shielding on the inside of the die to limit the signal strength from all tags but the bottom one. Tags were mounted on the inside and insulated via spacers from an inner aluminum-lined shielding cube. This approach, however, yielded only 80% recognition rate even under ideal conditions. In most cases, the antenna recognized more than one tag, making it difficult to infer with certainty which side was being read. As the tags we used were rather big (i.e., 4x4cm and 2x1cm, respectively), and since the read range of an RFID tag is proportional to the size of its antenna coil, we concluded that smaller tags would yield much better results. In addition to that, smaller tags would also allow for a smaller form factor than our initial prototypes.

3   An Augmented Die with Perfect Recognition Rate

We began work on the next version of our augmented dice using the newly available Philips I-Code1 tags, which feature a size of only 9mm in diameter and very short read ranges. Consequently, we were able to move tags much closer together than before and thus reduce the physical dimensions of the dice. As with our previous

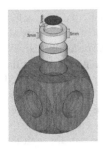 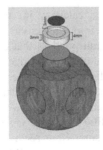  

Fig. 1. The explosion models of the first and the second versions of the 30mm dice (leftmost and left), the third version of the 30mm prototype (right), and the 16mm prototype (rightmost)

Table 2. Characteristics of the four prototypes

Parameter	30mm die (3 prototypes)			16mm die
Hole diameter	15mm	15mm	10mm	10mm
Hole depth	7mm	5.5mm	3mm	2mm
Insulation Material	Aluminum foil	Aluminum foil	n/a	n/a
Insulation from	Cylindrical	Cylindrical	n/a	n/a
Spacer material	Wood	PVC	n/a	n/a
Spacer height	5mm	4mm	n/a	n/a
Cap material	Wood	Wood compound	Wood compound (opt.)	Wood compound (opt.)
Antenna-to-surface distance	0mm	5mm	14mm	22mm

version, only standard off-the-shelf RFID components were used: a FEIG ID ISC.MR101 mid-range reader (HF 13.56MHz), a FEIG ID ISC.ANT100, 10x10 cm antenna, and passive Philips I-Code1 tags (HF 13.56MHz).

The basic recognition principle remained unchanged: by ensuring that only the tag at the bottom of the die is detected, we can unambiguously infer which face of the die is on top. While the read range of the new tags was now much lower, it turned out to be still too high when we simply placed the tags directly on the die surface – more than one tag was detected. As before, our idea thus was to reduce the read range with the help of metallic insulators. We successively constructed three 30mm dice, followed by one 16mm die, all made of spruce wood, with each new die generation iteratively evolving from the previous. Each prototype was subject to an extensive test series similar to [4] to evaluate its performance.

In the first 30mm prototype (see Fig. 1 leftmost and Tab. 2) we inserted aluminum foil cylinders into circular holes of 7mm depth and used wooden spacers to separate the aluminum from the RFID tag. The spacer had a height of 5mm and such a diameter that it would just fit into the drilled hole. A 2mm thin wooden cylinder was put as a cap on the top of each hole to fill the remaining gap. The values were chosen more or less randomly to get a first impression of the behavior. The resulting die performed worse than our previous models: the aluminum cylinders shielded the tags too much, i.e., even the bottom tag would not be detected by the table antenna.

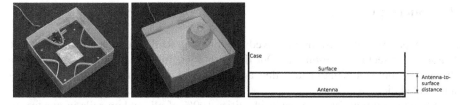

Fig. 2. The antenna of the dicing ground with a metallic foil in the center (left), the dicing ground of the 30mm prototype, and the cross-section of the dicing ground construction (right)

For our second die, we reduced the depth of the holes to 5.5mm and used a circular PVC insulation layer instead of a cylindrical, to reduce the shielding effect (see 2nd image from the left in Fig. 1). Initial measurements were significantly better, but still far from perfect: while the tag at the bottom was now always recognized, one or two other tags were as well. We thus attempted to increase the distance between the antenna and the die, by raising the tabletop surface slightly above the antenna (see Fig. 2 right). After a few tries, we managed to find a solution that turned out to work perfectly: adjusting the antenna-surface-distance to 5mm finally resulted in a recognition rate of 100% according to our test series of several hundred rolls (cf. [4]).

Given these results, we wanted to investigate if we could build a die completely without insulation layers and spacers, by only working with the distance between the antenna and the surface. Using drilled holes of 3mm depth and 10mm diameter, we directly placed the RFID tags inside and covered them with simple stickers. Using the trial-and-error approach as before, we found the optimal distance to be 14mm, again yielding a 100% recognition rate. Another advantage of this approach is the much simpler construction process as well as the reduction of potential imbalances due to construction flaws (i.e., preventing that one side has a higher probability of being rolled); the probabilistic correctness of the dice was also tested by us.

Having achieved perfect recognition rates with the 30mm die, shrinking the die to the more common 16mm size seemed straightforward. However, initial testing with the 16mm die revealed recognition problems at the borders of the surface – the reliable detection of the bottom tag was only possible in the center of the antenna. We realized that the smaller height of the die had moved the side tags closer to the antenna surface. Since the electromagnetic field at the edge of the antenna runs nearly parallel to the surface, the lower height had moved the side tags into antenna range again. In many cases, the reduced height even allowed the tag on the top side of the die to be identified. Simply increasing the distance between antenna and surface further did not help: at a height of 22mm, no tags were detected near the edges of the antenna anymore, but both the top and the bottom tag were still identified when the die was placed squarely in the antenna center.

To help even out the antenna field, we used two approaches: first, in order to weaken the field strength at the center, we placed a 35x35mm aluminum foil as an insulator at the center of the antenna (see Fig. 2 left). Second, to avoid the problematic border region, we added a physical barrier that restricted the tabletop surface to 90x90mm (compared to 100x100mm before, see Fig. 2 center). These modifications finally yielded a recognition rate of 100% using the 16mm die, though at the cost of a slightly smaller dicing area.

4 Conclusions

In this paper we presented the improved version of an RFID-based augmented die that features a perfect recognition rate. Our final prototype fully resembles an off-the-shelf die with 16mm side length and is thus an appropriate replacement of traditional, non-augmented dice.

While our current setup correctly identifies 100% of all random rolls in our test, it comes at the expense of a carefully constructed "tabletop surface." Increasing this area will most likely involve another careful round of tuning. Previous investigations into bigger (off-the-shelf) antennas, as well as into the use of antenna arrays, showed that the created field is too heterogeneous. Additionally, due to the nature of RFID, our setup is sensitive to the immediate environment, especially the table it is placed on. A solution could be to include a shielding construction around the whole dicing ground, but this would come at the price of increased size and a more expensive construction.

Admittedly, using RFID for constructing augmented dice is a "hack," as this technology was never designed for precise localization. The high sensitivity of the RF field requires an unwieldy trial-and-error process. Furthermore, we have yet to confirm whether our dice are capable of being rolled several thousand times without compromising the perfect recognition rate, which would be the prerequisite for real-world applications.

Nonetheless, in our opinion, the benefits of using RFID technology for external detection outweigh its disadvantages: an RFID-based solution is maintenance-free and the detection devices can be invisibly integrated into the environment (e.g., a game board). The continuously decreasing costs for standard RFID equipment, as used in this project, further strengthen this assumption. In our previous work we concluded, "if we are able to construct an even smaller version of our dice, e.g., 1x1 cm in size, we could close the gap between the real and virtual worlds in a truly pervasive and unobtrusive way." We hopefully have come significantly closer.

References

1. Benford, S., Magerkurth, C., Ljungstrand, P.: Bridging the physical and digital in pervasive gaming. Communications of ACM 48(3), 54–57 (2005)
2. Bohn, J.: The Smart Jigsaw Puzzle Assistant: Using RFID Technology for Building Augmented Real-World Games. In: Proceedings of 1st International Workshop on Pervasive Gaming Applications (PerGames 2004), Vienna, Austria (April 2004)
3. Floerkemeier, C., Mattern, F.: Smart Playing Cards – Enhancing the Gaming Experience with RFID. In: Proceedings of PerGames 2006, Dublin, Ireland (May 2006)
4. Hinske, S., Langheinrich, M.: RFIDice – Augmenting Tabletop Dice with RFID. In: Proceedings of PerGames 2007, Salzburg, Austria (June 2007)
5. Magerkurth, C., Memisoglu, M., Engelke, T., Streitz, N.: Towards the next generation of tabletop gaming experiences. In: Proceedings of the 2004 conference on Graphics interface (GI 2004), School of Computer Science, University of Waterloo, Waterloo, Ontario, Canada, pp. 73–80 (2004)

ASEBA-Challenge: An Open-Source Multiplayer Introduction to Mobile Robots Programming

Stéphane Magnenat[1], Basilio Noris[2], and Francesco Mondada[1]

[1] LSRO laboratory, EPFL, 1015 Lausanne, Switzerland
stephane at magnenat dot net
http://mobots.epfl.ch/aseba.html
[2] LASA laboratory, EPFL, 1015 Lausanne, Switzerland

Abstract. We present in this paper a realistic looking robotic survival challenge simulation. Using a model of the e-puck, an open-source mobile robot designed for educational purposes, our simulation allows several players to program the behaviour of e-pucks competing for food. The simulation was tested and well accepted by a hundred children between 7 and 16 years of age. We think that this type of simulations holds a great pedagogical potential because of their inherent fun.

1 Introduction

Teaching robots programming is complicated. Indeed, to be able to successfully program even the simplest behaviour, one has to understand the basics of programming as well as the basics of robotics. The firsts encompass concepts such as variable, execution flow, loops, and so on. The seconds encompass concepts such as sensors, actuators, mobility, perception-action loops, and so on. Yet teaching robots programming, but also teaching programming *through* robots, holds a tremendous pedagogical potential because of the innate human empathy towards animated artifacts, in particular from young people. For example, in our university we use this interest and teach embedded programming to micro-engineering students using robots. We also run a yearly robotic contest.

In this paper we present ASEBA-Challenge, an open-source multiplayer game tailored at teaching mobile robots programming. We also present the result of its deployment in a general public event where it was used by hundred children between 7 and 16 years. ASEBA-Challenge is composed of two parts: a shared 3d arena where simulated robots evolve, and one integrated development environment per player in which they can program and debug their robots. Our goal with this setup is to push down the minimal amount of burden needed to program the robots, and thus to maximize the fun o of the players and the educational value.

ASEBA-Challenge is part of the ASEBA technology, which also works on physical robots of different complexities. In particular, we simulate the e-puck mobile robot which exists physically and the controller can be ported to it with minor changes (the real sensors are less idealistic). Therefore we provide a smooth educational path for people interested in real-world robotics.

P. Markopoulos et al. (Eds.): Fun and Games 2008, LNCS 5294, pp. 65–74, 2008.

2   Related Work

In this section we present some noteworthy approaches that teach programming through mobile agents, physical or virtual. Our aim is not to give an exhaustive survey of the field, but rather to plunge ASEBA-Challenge into context.

The Logo programming language is an early attempt to teach programming with fun [3]. At its root, Logo is a user-friendly dialect of Lisp, but is mostly known for its use in education through its turtle graphics. In this mode, it allows drawing of vector graphics by procedural programming of a virtual turtle. The turtle holds a pen and its movements produce graphics. It is easy to produce nice looking graphics and Logo is motivating for students.

The Lego Mindstorms is probably the easiest way to build physical robots [5]. The Mindstorms consists of a Lego brick enclosing a microcontroller and batteries. It can simultaneously connect to three motors and three sensors out of a large set, including touch, sound, light, ultrasonic, etc. The Mindstorms is an ideal tool for introducing children to robotics, as it allows them to build robots of increasing complexity with bricks they are familiar with. Furthermore, the Mindstorms set provides a graphical programming environment. Unfortunately, being a set of physical devices, it is expensive and is subject to robustness and noise issues.

More recently, the availability of quality game engines including physical simulators, scripting, and display opened new educational possibilities. By allowing children to program worlds they are already familiar with, modding a video games [2] holds a good potential for education. This approach being recent, it still lacks pedagogical maturity: the development tools typically do not provide any debugger, and the games do not provide pedagogical tutorials custom tailored at modding.

Rat's life[1] is a robot programming contest, based on the Webots simulator [7] and the e-puck robot. Like ASEBA-Challenge, it allows players to compete in a virtual arena using a model of the e-puck. Unlike ASEBA-Challenge, the robots must be programmed in C, which is more complex and less user-friendly than our script. Moreover, only two players can compete concurrently and the edit/test cycle of the robot behaviour is much slower. Rat's life is using more standard technologies than ASEBA-Challenge and one can easily build its arena with Lego. Porting is easy, but at the price of a reduced user-friendliness. It also radiates less fun than ASEBA-Challenge, lacking the artistic touch of a video game that is important to attract and retain the attention of players.

Ceebot from Epsitec[2] is one of the closest works to ASEBA-Challenge. In Ceebot, the player also programs a simulated robot in a 3d environment. Ceebot comes with an elaborate tutorial of high educational quality. While Ceebot has a more sophisticated language (including objects, ...) and environments than ASEBA-Challenge, it lacks the multiplayer aspect and the portability to a physical robot.

---

[1] http://www.ratslife.org
[2] http://www.ceebot.com/ceebot/index-e.php

Each of these approaches brings a creative solution to streamline the learning of programming, yet none of them combine the fast develop/test cycle of an integrated development environment, the social dynamics of a multiplayer game, and the deep motivation inherent to robotics. ASEBA-Challenge combines the three.

3   ASEBA-Challenge

ASEBA-Challenge is a mobile robots simulation game where several robots compete for limited food resources in a closed arena. Each robot starts with a given amount of energy that decreases over time. When the robot feeds, the energy increases, as do its chances of survival. Points are earned by staying alive as long as possible. When the energy of a robot reaches zero, the points earned are halved and its energy is reset to the initial value. When the game starts, the robots are immobile at a random location in the arena.

The player connects to a robot and programs its behaviour using a set of simple instructions and conditional switches. The player can lay down the first blocks of behaviour in a single player environment. Once the basic elements are accomplished, such as endowing the robot with obstacle avoidance abilities, the player can connect to a multiplayer arena to test and fine-tune the performance of the robot against the other players.

3.1   Underlying Technologies

ASEBA-Challenge is based on three open-source technologies we have developed: ASEBA, the e-puck robot, and the Enki simulator.

ASEBA is a framework to ease the development of robots controllers. Its core is a tiny virtual machine with embedded debugging logic, small enough to run on any 16 bits microcontroller or better. This virtual machine provides dynamism (loading the program is very fast) and safeness (no script mistake can crash the robot). An integrated development environment interacts with several of those virtual machines concurrently through events, which makes ASEBA suitable for developing controllers for multi-processors robots [6] or collective robotics experiments. In ASEBA-Challenge, each robot runs one virtual machine.

The e-puck is an open-source/open-hardware educational differential wheeled robot[3] (Figure 2, right). It consists of a cylinder of about 7 cm in diameter and embeds a large number of sensors: height infrared around its body, three microphones, a three axis accelerometer, and a VGA camera. It also provides a loudspeaker and a LEDs ring. At the time of writing, a fully assembled and tested e-puck is typically available from vendors at the price of 950 CHF.

Enki[4] is an open-source robot simulator that we use to simulate the e-puck. Enki provides collision and limited physics support for robots evolving on a flat

---

[3] The e-puck mechanical and electrical schematics, blueprints, and source code are freely available at http://www.e-puck.org

[4] http://home.gna.org/enki

surface. It includes a realistic model of the e-puck infrared sensors, as well as a simplified model of its camera.

3.2   Arena

In the development of an environment for mobile robot programming, aesthetic considerations are seldom of paramount importance. However, our goal is to introduce children and young people to robots programming in an entertaining way. For this reason we opted for a realistic looking, yet minimalist environment. The game arena consists of a closed space with four food stations and a number of energy-hungry e-pucks (see Figure 1).

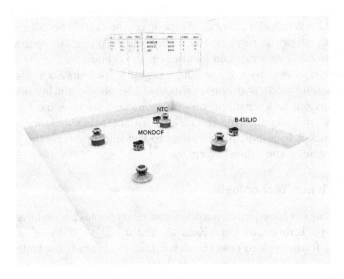

Fig. 1. The ASEBA-Challenge arena. A number of e-pucks searching for the food sources.

In developing the graphics and layout of the simulated environment, we wanted to have a clean and easily readable interface while attaining a high level of realism. Moreover we wanted the system to run in real-time on any type of machine. We modeled the main elements of the environment (namely the e-puck robot, the arena, and the food stations) using a commercial 3d modeling software (Newtek Lightwave3d[5]). The e-puck model was constructed from scratch using the technical design files as blueprints and counts 1671 polygons. As we were not aiming for fancy graphical effects but for a believable minimalist environment, we opted for a static lighting environment, and computed for each model the radiosity [4] response to the global lighting. Figure 2 shows the e-puck in the different stages of development. Once the color texture and radiosity maps are generated and composed together, we use simple OpenGL 1.1 texture mapping to display them in real-time. The shadow for the e-puck and food stations is added

---

[5] http://www.lightwave3d.com

Fig. 2. Development steps for the creation of the e-puck model. Left to right: wireframe of the model; texture map; radiosity map; texture and radiosity maps combined; photo of the real robot.

as an alpha-layered polygon with radiosity map attached to the bottom of the model. The whole system counts five 1024x1024 textures (color and shadow maps for the e-puck and food stations, radiosity for the arena). A standard computer can load a score of robots with no apparent drop in performance.

These choices allow ASEBA-Challenge to target a large public (because of reasonable graphics cards requirements) while being attractive enough to retain the attention of children for a long time. Moreover, a realistic looking robot facilitates the identification with a physical robot.

3.3   Integrated Development Environment

When learning programming, it is important to have a gentle, tolerant, and failsafe environment. In ASEBA-Challenge, players program their robots through an integrated development environment, which provides the following features (Figure 3):

- **Failsafe.** No script mistake can crash neither the environment nor the robot.
- **Syntax highlighting.** The script editor highlights the syntax and colors errors in red. This increases the readability of the scripts.
- **Instant compilation.** The environment recompiles the script while the player is typing it. The result of compilation (success or a description of the error) is displayed below the editor, which permits the correction of errors as soon as they appear.
- **Variables inspection.** The environment lists the variables available on the robot along with their values. The player can update this list in a single click.
- **Debugger.** The environment integrates a debugger. It gives the current execution status, supports continuous execution, step by step, and breakpoints. A right click inside the script editor allows to set or clear a breakpoint on a specific line.

3.4   Programming Language

Players program their robots by writing scripts in a simple language. Syntactically, this language resembles *matlab*. This similarity enables players of

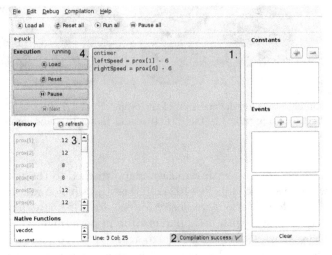

Fig. 3. Screenshot of the integrated development environment. The enclosed elements are the following (clockwise): 1. Editor with syntax highlighting; 2. Message bar from instant compilation; 3. Variables and their values; 4. Debug commands.

ASEBA-Challenge to feel at ease with most scripting languages. Semantically, this language is a simple imperative programming language with a single basic type (16 bit signed integers) and arrays. This simplicity allows players to program behaviours with no prior knowledge of a type system, integers being the most natural type of variables to the general public.

The rationale behind building a language/compiler from scratch is to have the full control over the language syntax and semantic, over the build process, and over the generated bytecode. This allowed us to implement the aforementioned integrated development editor, including the remote debugging of the robot, with relative ease.

We will now take on describing the features of ASEBA script that are useful from an educational point of view[6]:

– **Comments.** Comments begin with a **#** and terminate at the end of the line.

```
# this is a comment
var b    # another comment
```

– **Variables.** Variables refer either to single scalar values or to arrays of scalar values. The values are comprised between -32768 and 32767, which is the range of 16 bit signed integers. We can access arrays elements using the usual square parenthesis operator; arrays indexes begin at zero.

```
var a
var b = 0
var c [10]
var d [3] = 2, 3, 4
```

---

[6] The complete list of features is available at http://mobots.epfl.ch/aseba.html

- **Expressions** and **assignations.** Expressions allow mathematical computations and are written using the normal mathematical infix syntax. Assignations use the keyword = and set the result of the computation of an expression to a scalar variable or to an array element. ASEBA provides the operators +, -, *, /, % (modulo), << (left shift), and >> (right shift). The most precedent operators are *, /, %; followed by + and -; followed by << and >>. To evaluate an expression in a different order, we can use a pair of parenthesis to group a sub-expression.

```
a = 1 + 1
b = (a - 7) % 5
b = b + d[0]
c[a] = d[a]
```

- **Conditionals.** ASEBA provides the if conditional and the operators ==, !=, >, >=, <, and <=.
  The block following the if is executed if the condition is true, and the code following the else if it is false.

```
if  a - b > c[0]  then
      c[0] = a
else
      b = 0
end
```

- **Loops.** Two constructs allow the creation of loops: while and for.
  A while loop repeatedly executes a block of code as long as the condition is true. The condition is of the same form as the one if uses.

```
while  i < 10  do
      v = v + i * i
      i = i + 1
end
```

A for loop allows a variable to iterate over a range of integers, with an optional step size.

```
for  i  in  1:10  do
      v = v + i * i
end
for  i  in  30:1  step  -3  do
      v = v - i * i
end
```

4   Results

We presented ASEBA-Challenge at the EPFL Robotics Festival the 19th of April 2008 (Figure 4). During a whole day, more than a hundred of children participated to the challenge in groups of around 30 people. Although the festival was a general public event, because of its location we had the feeling that a large

Fig. 4. ASEBA-Challenge deployment at the EPFL Robotics Festival the 19th of April 2008. Photos: Alain Herzog.

```
# obstacle avoidance using the        # food sources homing using
# proximity sensors                   # a simple three pixels camera

ontimer                               ontimer
var distanceToWall = prox[0] +          leftSpeed = -10
prox[1] + prox[6] + prox[7]             rightSpeed = -5

if distanceToWall < 48 then           if camB[0] > 55 then
    leftSpeed = 10                        leftSpeed = -10
    rightSpeed = -10                      rightSpeed = 10
else                                  end
    leftSpeed = 10                    if camB[2] > 55 then
    rightSpeed = 10                       leftSpeed = 10
end                                       rightSpeed = -10
                                      end
                                      if camB[1] > 55 then
                                          leftSpeed = 10
                                          rightSpeed = 10
                                      end
```

Fig. 5. Examples of codes children wrote at the EPFL Robotics Festival. Distances to walls are in cm, camera values are in percentage of the color component intensity, and wheel speeds are in cm/s. These units correspond to the simple mode of ASEBA-Challenge. The latter can also be compiled with realistic sensors responses corresponding to the physical e-puck.

proportion of the children had at least one parent of engineering profession. The children were of both sexes and aged between 7 and 16 years (avg. 12 years). Children programmed their robots either alone or in pairs on a computer station. A staff of 6 computer scientists introduced and supervised the event giving explanations whenever the need arose. Albeit children initially developed their robots inside their own arena, the best robots were allowed to compete in two arenas projected on the front of the room. All the participants were able to program the basic behaviours into the robots (obstacle avoidance, see Figure 5, left) following instructions and with help from the support staff in case of block, and about half of them managed to implement the more advanced behaviours (going to food sources, see Figure 5, right) by their own means. Three children played with the real e-puck and were able to program it, including advanced sensors such as the accelerometer. A good number of people inquired on the availability of the software.

4.1   User-Friendliness

Most of the players enjoyed endowing the robots with the ability to navigate the arena and look for food. The players were initially puzzled because the goal was not to manually control the robot, but to give it an autonomous behaviour. This problem seemed to be made worst because of the Braitenberg style [1] examples from the tutorial; and switching explanations to an `if condition then action` style of programming helped the players to understand faster. However, the players soon overcame this difficulty and most of them acquired a sort of fondness for their robot; the term pet was mentioned more than once. One frequent remark was that the programming language should be in french[7]. The assistants had to translate commands such as `if`, `else`, and the names of variables for the youngest children. Some children made remarks on the presence of unused panels in the integrated development environment. These panels were designed for the research use of the integrated development environment, they were not necessary for ASEBA-Challenge.

We have also noticed that one of the most frequent difficulty was the abstraction from the robot sensors values to the variables content. To improve the pedagogical experience, we think that we should add a schematic graphical display of the sensors values. Technically, we could achieve this by adding a plugin interface to the integrated development environment.

As newcomers entered the contest every hour, we gave them a short talk describing the setup, the robot, and the goal. In overall, people managed to get the basic behaviours working in 45 minutes and the more complex ones in one hour and an half.

4.2   Interaction

During the later part of the game, when players had mastered the basic elements of ASEBA-Challenge, a plethora of interesting behaviours appeared.

Some players started using the robot colored ring to trick other robots into escaping from or following them. As most robots were looking for red and blue objects as source of food, the simpler robots were heavily affected by the behaviour of the naughtier ones. This unleashed a response from the other players who had then to cope both with the environment and the other players, requiring their programs to be more dynamical and complex.

Some children also played with several robots in the arena on their own computer, to implement social games with their robots. For instance, a girl programmed several robots to change their colors when they got close to each

---

[7] EPFL is in the french-speaking part of Switzerland.

other. We think that the interest of children towards behaviours involving multiple robots should be further encouraged, for instance by making a derived game where children could play with several robot each.

5   Conclusion

We presented an open-source challenge game in a mobile robots feeding/survival simulation. The robots simulation is realistic looking and sufficiently easy to understand even for children as young as 7 years of age. The interaction between the robots makes the game stimulating in multiplayer mode.

Moreover, the availability of a physical robot allows further pedagogical experience for interested children. While this robot is more expensive than, for instance, a Lego Mindstorms; its union with a realistic looking simulation environment can expose more children to programming while providing only a small amount of physical devices. This can reduce the overall cost, despite the higher price of the individual robot.

Finally, we observe that children enjoy the nice looking graphics and the thrilling gameplay of ASEBA-Challenge. We think that such games hold a great pedagogical potential because of their inherent fun.

Acknowledgments

We thank the participants and the staff of the robotics festival. In particular: Mara Dalla Valle, Cécile Grivaz, Jacques Paul Grivaz, Solaiman Shokur, Jean-Marc Koller, Philippe Retornaz, Martin Voelkle, and Emmanel Eckard. We also thank the four anonymous reviewers for their insightful comments. Finally, we thank Fanny Riedo for correcting the manuscript.

References

1. Braitenberg, V.: Vehicles. MIT Press, Cambridge (1984)
2. El-Nasr, M.S., Smith, B.K.: Learning through game modding. Comput. Entertain. 4(1), 7 (2006)
3. Harvey, B.: Computer Science Logo Style. MIT Press, Cambridge (1997)
4. Jensen, H.W.: Global Illumination Using Photon Maps. In: Rendering Techniques 1996 (Proceedings of the Seventh Eurographics Workshop on Rendering), pp. 21–30. Springer, Heidelberg (1996)
5. Klassner, F.: A case study of lego mindstorms'[TM] suitability for artificial intelligence and robotics courses at the college level. In: SIGCSE 2002: Proceedings of the 33rd SIGCSE technical symposium on Computer science education, pp. 8–12. ACM Press, New York (2002)
6. Magnenat, S., Longchamp, V., Mondada, F.: Aseba, an event-based middleware for distributed robot control. In: Workshops DVD of International Conference on Intelligent Robots and Systems (IROS) (2007)
7. Michel, O.: Webots: Symbiosis between virtual and real mobile robots. In: Heudin, J.-C. (ed.) VW 1998. LNCS (LNAI), vol. 1434, pp. 254–263. Springer, Heidelberg (1998)

Test-Bed for Multimodal Games on Mobile Devices

Marcello Coiana[1], Alex Conconi[2], Laurence Nigay[3], and Michael Ortega[3]

[1] Arcadia Design,
Loc. Is Coras – CP. 360 0928 Sestu, Italy
marcello.coiana@arcadiadesign.it
[2] TXT e-solution,
Via Frigia 27 20126 Milano, Italy
alex.conconi@txt.it
[3] Grenoble Informatics Laboratory (LIG), University of Grenoble 1,
38042 Grenoble, France
{laurence.nigay,michael.ortega}@imag.fr

Abstract. We present a test-bed platform for the iterative design of multimodal games on a mobile phone or a PDA. While our test-bed platform is general to multimodal systems, in this paper we focus on games on mobile devices, since games are intrinsically multimodal, enriching thus the gaming experience and potential for interaction innovations. As part of a player-centered design approach, our goal is to be able to quickly test various forms of multimodal interaction before beginning with the development of the final multimodal game on mobile devices. We adopt a micro-approach for our game test-bed, focusing on multimodal interaction for generic tasks, including moving of an object or a character. Our test-bed facilitates the efficient exploration of the multimodal design space and enables controlled experiments of the designed interaction in-lab and/or in-situ.

Keywords: Game, Multimodality, Mobile Device, Test-Bed Platform.

1 Introduction

The first commercialization of many user interface innovations appeared in games, even though they were invented in research environments [7]. Nowadays, these innovative modalities and multimodal interaction techniques, are evident in current high-end platform games (e.g. Nintendo Wii). While in such platform games, innovative modalities and multimodality are becoming more and more popular, multimodality in mobile games is still in its infancy. In the few studies focusing on multimodal mobile games, the considered modalities are mainly reduced to speech and graphics [16] as well as location (i.e., a passive/perceptual modality) as in the pervasive mobile game ARQuake [13]. Moreover except for a few mobile phones that include sensors such as accelerometers, proximity sensors and tactile screen with two-handed interaction as in the recent iPhone [10], multimodality on mobile devices is far from being mature.

P. Markopoulos et al. (Eds.): Fun and Games 2008, LNCS 5294, pp. 75–87, 2008.

However, as the mobile game market tends to follow the more mature console/PC game market and with the recent growing diffusion of multimodal phones, game developers will be more and more interested in following this new trend. Moreover the players will become more demanding in terms of involvement in the mobile games as they are used to interacting with different modalities in PC/console games. Game performance must match or exceed the users' expectations. As a consequence, in order to anticipate the users requirements, and in order to be ready for the market challenge, the game developers need a prototyping platform to experiment on new modalities and forms of multimodality inside their mobile games. In this paper we address this issue by presenting a game test-bed that allows the rapid development of prototypes as part of an iterative user-centered design. Our game test-bed enables the game designers to experiment on new pure or combined modalities inside their games on mobile devices, while overcoming the current interactive limitations of mobile devices. Therefore the test-bed enables the game designers/developers to focus on the experience of the player before developing the final game running on mobile devices. When studying game designer practices, we learned that the experience is key. Since many modalities are available on PC, our test-bed for multimodal mobile games establishes a bridge between two platforms - the PC and the mobile device. The design, development and evaluation of our test-bed have been conducted as part of a multidisciplinary European project, OpenInterface [12] that involves game designers, HCI designers, software developers as well as psychologists and ergonomics.

The structure of the paper is as follows: We first explain the adopted iterative user-centered design approach and the key role of the test-bed in order to fully understand the scope of our mobile game test-bed. We then provide an overview of the underlying software framework used to develop the test-bed, namely OpenInterface, and then present the mobile game test-bed. We finally present an illustrative example of the test-bed, the Funny rabbit game.

2 Player-Centered Design Approach and Test-Bed

Following the ISO standard human-centered design process for interactive systems (ISO 13407 Model, 1999), we adopt an iterative user-centered design approach for designing mobile games. Such an approach for the design of games involves many different types of expertise. Two of the most common groups involved in user interface design are human factors specialists and programmers [1]. For games, graphic and game designers are also involved. The user-centered design approach aims at bringing all these types of expertise together. The four main activities of the design approach, namely 1- Specify the context of use 2- Specify the user requirements 3- Produce design solutions 4- Evaluate designs against requirements, are iterative. For games, the process is truly iterative as shown in Figure 1, and the need for intensive playtest is crucial. The game is evolving from an initial starting point as the designer is designing and balancing the game play of the title [6]. We address this issue of "evaluating designs against requirements" by providing a test-bed for playtesting mobile games. Our test-bed allows the rapid prototyping of the mobile games for performing test with players. Such an approach is also called a player-centered design approach [8] or experience-centered design approach.

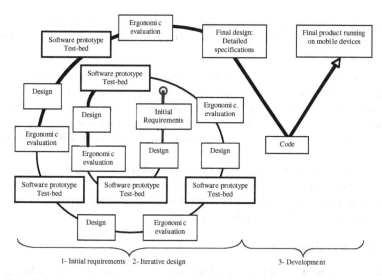

Fig. 1. Overall design and development process. The game test-bed supports the iterative user-centered design. The process comprises three main phases: 1-Initial Requirements 2-Design phase based on prototypes that are iteratively evaluated, modified and refined to lead to detailed specifications. 3- Development based on a more classical approach from software engineering as in the IntuiSign design and development process [14].

Although there is no common agreement on what kind of usability evaluation methods can and should be used to enhance the design of games, player experience will be particularly influenced by input and output modalities and interaction techniques [2]. Multimodality plays a central role in games since the only incentive to use a game is the pleasure derived from the interaction. In addition the flexibility of multimodal interaction enables us to support various player types that also enhance playability [8]. Moreover it has been shown that multimodality in games also enhances the interaction robustness by compensating the weakness of one modality by the strengths of other modalities, making the mobile game more enjoyable in any given environment [11].

To be able to experience a rich set of innovative pure or combined modalities, the game test-bed enables the rapid development of multimodal prototypes. While the test-bed enables us to explore multiple design solutions in terms of multimodal interaction and to experience them with players manipulating a mobile device, the final version of the game will then be developed on mobile devices: this is modeled in Figure 1 by the right branch. The resulting overall design and development process corresponds to the structure of the IntuiSign design and development process [14], an attempt to integrate the well-know user-centered iterative design in a process that fits within the industry constraints.

3   OpenInterface Framework for Multimodal Interaction

For developing the mobile game test-bed, we base ourselves on the OpenInterface framework, an environment for the rapid development of multimodal interactive systems. The OpenInterface (OI) framework is made of an underlying platform, namely OpenInterface platform, and the OpenInterface Interaction Development Environment (OIDE).

- The OI platform [3] is a component-based platform that handles distributed heterogeneous components based on different technologies (Java, C++, Matlab, Python, .NET). It allows the integration of existing interaction techniques written in different languages. The platform includes a tool for creating new components (i.e., interaction techniques) from existing code without modifying the original code.
- The OIDE is a component-based system built on top of the OI platform. OIDE adds development tools offering access to interaction capabilities at multiple levels of abstraction. The OIDE includes a component repository as well as construction, debugging, and logging tools.

3.1 Component Repository

The OIDE component repository includes modalities both developed "in-house" (e.g., speech recognition, video "finger tracker", accelerometer-based gesture recognition) and also accessible via proxies to other component sets (e.g., Phidgets, ARToolkit). Our components include device drivers, interaction techniques, multimodal fusion mechanisms, development services and developer-defined combinations. OIDE supports descriptions, querying and access in an extensible set of description schemas. Within the vast world of possibilities for input modalities (from the user to the system) as well as for outputs (from the system to the user), we distinguish two types of modalities: the active and passive modalities [5]. For inputs, active modalities are used by the user to issue a command to the computer (e.g., a voice command or a gesture recognized by a camera). Passive modalities refer to information that is not explicitly expressed by the user, but automatically captured for enhancing the execution of a task. For example, in the "Put that there" seminal multimodal demonstrator of R. Bolt [4], that combines speech and gesture, eye tracking was used for disambiguating among multiple objects on screen. For games, examples include location-aware games and more generally pervasive mobile games [13]. A huge variety of passive modalities can be used in games including emotion, bio-signal processing and eye-movement.

3.2 Construction and Logging Tools

Figure 2 illustrates the OIDE Graphical Editor in which components accessible via the repository can be inspected, configured, linked to other components and to external services or to application functionality, in the assembly view. The result can be either an individual technique or a fully functional user interface to an application. In the example of Figure 2, a Speech recognition component and a Wiimote component are both connected to a fusion component. The latter combines the received events in a complementary way in order to obtain a complete task "Go there", combining speech and gesture with the Wiimote. The graphically specified pipe-line of OpenInterface components therefore defines a generic multimodal technique that can be then be connected to an application.

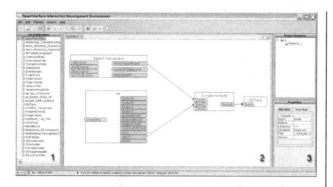

Fig. 2. Overview of the OIDE graphical editor: 1-Palette of components (modalities, devices, fusion and transformation components). 2- Editing zone for assembling the components and defining an OI component pipeline 3- A component information panel.

Fig. 3. OIDE Debugging and Logging tools. In the example, the Shake accelerometer events are logged in order to tune the interaction with the mobile game.

The logging tool is responsible for recording multiple component-specific formatted data streams while an OI application is executing [9]. A generic "oscilloscope" display, that can be configured while in use, can be used to display data streams at runtime. In Figure 3, the oscilloscope shows data at the lowest level of abstraction, direct from the device itself (in the example, the SHAKE device) but it is also possible to display application-level data (as shown in Figure 7).

4   Game Test-Bed on Mobile Devices

Focusing on multimodal interaction, the game test-bed is based on the OpenInterface (OI) framework described in the previous section. Therefore the test-bed demands for an architecture that links the OI platform running on a PC with the functional core of mobile games running on devices such as PDAs or Smartphones. Test-bed applications are expected to be flexible and open, to allow fast prototyping for experimentation, but also consistent and adequately performing, in order to address actual use cases. This tradeoff requires careful architectural choices. Besides this main functional requirement (i.e., support the communication between the OI platform and game functional core), some non-functional requirements apply, namely technical constraints (e.g., compatibility with the OI framework and with legacy functional core technology) and business constraints (e.g., support most widespread mobile phones). Furthermore we identify and address quality attributes including usability (provide an easy to use RAD framework for developers of the game functional core and interaction), modifiability (take into account that test-bed scenarios may involve unpredictability) and performance (avoid user interface sluggishness and provide stable and acceptable response times).

Our architecture is based on a layered protocol stack approach, as shown in Figure 4. We designed two additional components running inside the OI platform (also called OI

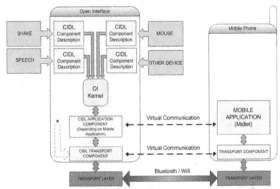

* Any other component can use the Transport Component to communicate with remote devices using the protocol described in the transport layer.

Fig. 4. Test-bed architecture connecting the OpenInterface platform running on a PC with a game application running on a mobile device

runtime kernel above): the Application Component and the Transport Component. The Application Component acts as a proxy for the mobile application. It is connected with other OI components through the OI platform pipe. Whenever an event from any connected component occurs, the Application Component parses such an event and sends a corresponding message to the mobile application through the Transport Component. The CIDL (i.e. the OpenInterface XML description) of the Application Component provides sinks and sources that manage the communication with the other OI components handling the input and output multimodal interaction. For example Figure 4 presents a setup that includes the SHAKE device, a Speech Recognition engine and a traditional mouse, all plugged into the OI platform. Such devices and modalities have been selected and assembled using the OIDE editor of Figure 2. An additional sink/source pair in the Application Component is connected to the Transport Component.

The Transport Component defines an interface for transferring messages from the OI platform to the mobile game and vice versa. Specific implementations of the Transport Component adopt different physical transport layers, such as Bluetooth or TCP/IP over WiFi. It is worth noting that the abstract transport layer interface also allows non physical connection, when the OI platform and the test-bed functional core are running on the same machine.

The communication protocol between the Application Component and the Mobile Application is message based. Messages are built by the Application Component in accordance with a protocol that the mobile application understands. When designing the message protocol, we identified three main approaches based on the level of abstraction of the exchanged messages:

- Low level: Send raw input from devices and modalities to the mobile application;
- High level: Send application-dependent events to the mobile application. This requires abstracting modality-dependent events in order to obtain application-dependent events (e.g. "Quit Game", "Move Player Up", "Open Inventory");

- Mid level: Send modality-independent and application-independent events to the mobile application. This solution implies abstracting the modality-dependent events into generic meta-events (e.g. "ESC", "UP", "START") creating hence an enhanced virtual gamepad.

On the one hand, the low level approach has the downside of deporting to the mobile application the computational charge of processing the (potentially heavy) raw data flow. On the other hand, the high level approach requires no processing. Representing however each event for every application makes the Application Component become too complex. It also implies a strong interdependence between the Application Component and the mobile application which goes against the modifiabity quality attribute. The mid level approach appears to be the optimal tradeoff: It performs the data flow processing inside the OI platform on the PC, but the internal logic of the OI component pipeline is not too tightly bound to the mobile application functionalities. Nevertheless a mixed approach combining the three above approaches is possible since the OI platform pipe allows stacking events at different levels of abstraction. These levels of abstraction are defined by the power of abstraction (multimodal inputs) or concretization (multimodal outputs) of the function performed by the OI component pipeline. The notion of level of abstraction expresses the degree of transformation that the interpretation and rendering functions realized by the OI component pipeline perform on information.

5   Illustrative Example: Funny Rabbit

From a game designer's point of view, the development of a game begins with a brilliant idea and ends with the definition of the smallest detail of interaction to increase the player's experience and engagement in the game. Our test-bed is dedicated to the design of the interaction, after sketches and storyboards that will be used in the beginning of the development.

For designing the interaction, we apply a hierarchical task analysis, compatible with the approach of the game tools that organize a game in missions, objectives, goals, triggers and so on. The game can be described in terms of interactive tasks and subtasks, breaking down the steps of a task performed by a player. Tasks and subtasks describe goals and actions. For example a task can be a main goal and its subtasks the actions needed to reach this goal:

$$Game = \{task1, ... taskn\} \ Taski = \{subtask1 , ... subtaskn\}$$

For performing each elementary subtask of a given task (abstract task), interaction modalities must be selected that leads us to define concrete tasks. For example an abstract task is <Move a character to the left> and a concrete task <Press left direction key>. In a standard mobile game, each task is performed by the player in a standard way with only one modality namely mod1(Keyboard): $task1->mod1 ... taskn->mod1$.

In this way, the design process is more focused on the abstract tasks rather than the concrete tasks. This happens because the way the tasks are performed by the player (concrete tasks) is given for granted for a game designer: for instance the movement of an object or a character is specified using the direction keys or the joypad. On the contrary, with our game test-bed, the design process focuses on both the abstract and concrete tasks. For an elementary abstract task, several pure or combined modalities can be chosen for defining the corresponding concrete task:

$$task1 \quad ->mod1 \ldots \quad task1->modn$$

Our test-bed allows the designer to explore different modalities for a given task. For performing each elementary task (abstract task), several pure or combined modalities can be designed (concrete task). To do so, the player's experience is always at the centre of the whole design process as shown in Figure 1. Questions raised during the iterative design process include: Is the player satisfied? Is the player engaged in the game? Is it fun? Is it cool? These issues are addressed for each task during the design. Concrete tasks are not given for granted anymore, leading to new unexpected experiences for the player and opening new doors to the creativeness of the game designer. We illustrate this design process and the use of the test-bed in the context of our Funny rabbit game of Figure 5. We show how a task can be extracted from a standard game on mobile devices to study different forms of multimodality for performing it.

In terms of the overall architecture of the test-bed, the functional core (logic of the game) of Funny rabbit is running on the mobile phone. Moreover the graphical outputs are also managed outside the OpenInterface framework, the corresponding code running on the mobile phone. To consider a game as close as possible to the state of the art in games, Funny rabbit is a 3D rendered graphic game. The player controls the movement of a 3D character, chooses which object to interact with, and examines 3D objects with 2 degrees of freedom. These are commonest tasks of a game. Thus, even though we illustrate the test-bed by considering the Funny rabbit game, the designed concrete tasks can be used for another game since they are concrete but generic.

The main task or goal of Funny rabbit is <find the rabbit that is hidden in a chest>. Such high level task is decomposed into three subtasks, illustrated in Figure 6: (1) move (the character), (2) select (the chest), (3) examine (the objects inside the chest).

For the design, we need to proceed further in the hierarchical task analysis and refine the three above tasks in terms of elementary abstract tasks. For example the task <move> is divided into four subtasks: Up, Down, Left and Right. Having identified elementary abstract tasks, we now focus on concrete tasks by considering the modalities to perform such tasks. We start the design of the concrete tasks by considering a first set of interaction devices. For Funny rabbit, we have so far

Fig. 5. The Funny rabbit game   **Fig. 6.** The three tasks Move, Select and Examine

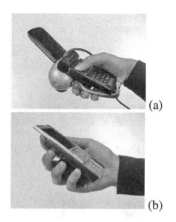

(a)

(b)

Fig. 7. Funny Rabbit: Movement of the player with the webcam

Fig. 8. (a) The webcam with Nokia N93 for moving the 3D character. (b) The SHAKE with Nokia N95 for 3D object examination.

considered the following input devices: a microphone, a SHAKE and a webcam. All of these devices are external to the mobile device (Nokia N93). Based on these three devices, different interaction modalities can be designed. We consider speech commands, 3D movements with the SHAKE and 3D movements recognized by the camera coupled with ARToolkit, as shown in Figure 7. In Funny rabbit, an example of use of these three modalities is the webcam with ARToolkit to move the 3D character (Figure 8-a), speech to issue commands like SELECT, and the accelerometer sensor of the SHAKE for 3D object examination (Figure 8-b).

The three concrete tasks have been specified using the OIDE graphical editor of Figure 3. The resulting OI component pipeline is shown in Figure 9: The OI components "SpeechRecognition" and "Shake" correspond to two modalities, respectively speech command and 3D gesture. Two OI components implement the 3D movement using the webcam. One component "ARToolkit" is generic and corresponds to the ARToolkit functionalities (proxy to access the component sets of the ARToolkit). The second component "Adapter" transforms the ARToolkit events in terms of control commands. Since we reuse a component that was developed to control an helicopter in another game, its port is called HeliControl by the developer of the component. For this modality, we did not develop a specific component but reuse existing ones in the palette of components. The OI component "MultiBTComponent" corresponds to the Transport component of Figure 4 and implements a Bluetooth transport layer. The OI component "EventAdapter" plays the role of the Application component of Figure 4.

The pure or combined modalities that define the concrete tasks can be easily adapted by graphically modifying the OI component pipeline of Figure 9. Indeed several other design possibilities for the concrete tasks could be specified and tested for Funny rabbit. The design solution of Figure 9 is based on continuous input for moving the character: this implies that for every single step of the character an input event is required; thus for keeping the character moving up, the player needs to keep

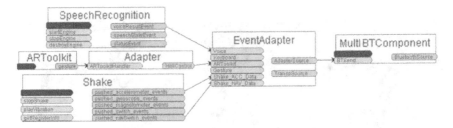

Fig. 9. OI component pipeline that defines the three concrete tasks of Figure 6

Fig. 10. OI component pipeline that defines the selection of an object by using speech

the webcam in the up position, like a virtual airplane cloche. Another design possibility to explore is discrete input implying to manage different movement states of the character: one event will then modify the state of the character. For instance an event "up" will switch the state into -following the north direction- until the player changes the state by a new event, for instance an event "stop". In this example, we change the elementary tasks of Funny rabbit and not the main three tasks of Figure 6. While modifications of the three main tasks will require changing the game (the functional core of the game) running on the mobile phone, modifications of the elementary tasks will be done within the OI framework. For example, speech commands are assigned to change the movement states of the character and the navigation switch of the SHAKE is assigned to stop any movement of the character. Since the modality based on the webcam is then no more used for moving the character, it can be assigned to examine 3D objects. Such design solution is specified by graphically assembling OI components and can be then tested with players.

The level of abstraction of the OI components manipulated in the OIDE graphical editor allows the user to focus on the interaction modalities and their combination. For example, the game designer wants to specify the way to select an object from a list: s/he starts with a voice command. The corresponding OI component pipeline specified with the help of a software developer is shown in Figure 10. Coming back home, s/he remembers that s/he has to pay the bills, so s/he opens the drawer where s/he kept them. While s/he is doing this movement, s/he likes the idea of selection associated to that action. So, the following day s/he wants to do the same with the selection task in the game, and adds a 3D gesture recognition engine that recognizes the opening gesture, using the OIDE graphical editor. To do so, in addition to the ready to use OI component for 3D capture ("Shake" component), a new OI component must be developed by programmers for recognizing the opening gesture ("Opening Gesture" component). A generic OI component for gesture recognition, based on an editor to specify by examples the gestures to be recognized, is under construction. Then the game designer enriches the pipeline with the new component

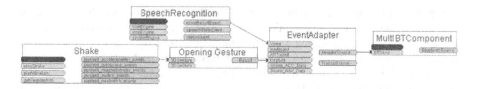

Fig. 11. OI component pipeline (extension of the one of Figure 10) that defines the selection of an object either by using speech or by performing an opening gesture using the SHAKE

as shown in Figure 11. Since the designer likes this way of interacting, s/he also asks the graphical department to make a graphical interface that looks like a drawer. The new prototype will then be evaluated with the help of human factors specialists. Another design solution based on combining the two modalities could also make the interaction more challenging, by combining the opening gesture with a voice command (a magic word for example). Such a design solution simply implies adding a fusion component (Figure 2) before the EventAdapter component in Figure 11.

This simple scenario illustrates the iterative player-centred design of the multimodal interaction of the game and highlights the multidisciplinary character of our design approach as well as the use of our test-bed for quickly developing different prototypes.

6 Conclusion and Future Work

Focusing on multimodal interaction for mobile games, we have presented a test-bed that allows the rapid development of prototypes as a central tool for an iterative player-centered design approach. The key features of our test-bed include:

- The rapid development of design solutions for multimodal interaction, including the combination of existing modalities on mobile devices such as the direction keys of the mobile device keyboard with new innovative modalities,
- The extension of existing mobile games with innovative pure or combined modalities that may not be available today on mobile phones,
- The support for an iterative player-centered design approach involving multiple expertise.

The first informal in-lab evaluation of the Funny rabbit game with a group of 16 users confirms that it is crucial to let players manipulate and experience the game. The evaluated test-bed includes many equivalent modalities for the abstract tasks such as moving the 3D character. For example first feedback was "it is fun" "it is cool". We plan to perform further experiments based on a game scenario including in-field evaluation, carrying the computer in a backpack.

There are several directions for future work on the test-bed for mobile games. We need to further study the design trade-off in the test-bed that leads to us having some input/output modalities managed in the OpenInterface framework and some running directly on the mobile phone with no link with the framework. For example in the Funny Rabbit game, the 3D graphical display is managed outside the OpenInterface framework, running on the mobile phone. This design trade-off has direct impact on the interaction design possibilities since modalities not managed within the framework cannot be combined with other modalities for exploring complementary or redundant usage of modalities. In addition this design trade-off is also based on interaction performance, minimizing the exchanged messages between the framework and the mobile application. This is especially important for the case of continuous feedback (tightly coupled interaction as in Shoogle [15]): indeed the mobile application must send messages to the OpenInterface framework for rendering information. That is why we did not manage the graphical display of the game in the framework. Nevertheless other continuous feedback can be managed in the framework. For example let us consider the case where the player moves a character on screen by tilting the mobile phone while obtaining vibrotactile feedback on the movement speed. In order to produce timely haptic responses, the mobile application must send messages to the OI framework and in particular to the OI component dedicated to the vibrotactile display for presenting the current computed speed.

Finally, in order to show the path from research results to industry requirements, a further step ahead needs to be done: the development of a final product from a prototype, as highlighted in our design and development process of Figure 1. The high level of abstraction of the multimodal interaction that the OpenInterface framework offers to developers, allows a smooth transition from a prototype to a well-engineered system that can satisfy the constraints of the current technology in terms of mobile devices and network performances. To show this smooth transition, we developed a game running on commercially available mobile devices, namely a game validator, that is a sub-part of our prototypes validated using our test-bed.

Acknowledgments. This work is funded by the OpenInterface (OI) European FP6 STREP FP6-035182. The authors thank the contribution of their OI colleagues.

References

1. Bailey, G.: Iterative methodology and designer training in human-computer interface design. In: Proc. of CHI 1995, pp. 198–205. ACM Press, New York (1995)
2. Bernhaupt, R., Eckschlager, M., Tscheligi, M.: Methods for Evaluating Games – How to Measure Usability and User Experience in Games? In: Proc. of ACE 2007, pp. 309–310. ACM Press, New York (2007)
3. Benoit, A., et al.: Multimodal Signal Processing and Interaction for a Driving Simulation: Component-based Architecture. Journal on Multimodal User Interfaces 1(1), 49–58 (2006)
4. Bolt, R.A.: Put-that-there: Voice and gesture at the graphics interface. In: Proc. of SIGGRAPH 1980, vol. 14(3), pp. 262–270 (1980)
5. Bouchet, J., Nigay, L.: ICARE: A Component-Based Approach for the Design and Development of Multimodal Interfaces. In: Extended Abstracts of CHI 2004, pp. 1325–1328. ACM Press, New York (2004)
6. Cherny, L., Clanton, C., Ostrom, E.: Entertainment is a human factor: a CHI 1997 workshop on game design and HCI. ACM SIGCHI Bulletin 29(4), 50–54 (1997)
7. Crawford, C.: Lessons from Computer Game Design. In: Laurel, B. (ed.) The Art of human-computer interface design, pp. 103–111. Addison-Wesley Pub. Co., Reading (1990)

8. Ermi, L., Mäyrä, F.: Player-Centred Game Design: Experiences in Using Scenario Study to Inform Mobile Game Design. Game Studies 5(1) (2005), http://gamestudies.org
9. Gray, P., Ramsay, A., Serrano, M.: A Demonstration of the OpenInterface Interaction Development Environment. In: UIST 2007 demonstration (2007)
10. iPhone, http://www.apple.com/iphone
11. Kue-Bum, L., Jung-Hyun, K., Kwang-Seok, H.: An Implementation of Multi-Modal Game Interface Based on PDAs. In: Proc. of ACIS SERA 2007, pp. 759–768. IEEE, Los Alamitos (2007)
12. OpenInterface European project. IST Framework 6 STREP funded by the European Commission (FP6-35182), http://www.oi-project.org
13. Piekarski, W., Thomas, B.: ARQuake: The Outdoor Augmented Reality Gaming System. In: Communications of the ACM, vol. 45(1), pp. 36–38. ACM Press, New York (2002)
14. Schlienger, C., Chatty, S.: An Iterative and Participatory HCI Design Process in the Industry Context: Bringing together Utility, Usability and Innovation... within Budget. In: Interfaces Magazine, vol. 72. HCI Publications (2007)
15. Williamson, J., Murray-Smith, R., Hughes, S.S.: Multimodal Excitatory Interaction on Mobile Devices. In: Proc. of CHI 2007, pp. 121–124. ACM Press, New York (2007)
16. Zyda, M., et al.: Educating the Next Generation of Mobile Game Developers. IEEE Computer Graphics and Applications 27(2), 96, 92–95 (2007)

Dynamic Game Balancing by Recognizing Affect

Tim J.W. Tijs[1], Dirk Brokken[2], and Wijnand A. IJsselsteijn[3]

[1] User-System Interaction Program, Department of Industrial Design
Eindhoven University of Technology, P.O. Box 513, 5600MB, Eindhoven, The Netherlands
t.j.w.tijs@tue.nl
[2] Philips Research Laboratories Europe
High Tech Campus 34, 5656AE, Eindhoven, The Netherlands
dirk.brokken@philips.com
[3] Human-Technology Interaction Group, Department of Technology Management
Eindhoven University of Technology, P.O. Box 513, 5600MB, Eindhoven, The Netherlands
w.a.ijsselsteijn@tue.nl

Abstract. Dynamic game balancing concerns changing parameters in a game to avoid undesired player emotions, such as boredom and frustration. This is e.g. done by adjusting the game's difficulty level to the (increasing) skill level of the player during the game. Currently, most balancing techniques are based on in-game performance, such as the player's position in a race. This is, however, insufficient since different types of players exist, with different goals, preferences and emotional responses. Therefore, to deal effectively with a player's emotions, a game needs to look beyond the player's performance. This paper provides an overview of two groups of potentially useful sources for dynamic game balancing: Overt behavior and physiological responses. In addition, we present EMO-Pacman, a design case that aims to implement these new balancing techniques into the game Pac-Man.

Keywords: Computer games, emotionally adaptive games, game balancing, affective loop, psychophysiology, emotions.

1 Introduction

To be enjoyable, a computer game must be balanced well. Adams & Rollins [1] list a number of requirements for a well-balanced game. For instance, a game must provide meaningful choices, the role of chance should not be so great that player skills become irrelevant, and players must perceive the game to be fair. Concerning the fairness of a (player-versus-environment) game, it is of key-importance that the game's difficulty is adjusted to the player's abilities. This is what many believe to be at the core of game balancing: Changing parameters in order to avoid undesired player emotions such as frustration (because the game is too hard) or boredom (because the game is too easy) [2]. Since the player's abilities tend to increase throughout the game, the game's difficulty level should be adapted continuously. Hence the need for dynamic game balancing.

P. Markopoulos et al. (Eds.): Fun and Games 2008, LNCS 5294, pp. 88–93, 2008.
© Springer-Verlag Berlin Heidelberg 2008

Currently, a number of heuristic techniques are used for dynamic game balancing, which try to assess the game's perceived difficulty level given a particular game state. Examples of these heuristics are I) the rate of successful shots or hits, II) number of life points, III) time left to complete a task and IV) the player's current position in a race. Regarding the latter heuristic, a commonly applied adaptation technique is rubber banding [3]: When falling behind, the player suddenly gets a boost in speed, which allows for catching up again (and/or the competing cars are slowed down).

However, game adaptation that is solely based on in-game performance can only have limited success, because there are many different types of players [4]. Each type of player has his/her own goals, preferences and emotional responses when playing a game. Therefore, taking the emotional (or affective) state of the player into account is expected to increase interest and fun; games can become *emotionally adaptive*. Results and approaches from research disciplines such as psychophysiology and affective computing can help in realizing this.

2 Emotionally Adaptive Games

Three types of methods for measuring affect can be distinguished [5]: Through self-reporting, by analyzing overt behavior and by analyzing physiological responses. For game balancing in a real-time environment, self-reporting is too obtrusive. However, self-reporting can be used to validate the results of the other two types. Regarding overt behavior[1], a number of potentially interesting techniques have previously been studied in an affective computing context. Techniques and studies focused on overt behavior that seem particularly useful for dynamic game balancing are provided in Table 1. A more detailed overview can be found at [6]. The relations between affect and physiological responses are investigated in the field of psychophysiology. A number of relevant techniques and studies can be found in Table 1; more detailed overviews can be found in e.g. [7] and [8].

Table 1. Potential sources for real-time analysis of affect

Overt behavior / expressions
Posture analysis, force exerted on game controls, facial emotions, gestures analysis, speech analysis.

Physiological responses
Heart rate (HR), Heart rate variability (HRV), Respiration rate (RSPRATE), Coherence between respiration rate and heart rate (RSP-HR_COH), Blood pressure, Blood volume pulse (BVP), Activity of the corrugator supercilii muscle, (CORR: for moving the eyebrows), Activity of the zygomaticus major muscle, (ZYG: for moving the cheeks), Activity of the orbicularis oculi muscle (OO: for moving the eye-lids), Skin conductance level (SCL), Skin conductance responses (SCR), Eye movements (EOG), Pupil size, Eye blink rate, Brain activity at various frequencies (EEG), Evoked Response Potential (ERP).

---

[1] In this category, we also include behavioral phenomena that are less overt, such as keyboard force (which is measured through sensors).

Fig. 1. The emotionally adaptive games loop, inspired on [9] and [16]

From an emotion-perspective, effective human-computer interaction can be realized using an "affective loop" [9]. Fig. 1 shows an affective loop that is tailored to the games domain. By providing the right game mechanics (e.g. audiovisuals, narrative, challenge), the game influences the player's experience, behavior and emotional state. During play, the emotional state of the player (measured in terms of *emotion-data*, such as the types mentioned in Table 1), is continuously being fed back to the game so that the game can adapt its mechanics (e.g. difficulty level) accordingly in real-time. All of this is done with the aim to optimize the experience.

Previous research attempts to create emotionally adaptive software have mainly focused on tutoring systems / productivity software (see e.g. [10]). Fewer attempts have been made to incorporate a closed-loop mechanism in a games context. Several authors [11, 12] have created games that improve player performance by adapting the difficulty level to the player's physiological state. Concept validation claims of these two studies were, however, based on a limited number of subjects. Besides these attempts, a number of biofeedback games have recently been developed, integrating the player's physiological data into the game (e.g. [13,14]). These games focus on stress manipulation rather than optimization of gameplay experience. Closest to the concept described in Fig. 1 probably is the work by Saari and colleagues. They created the Mind-Based Technology framework for psychological customization [15] and, based on this, initiated a framework for emotionally adaptive games (e.g. [16]).

To obtain empirical support for the emotionally adaptive games concept, an emotionally adaptive version of the game Pac-Man is currently being developed in the EMO-Pacman project, as described in the next section of this paper.

3   EMO-Pacman

EMO-Pacman (explained in more detail in [17]) is a two-stage attempt to create a game (adapted from Pac-Man, [18]) that adjusts its speed to the player's current emotional state. In the first stage of the project, we investigated the relations between the individual elements of the emotionally adaptive games framework (Fig. 1). The main research question in this stage was "What game mechanic setting causes what kind of emotional state, and what emotion-data is this accompanied by?"

To investigate this, a user test was conducted involving 24 adult subjects. One game mechanic, *game speed*, was manipulated, consisting of 3 levels (referred to as slow-mode, fast-mode and normal-mode). Changes in speed affected both the player's character (Pac-Man) and his/her opponents (ghosts). Speed was selected as an

Table 2. Effects of game speed on emotion-data

Significant (p < 0.05) results	
Feature	**Speed mode identified (desired action)**
Mean SCL	slow (speed up)
Number of SCR	slow (speed up)
Mean HR	slow (speed up)
Mean RSPRATE	slow (speed up)
Mean ampl. of the CORR signal	fast (slow down)
Mean ampl. of the ZYG signal	fast (slow down)
Mean key-press force	slow (speed up) & fast (slow down) & normal (none)

No significant results

Mean value of the CORR signal, mean value of the ZYG signal, mean value of the BVP signal, mean ampl. of BVP signal, mean RSP-HR_COH, HRV: mean power perc. of the 0.04-0.15Hz spectrum.

independent variable since it is relatively simple to manipulate, and speed changes were expected to have a strong influence on the player's emotional state. Different from the original Pac-Man version, the objective was not to stay alive and finish all levels. Instead, the objective was to score as many points. The player gained points by letting Pacman eat objects (scared ghosts, points, fruit) and lost points when Pacman was eaten by one of his opponents (angry ghosts). During the test, the game was paused twice to let the player report on their emotional state (bored / frustrated / enjoyed). In parallel, a series of emotion-data features was recorded during game play (see Table 2), explained in more detail in [17].

From the results, it seems that the "too easy - boredom" and "too hard - frustration" combinations do not always apply, because 2 participants reported frustration in the slow-mode and 2 others reported boredom in the fast-mode. Nevertheless, a strong majority (83%) reported boredom in the slow-mode. Although the fast-mode was considered enjoyable by some (58%) and frustrating by others (33%), almost all participants (96%) indicated in the post-game interview to prefer the normal mode over the slow- and fast-mode. Therefore, we conclude that I) the slow-mode was considered boring, II) the fast-mode was enjoyable for some but frustrating for others and III) the normal-mode was the most enjoyable mode. A series of t-tests was performed to investigate the influence of the factor game speed on the emotion-data, as shown in Table 2.

From the preliminary results of this experiment, displayed in Table 2, we can e.g. conclude that the players' mean skin conductance level (SCL) during the slow-mode was significantly different from that during the other two speed-modes (i.e. slow and fast).

4 Discussion and Further Work

As argued for, we believe that games can strongly benefit from analyzing the user's affective state when playing a game. The research fields of e.g. affective computing and psycho(physio)logy offer several potentially useful techniques for continuous analysis of a player's emotional state. The first experiment in the EMO-Pacman project has provided some preliminary empirical evidence for this. The project's ultimate goal is to create an emotionally adaptive game demonstrator. The results from Table 2 can be useful in creating such a classifier. For instance, when a player's skin conductance level drops low during Emo-Pacman, this may indicate boredom because I) the strong majority of subjects in the first experiment found the slow-mode boring, and II) on average (over 24 subjects) the SCL values were significantly lower during this speed mode than during the other two modes. Even though differences in physiological responses between individuals and within individuals over time are not uncommon (see e.g. [19]), the results from Table 2 can be used as a starting point.

One of the main challenges ahead is to create a properly functioning decision making system. For instance, how to respond when two emotion data features indicate boredom but two others do not? In this context, AI-based techniques (e.g. [20]) are expected to be more powerful than only performing statistical tests. Therefore, as a first step in the next phase, a classifier will be tested with the present dataset. In case the results of this test will prove unsatisfactory (e.g. insufficient data/accuracy), unused additional features from the gathered dataset will be analyzed. For instance, the subjects' faces were recorded with a webcam during the experiment (providing possibilities for facial emotion tracking). In addition, other possibilities lie e.g. in analyzing the initial/previous physiological states [21][2] of the players, analyzing the amplitude / recovery time of their skin conductance responses and looking at the variance, skewness and kurtosis of the emotion-data ([22] and [23] provide more detailed feature analysis descriptions).

Acknowledgments

The authors would like to thank Gert-Jan de Vries, Jack van den Eerenbeemd, Paul Lemmens and Floris Crompvoets of Philips Research Laboratories and the FUGA project for contributing to this work.

References

1. Adams, E., Rollings, A.: Game Design and Development; Fundamentals of Game Design. Pearson Education, NJ (2007)
2. Koster, R.: Theory of Fun for Game Design. Paraglyph Press, Phoenix (2004)
3. Pagulayan, R.J., Keeker, K., Wixon, D., Romero, R., Fuller, T.: User-centered design in games. In: Jacko, J., Sears, A. (eds.) Handbook for Human–Computer Interaction in Interactive Systems, pp. 883–906. Lawrence Erlbaum Associates Inc, Mahwah (2002)
4. Bartle, R.A.: Hearts, Clubs, Diamonds, Shades: Players who suit MUDs, http://www.mud.co.uk/richard/hcds.htm
5. Öhman, A.: The Psychophysiology of Emotion: An Evolutionary-Cognitive Perspective. In: Ackles, P.K., Jennings, J.R., Coles, M.G.H. (eds.) Advances in Psychophysiology, vol. 2, pp. 79–127. JAI Press, Greenwich (1987)

---

[2] For example, a high (140 BPM) heart rate might not increase as much by an arousing game effect as a normal heart rate.

6. The HUMAINE portal; Research on Emotions and Human-Machine Interaction, http://emotion-research.net
7. Ravaja, N.: Contributions of Psychophysiology to Media Research: Review and Recommendations. Media Psychology 6, 193–235 (2004)
8. Allanson, J., Fairclough, S.H.: A research agenda for physiological computing. Interacting with Computers 16(5), 857–878 (2004)
9. Sundström, P., Ståhl, A., Höök, K.: eMoto - A User-Centred Approach to Affective Interaction. In: Tao, J., Tan, T., Picard, R.W. (eds.) ACII 2005. LNCS, vol. 3784. Springer, Heidelberg (2005)
10. Schaefer, F., Haarmann, B.W.: The Usability of Cardiovascular and Electrodermal Measures for Adaptive Automation. In: Westerink, J.H.D.M., Ouwerkerk, M., Overbeek, T.J.M., Pasveer, W.F., De Ruyter, B. (eds.) Probing Experience: From Assessment of User Emotions and Behavior to Development of Products. Philips Research Book Series, vol. 8, pp. 235–243 (2008)
11. Takahashi, M., Tsuyoshi, A., Kuba, O., Yoshikawa, H.: Experimental Study Toward Mutual Adaptive Interface. In: Proceedings of the 3rd IEEE International Conference on Robot and Human Communication, Nagoya, Japan, pp. 271–276 (1994)
12. Rani, P., Sarkar, N., Liu, C.: Maintaining Optimal Challenge in Computer Games Through Real-Time Physiological Feedback. In: Proceedings of the 1st International Conference on Augmented Cognition, Las Vegas, NV (2005)
13. Journey to Wild Divine, http://www.wilddivine.com
14. Bersak, D., McDarby, G., Augenblick, N., McDarby, P., McDonnell, D., McDonald, B., Karkun, R.: Intelligent Biofeedback Using an Immersive Competitive Environment. In: Abowd, G.D., Brumitt, B., Shafer, S. (eds.) UbiComp 2001. LNCS, vol. 2201. Springer. Heidelberg (2001)
15. Saari, T.: Mind-Based Media and Communications Technologies. How the Form of Information Influences Felt Meaning. Acta Universitatis Tamperensis 834. Tampere University Press, Tampere (2001)
16. Saari, T., Ravaja, N., Turpeinen, M., Kallinen, K.: Emotional Regulation System for Emotionally Adapted Games. In: Proceedings of FuturePlay 2005, Michigan State University, MI (2005)
17. Tijs, T.J.W., Brokken, D., IJsselsteijn, W.A.: Creating an Emotionally Adaptive Game (submitted)
18. Overmars, M., McQuown, B.: Pac-Man. GM6 [computer software]
19. Lacey, J.I., Lacey, B.C.: Verification and extension of the principle of autonomic response stereotypy. Am. J. Psychol. 71, 50–73 (1958)
20. Yannakakis, G.N., Hallam, J.: Towards Optimizing Entertainment in Computer Games. Applied Artificial Intelligence 21, 933–971 (2007)
21. Berntson, G.G., Cacioppo, J.T., Quigley, K.S.: Autonomic Determinism: The Modes of Autonomic Control, the Doctrine of Autonomic Space, and the Laws of Autonomic Constraint. Psychological Review 98(4), 459–487 (1991)
22. Picard, R., Vyzas, E., Healey, J.: Toward Machine Emotional Intelligence: Analysis of Affective Physiological State. IEEE Transactions on Pattern Analysis and Machine Intelligence 23(10), 1175–1191 (2001)
23. Van den Broek, E.L., Schut, M.H., Westerink, J.H.D.M., Van Herk, J., Tuinenbreijer, K.: ECCV 2006 Workshop on HCI. In: Huang, T.S., Sebe, N., Lew, M., Pavlović, V., Kölsch, M., Galata, A., Kisačanin, B. (eds.) ECCV 2006 Workshop on HCI. LNCS, vol. 3979, pp. 52–63. Springer, Heidelberg (2006)

Alone or Together: Exploring the Effect of Physical Co-presence on the Emotional Expressions of Game Playing Children Across Cultures

Suleman Shahid, Emiel Krahmer, and Marc Swerts

Department of Information and Communication Sciences,
Faculty of Humanities, University of Tilburg,
Tilburg, The Netherlands
{S.Shahid,E.J.Krahmer,M.G.J.Swerts}@uvt.nl

Abstract. In this paper, we investigate the influence of physical co-presence on the emotional expressions of game playing children. We show that the emotional response of children belonging to different age groups and different cultural backgrounds varies when they play a game alone or together with their friends. A simple but quite effective number guessing game was developed to use as a tool for inducing emotions in an ethical way, which was played by Pakistani and Dutch individuals and pairs. The audiovisual emotional data thus collected was used in two perception tests in which Dutch viewers observed and classified the emotional response of Pakistani and Dutch children. Results show that the correct classification in both cultures is higher for children playing games in pairs, thus children in pairs are more expressive than individuals. Furthermore, both Pakistani individuals and pairs are more expressive than Dutch ones.

Keywords: Social gaming, Physical co-presence, Positive and Negative emotions, Cross-cultural comparison.

1 Introduction

Emotions are often seen as deeply personal experiences and many researchers believe that an important function of emotional facial expressions is to display the internal state of the individual [1]. However, there are also researchers who emphasize that these emotional expressions primarily serve as social signals [2]. In general, researchers subscribing to both perspectives will accept that non-verbal expressions of emotions, either via voice or via facial expressions, do play a role in social communication, but the general trend in research has been to study the expression of emotions by looking at individuals, mostly without taking the social context into account [3]. With a few notable exceptions, the focus of emotion research has either been on posed expressions or on expressions elicited in non-social situations [4].

Furthermore, regardless of such different perspectives (social vs. non-social) taken by researchers, a fundamental issue in this area of research has always been to develop methods for inducing emotions in a natural and ethical way, which is still a challenging task [5]. An important drawback of previous induction procedures is that

P. Markopoulos et al. (Eds.): Fun and Games 2008, LNCS 5294, pp. 94–105, 2008.

they tended to be designed and used for non-social situations, so that results gained from these techniques are not easy to generalize because of their artificially controlled settings [6]. Moreover, such methods may be effective in one particular culture or age group, but may not generalize to people with other backgrounds. So, there is a clear need for developing innovative techniques that meet different criteria: ideally, they should (1) lead to emotions in a natural and ethical way, and (2) be applicable across cultures and groups. In this paper, we explore the possibility of using games as a tool to induce emotions, which meets the criteria above.

Generally games are regarded as interactive, result oriented, competitive, dynamic and engaging in nature [7] and precisely these features can be exploited for using them as emotion inducers. Kaiser et al [6] reported that games give more control (to both players and experimenters) to create a natural ambience and go beyond traditional experimental settings of emotion induction. While playing games, people become engaged (both negatively and positively) and their level of engagement in games can lead to an intense emotional state (e.g., a state of flow) [8]. Moreover, it has been shown that there is a relationship between fun/enjoyment and emotions (expression of these emotions) [9] where fun in an activity can lead to an overall positive experience [10]. So the relation between emotions and games is interesting from a double perspective: on the one hand, games appear to present themselves as handy tools to induce natural emotions; on the other hand, the level of emotional involvement while playing games can be used as a metric to measure the fun and engagement in the games.

In our study, we look at the spontaneous expressions of two different emotions, one positive ("joy") and one negative ("disappointment"), elicited using the GamE (Games as a method for eliciting Emotions) paradigm, with a specific focus on the role of the social context on the expression of these emotions. Under the GamE paradigm, our objective is to design a number of games to be used as a tool for inducing emotions in a natural and ethical way [11] and the card game developed during this particular research is one example of this. One specific innovation is that we focus on facial expressions as potentially relevant correlates of the internal emotional state of game players. While there is a whole body of research into facial expressions as "windows to the human soul" [12], these have so far not been included in tests to systematically evaluate games.

In the following, we elaborate on two potentially important factors that may affect the way games are played and appreciated, namely social context and age. Regarding the former, it is of course known that many different factors may contribute to the social context, but here we limit ourselves to two important ones, namely *physical co-presence* and *culture*. If emotional expressions primarily serve to reflect the individual state of an individual, then we can hypothesize that it does not really matter whether emotional expressions are collected from children that play a game alone or from pairs of children that play the game together. However, if the expressions also have a considerable social aspect, we *would* expect to find differences in expressivity between individual players and pairs of players.

Even though certain expressions of emotion have been claimed to be universal, culture arguably also plays an important role in shaping the emotional reactions of people [13]. What is logical to do in a particular social setting of one culture might be impolite to do in a similar social setting of another culture. There are some studies, which compare the expression of emotions across cultures in social context [14] but overall most of the work has focused on intra-cultural aspects of emotions. As a result it is still largely unknown how a culture influences the overall experience and expressiveness of emotions in specific social contexts.

Besides these two aspects of the broader context, we also include one individual factor in our studies, namely *age*. An interesting albeit largely unexplored question is how children learn to "use" their non-verbal expressions in a social context. Generally speaking, adults are more stable in their expression of emotions than children, who are overall more expressive than adults. In particular, young children use emotions as a communication aid because of their limited verbal abilities. This raises the question how children "grow" towards more adult-like expressiveness, and whether this development process is the same for different cultures and contextual settings.

In this paper, we focus on 8 and 12 years old children from Pakistan (a south-Asian culture) and from the Netherlands (a western-European culture), who either play a card guessing game alone or in pairs (section 2). The data collected with the GamE paradigm was then used for two perception studies (described in section 3) where adults look at both Pakistani and Dutch individual children (who had either played the game alone, or with another child) to find out whether differences in expressiveness could be found.

2 Experiment 1: Data Collection

2.1 Setup (Game Design)

For inducing positive and negative emotions in children in a natural manner, we used the GamE paradigm. We developed a simple card game to use as a tool for inducing emotions in children. In the card game, children have to guess whether an upcoming number would be higher or lower than the previous (reference) number.

When the game starts, players see a row of six cards on the screen where the number of the first card is visible ('7' in the case of the example in Fig 1) and the other five cards are placed upside down so the numbers are hidden. All the numbers

Fig. 1. Loosing variant of the game

Fig. 2. Winning variant of the game

on the cards are between 1 to 10 and a number displayed once is not repeated in a particular game. Players have to guess whether the number on the next card will be higher or lower than the previous number. Once players have guessed the number, the relevant card is turned around and the correct answer is visible on the screen. Players are also informed about the correctness or incorrectness of their answer via a characteristic non-speech sound. If players make a wrong guess, the game is finished and they move to the next game. If players guess the number correctly then they are asked to guess the next number and players only win a game if they guess all numbers in the row correctly. In the case of winning a game, they receive a coin. At the end of the experiment, consisting of a number of games, players can exchange the coins they won with a prize.

The card games were developed using Microsoft® PowerPoint®. Appropriate colorful images were chosen for the game background and different animations were used to turn card around for making the game more attractive for children. While designing games, basic game design principles were kept in mind and on the one hand it was tried to make games a little bit uncertain but on other hand it was also tried to make some sequences predictable because a nice balance of these two makes games challenging [15] and can help in inducing emotions. During the experiment, children played six games, and could in theory win six coins. However, unknown to the children, each game was completely deterministic, and two different game alternatives were used. In the first alternative, a rational decision procedure would result in winning the game, and in the second alternative, being rational would result in losing the game. Figure 1 is an example of the loosing variant: the most probable outcome for the final card would be a "lower" number than 9, but guessing "lower" would make this a losing game. The two other losing games were: 8 – 3 – 9 – 7 – 2 – 1 and 1 – 9 – 4 – 8 – 3 – 2. One winning scenario is shown in figure 2 and two other winning scenarios were 9 – 2 – 8 – 1 -10 – 7, and 1 – 3 – 9 – 2 – 7 – 6. Winning and losing games were mixed in the sequence, starting and ending with a variant in which children were likely to win.

2.2 Participants

In total, 144 children played the game of which 96 children played the game in pairs, 48 Dutch children (24 pairs) and 48 Pakistani ones (24 pairs). The remaining 48 children (24 Dutch and 24 Pakistani ones) played the game individually. In both conditions (individual and pairs), half of the Dutch and Pakistani children were around 8 years old (group 4 in the Dutch elementary school system) and the other half were around 12 years old (Dutch group 8). In the case of pairs, always children of the same age were paired. Parents and teachers gave prior written permission for their child to participate, and signed a consent form stating that the recordings could be used for research purposes.

2.3 Procedure

The experiment was conducted in four elementary schools, two schools in Tilburg (the Netherlands) with Dutch participants and two schools in Lahore (Pakistan) with Pakistani participants. The procedure for both conditions (pairs and individuals) in all four schools was essentially the same. A separate room was chosen in all four schools where depending on the condition, children in pairs (self-selected pairs of the same age group) or individual children were invited and asked to sit on the chair(s) placed in front of a desk on which a laptop computer was placed. On the top of the laptop, a camcorder was placed in such a way that it could record the children's faces and the upper part of their body. Before the start of each experiment, the camera was adjusted to the children's height. Another computer was attached to the laptop to facilitate the experimenter in controlling the game. The experimenter was outside of the visual field of the game-playing children.

Once the children were in the room and had chosen the appropriate seat(s) for sitting, the experimenter welcomed the children and started a small talk discussion by asking a few questions to break the ice ("How old are you? Do you like to play games?" Etc.). After this introductory phase, the experimenter gave spoken instructions, telling the children about the game and the coins they could win. All the game rules outlined in the previous section were explained to the children (in Urdu and Dutch for Pakistani and Dutch children, respectively), and when they seemed to understand the rules, the experimenter started a practice game ("So you only have to say whether the next card is higher or lower. This is just an exercise and it doesn't really count"). After this exercise, the experimenter asked the children whether they had any questions, and if not the experimenter left the children's field of vision and started the first experimental game.

The experiment did not have a fixed duration because different children and pairs of children took different time and in the case of pairs, it sometimes involved a lot of discussion between the children, which also varied considerably from pair to pair. On average each session lasted for approximately 10 to 15 minutes. At the end of the game session, the experimenter congratulated the children and they could trade in their coins for an individual gift (a whistle or small plastic ball in the case of the Dutch participants and big size chocolates and key rings for the Pakistani participants).

Fig. 3. Representative stills for Pakistani players, with from left to right: 8 years old winning and 12 year old loosing individuals (top), 8 years old loosing and 12 years old winning individuals taken from pairs (bottom)

Fig. 4. Representative stills for Dutch players, with from left to right: 8 years old loosing and 12 year old winning individuals (top), 8 years old winning and 12 years old loosing Individuals taken from pairs (bottom)

2.4 Results and Discussion

Figures 2 and 3 show representative stills of winning and losing individual children, and individual children taken from couples. Note that in the latter case, the children were actually sitting next to another child with whom they were playing the game together. Overall, the game worked quite well, in that all individual and pairs of participants indeed made the logical choices that were expected in most of the cases, so that each individual child and pair of children lost at least two games and won at least two games. Furthermore, not even a single child noticed and reported that the game was in fact a deterministic simulation. The data gathered are rich and constitute a valuable collection of audiovisual emotional child speech, consisting of both decision-making dialogues (in the case of pairs), and audiovisual responses to winning or losing a game. Informal observations reveal clear emotional differences between individual players and players in pairs. There are also clear differences among different age groups and cultures and we attempt to quantify all these differences in a series of cross-cultural perception experiments described below.

3 Experiment 2: Cross-Cultural Perception Studies

3.1 Stimuli

From all of the individuals and pairs that participated in Experiment I, we selected the first response of their winning game (in which they made a correct prediction for the last card) and the first response of their losing games (in which the final guess turned out to be incorrect). In addition, from the clips of child-pairs, we selected randomly one child from each pair by zooming in on his/her face. In this selection, half of the children sitting on the right chair and half of the children sitting on the left chair were selected. We also tried to select equal numbers of boys and girls. The stimuli were cut from the moment the final card was turned until their primary response was finished. This resulted in 96 Dutch stimuli: 2[alone/together] x 2[win/lost] x 2[boy/girl] x 2[8/12 years old] x 6[instances]. In this similar fashion, the 96 Pakistani stimuli were developed. Stimuli were presented to participants in a random order, in a vision-only format to avoid participants from relying on auditory cues.

3.2 Participants

72 Dutch adults, with a roughly equal number of men and women, participated in the perception experiments.

3.3 Procedure

Two group experiments were conducted: Dutch viewers judging Pakistani children [36 participants] and Dutch viewers judging Dutch children [36 participants] with essentially the same procedure for both experiments.

For both experiment, groups of participants were invited into a classroom where the stimuli were projected on a white classroom wall using a beamer. Participants were told that they would see 96 stimuli in both cases (Dutch and Pakistani children).

In addition, they were instructed that the children had just won or lost a game and they, as viewers, had to guess from the children's facial expression whether they had won or lost the game. Each stimulus was preceded by a number displayed on the screen indicating the upcoming stimulus, and followed by a six second pause during which participants could fill in their score on the answer form. Before the actual experiment, there was a short training session in which 4 clips were shown (different from the ones shown in the actual experiment) to make participants familiar with the stimuli and the experimental task. If there were no further questions, the actual experiment started which lasted for approximately 18 minutes. During the experiment there was no interaction between participants and experimenter.

3.4 Statistical Analysis

All tests for significance were performed using a repeated measurement analysis of variance (ANOVA) with three within-subjects factors, namely Co-presence (levels: individual, individual from pairs), Age (levels: 8 years old, 12 years old) and Sex (levels: boy, girl), and with one between-subjects factor: Culture (levels: Dutch, Pakistani) and with percentage of correct classification as the dependent variable.

3.5 Results

Table 1 summarizes the results. The repeated measurement analysis of variance shows a significant main effect of co-presence (individuals vs. pairs) (F (1,70) = 716.753, $p < .001$, $\eta_p^2 = .911$). The average of correct classifications is higher for individuals taken from pairs ($M = .812$) than it is for individuals playing alone ($M = .605$). Another significant main effect was found of culture ($F(1,70) = 168.9, p < .001$, $\eta_p^2 = .707$). The average of correct classifications for Pakistani children ($M = .782$) is higher than for Dutch children ($M = .636$). Finally, no significant main effect of sex nor of age was found.

Besides these main effects, we discuss a number of significant two-way interactions. We found a significant interaction between culture and co-presence (F (1,70) = 24.177, $p < .001$, $\eta_p^2 = .257$). This interaction can be explained as follows: even though Pakistani children are overall more expressive than Dutch children (higher percentage correct), the difference between Pakistani individuals ($M = .66$) and Pakistani individuals from pairs ($M = .90$) is larger than the difference between Dutch individual ($M = .55$) and Dutch individuals from pairs ($M = .72$). We also found a significant interaction between Culture and Sex (F (1,70) = 7.774, $p < .01$, $\eta_p^2 = .11$). This interaction can be explained by the fact that both Pakistani boys and girls are more expressive than Dutch boys and girl, but this difference is overall higher between Pakistani and Dutch boys. Another interesting interaction was found between Culture and Age (F (1,70) = 46.782, $p < .001$, $\eta_p^2 = .40$). This interaction can be explained by the fact that the Pakistani children aged 8 and 12 are comparable in their expressiveness, while the Dutch 8-year olds are overall clearly more expressive (higher percentage correct) than the Dutch 12 year olds. No further significant interactions were found.

Table 1. Mean of correct classification results for Dutch observers judging stimuli from Dutch and Pakistani kids (individual and individual taken from pairs) in 2 age groups

Culture	Co-presence	Sex	Age	Mean (Std. Error)
Dutch	Individuals	Boy	8	.625 (.019)
			12	.461 (.018)
		Girl	8	.565 (.019)
			12	.554 (.017)
	Individuals taken from pairs	Boy	8	.760 (.014)
			12	.679 (.015)
		Girl	8	.719 (.019)
			12	.724 (.014)
Pakistani	Individuals	Boy	8	.617 (.019)
			12	.784 (.018)
		Girl	8	.595 (.019)
			12	.639 (.017)
	Individuals taken from pairs	Boy	8	.920 (.014)
			12	.870 (.015)
		Girl	8	.887 (.019)
			12	.941 (.014)

4 Conclusion and Discussion

In this paper we investigated how the emotional response of children belonging to different age groups and different cultural background varies when they play a game individually or in pairs. For collecting emotional data in a natural way, we developed a simple but effective game in which individual participants or pairs of participants have to guess whether a card will contain a higher or lower number than a reference card. The emotional data collected in this way was used in two perception experiments, in which Dutch viewers in Tilburg saw fragments (without sound) of Pakistani and Dutch children; they were instructed to guess from the facial expressions of children whether children had won or lost the game.

In general, the number of correct classifications was high, indicating that the cues from the facial expressions of the children were very clear regarding the question whether they had just lost or won a game. We found that the children playing the game in pairs were more expressive than the children playing the game individually; as a result, the correct classification for children taken form pairs was higher than for the individual ones. This finding, which was true for both cultures, confirms our major hypothesis that physical co-presence influences the emotional expressions of children, in line with previous findings (e.g. [16]) regarding the effect of presence on the emotional response of people. Another interesting finding relates to the overall expressiveness of the Pakistani children. Both Pakistani individuals and individuals taken from pairs were more expressive than their Dutch counterparts. This is in line with our previous findings [17], which show that Pakistani children (in both age groups) are more expressive than their Dutch counterparts. The pattern that Pakistanis are more emotional/expressive than Dutch was also found in totally different settings with adults [18].

Another interesting result related to the fact that the Pakistani 12 years old girls (especially the individuals taken from pairs) are not only more expressive than their Dutch counterparts but also more expressive than the 8 years old Pakistani girls and boys. This is an interesting finding, which, at first sight, seems to be incompatible with expectations based on the age theory [19] that younger children are more expressive than older ones, though it is consistent with the outcome of the work by [20] that girls are more expressive in showing their emotions than boys. This result is also in line with another study where it was shown that females were more expressive in the presence of a friend than in the presence of stranger [4]. Future analyses into this issue may reveal why it is that Pakistani 12 years old girls are the most expressive of the children we analysed, which could possibly be due to culture-specific display rules which dictate that Pakistani girls at a certain age are no longer supposed to be expressive in normal circumstances, which they may compensate for in game situations like the ones we analysed.

Other than the emotional differences after winning or losing a game, inspection of the recordings revealed that there were also differences in how Dutch and Pakistani children behaved during the time before the card was turned around, so when they were deciding whether the upcoming card would contain a higher or lower number. One salient difference was that Pakistani children often made praying gestures (forming a cup with the hands to pray, and finishing the prayer by wiping the hands across the face) while Dutch children never prayed. Gesturing was more common when children were playing game in pairs. Another interesting difference is that the interpersonal distance between Pakistani children appeared to be smaller than that between Dutch children; there was more touching, holding hands, putting head on shoulder with the Pakistani than with the Dutch children. This strong social bonding and interaction could be observed both during the decision making phase, and after the game result was known.

Overall, the card game developed under the GamE paradigm was quite engaging for children. Almost all children reported that they found the game full of fun because it was challenging, as it contained both winning and loosing situations with a fair amount of uncertainty. The game is also useful because it appears to generalize to multiple settings: it worked quite well in both cultures, across different age groups and in different social contexts and proved to be a good basic tool for inducing emotions without any artificial posing.

And finally, this research has provided reasons to include facial expressions in the evaluation metrics of games. Such expressions not only correlate with emotions but are especially useful when judging children, whose verbal skills are not as good as those of adults, which may be a disadvantage when one wants to evaluate a product (such as a game): children may not score well on observation techniques that work well for adults (e.g. when they have to complete scores on a form, or express things verbally through a thinking-aloud method), while their facial expressions may be spontaneous and clear.

5 Future Work

In the future, we plan to run the perception test in Pakistan with Pakistani viewers to explore whether there are any cross-cultural differences in perceiving the emotional response of Pakistani and Dutch children. Furthermore, the audio-visual data gained from these experiments offers a rich collection of not only facial expressions but also body movements, like hand gestures. We would like to explore to what extent such gestures contain additional information that is useful for judging the emotional responses of children.

Our results shows that there is a strong influence of physical co-presence on the emotional expression of children but in future we would like to see that how different combinations of pairs (e.g., a pair of two strangers, a pair consisting of one active and one passive partner, a pair of a child and a robot) would effect these emotional expressions of children. Last but not the least we would like to investigate the short term and long term effect of game playing sessions on children's mood.

Acknowledgments. We thank Sjoukje Hoebers and Remco Stultiens for their help in collecting some of the production and perception data. We thank the children who participated in this study and specially their parents who gave their consent for this research. We thank the principal and teachers of schools in Tilburg and Lahore for their cooperation, and we thank all our perception test participants. Finally, thanks to the four anonymous reviewers for their constructive comments on a previous version of this paper.

References

1. Ekman, P.: Strong evidence for universals in facial expressions: a reply to Russell's mistaken critique. Psychological Bulletin 115, 268–287 (1994)
2. Fridlund, A.: Human facial expression: an evolutionary view. Academic Press, New York (1994)
3. Manstead, A.S.R.: The social dimension of emotions. Psychologist (18), Part (8) (2005)
4. Wagner, H.L., Smith, J.: Facial expressions in the presence of friends and stranger. Journal of nonverbal Behaviour 15(4) (1991)
5. Cornelius, R.R.: The science of emotion. Research and tradition in the psychology of emotion. Prentice-Hall, Upper Saddle River (1996)
6. Kaiser, S., Wehrle, T.: Situated emotional problem solving in interactive computer games. In: Frijda, N.H. (ed.) Proceedings of the IXth Conference of the International Society for Research on Emotions, pp. 276–280. ISRE Publications, Toronto (1996)
7. Salen, K., Zimmerman, E.: Rules of Play, Game Design Fundamentals. The MIT Press, Massachusetts (2003)
8. Lazzaro, N.: Why We Play Games: Four Keys to More Emotion Without Story. In: Game Developer Conerence (GDC), San Fransisco, USA (2004)
9. Podilchak, W.: Distinctions of fun, enjoyment and leisure. Leisure Studies 10(2), 133–148 (1991)
10. Jackson, S.A.: Joy, fun, and flow states in sports. In: Yuri L. H. Emotions in Sport. Human Kinetics (1999)

11. Shahid, S., Krahmer, E., Swerts, M.: GamE: Game as a method for eliciting Emotions. In: Proceedings of Measuring Behavior 2008, Maastricht, the Netherlands (to appear, 2008)
12. Kappas, A.: The Fascination With Faces: Are They Windows to Our Soul? Journal of Nonverbal Behavior 21(3), 157–161 (1997)
13. Elfenbein, H., Ambady, N.: On the universality and cultural specificity of emotion recognition. Psychological Bulletin 128, 203–235 (2002)
14. Masuda, T., Ellsworth, P.C., Mesquita, B., et al.: Placing the face in context: Cultural differences in the perception of facial emotion. Journal of Personality and Social Psychology 94(3), 365–381 (2008)
15. Thompson, J., Berbank-Green, B., Cusworth, N.: Game Design: Principles, Practice, and Techniques - The Ultimate Guide for the Aspiring Game Designer. John Wiley & Sons, Hoboken (2007)
16. Wagner, H., Lee, V.: Facial behavior alone and in the presence of others. In: Philippott, P., et al. (eds.) The social context of nonverbal behavior, pp. 262–286. Cambridge University Press, New York (1999)
17. Shahid, S., Krahmer, E., Swerts, M.: Audiovisual emotional speech of game playing children: Effect of age and culture. In: Proceedings of Interspeech 2007 (IS 2007), Antwerpen, Belgium (2007)
18. Shahid, S., Krahmer, E., Swerts, M.: Real vs. acted emotional speech: Comparing Caucasian and South-Asian speakers and observers. In: Proceedings of Prosody 2008, Brazil (2008)
19. Thompson.: Emotion Regulation: A Theme in Search of Definition. In: The Development of Emotion Regulation, pp. 25–52 (1994)
20. Chapman, A.J.: Social facilitation of laughter in children. Journal of Experimental Social Psychology 9, 528–541 (1973)

Shared Fun Is Doubled Fun: Player Enjoyment as a Function of Social Setting

Brian J. Gajadhar, Yvonne A.W. de Kort, and Wijnand A. IJsselsteijn

Eindhoven University of Technology, Human Technology Interaction, IPO 1.20,
5600 MB Eindhoven, The Nethetlands
{B.J.Gajadhar,Y.A.W.d.Kort,W.A.IJsselsteijn}@tue.nl

Abstract. Although the social relevance of digital gaming has been discussed and investigated in cultural and sociological readings, social context has been largely neglected in terms of in-game player experience. In this paper we present a study in which player experience is empirically tested comprehensively, with the focus on the interplay between player enjoyment and social context. Self reports on the Game Experience Questionnaire and an aggression state questionnaire were explored for three play configurations: virtual, mediated, and co-located co-play. Additionally, effects of familiarity and winning vs. losing were tested. Results indicate that a co-located co-player significantly adds to the fun, challenge, and perceived competence in the game. Aggression was influenced by familiarity and performance. The effect of social context was mediated by the level of social presence. These findings illustrate that social context is an important determinant of player enjoyment and should be incorporated in models of player experience.

Keywords: Digital gaming, game experience, player experience, enjoyment, social presence, play setting, social setting, play configuration.

1 Introduction

Play is an intrinsically motivated, physical or mental leisure activity that is undertaken only for enjoyment or amusement and has no other objective [1]. Games present more structured and rule-based play modes, and are often more goal-directed. But both play and games are engaged in by people of all ages. In fact most people have played board games or card games with their parents, siblings, children, or friends. These traditional games are often seen as a constructive means for family/peer interaction.

As do traditional games, digital games offer opportunities for social interaction [2,3,4,5]. In fact, according to gamers, socializing is the number one motivation for playing digital games [3]. Yet besides playing with real and present friends, digital games also offer possibilities for playing against or with non-human co-players (i.e. computer agents) or mediated human co-players (i.e. online play). To date, little attention has been given to the nature and role of the exact social setting in explanations of player enjoyment. Apart from two psychophysiology-based studies on the effects of competing against a computer or a human [6,7] most studies concerning

P. Markopoulos et al. (Eds.): Fun and Games 2008, LNCS 5294, pp. 106–117, 2008.
© Springer-Verlag Berlin Heidelberg 2008

player experience focus only on one specific [4] or even a non-specified [8,9] social play configuration. They have left unaddressed whether enjoyment is equal in collocated multi-play versus other popular play settings that do not include a human co-player (i.e., computer agent as co-player) or lack the physical nearness of a human co-player (i.e., online play).

In spite of the clear social roles digital games play, the social component of gaming is often missing in theories and models of player experience and digital gaming platforms are not valued to their full extent as a medium which brings people together [e.g., 8,9,10]. However, some researchers in the field have argued that player enjoyment will differ between settings that differ in potential for social interaction [11]. Physical play settings are a complex mix of social (with friends vs. with strangers), spatial (at home vs. at the Internet café) and media (side-by-side vs. online) characteristics. It is hypothesized that the impact of socio-spatial setting on player experience is substantial, and mediated by the social presence of the co-player [11]. Social presence is defined as the subjective counterpart of objective closeness in communication: 'the sense of being with another' [12] and is mainly applied in respect to communication technology. Recently, the concept was also introduced in digital gaming research [5].

The current study aimed to empirically test the influence of a co-player presence on player enjoyment, by systematically varying social play settings with increasing levels of objective co-player presence or closeness. The mediating role of social presence, the subjective sense of being with another, was also explored. Moreover, player enjoyment was treated and measured as a multidimensional construct, giving detailed insight into player experience and how it is shaped by situational characteristics.

1.1 Digital Game Enjoyment

Player experience is a broad term which can be roughly subdivided into player involvement and player enjoyment. Player involvement describes a player's focus and interest during digital play in terms of flow, immersion and engagement [13]. We regard digital game enjoyment as a generic term that indicates the amount of pleasure or displeasure and includes concepts such as positive affect, competence, challenge, frustration and aggression. Explicitly treating player enjoyment as a multidimensional construct, will give a better understanding of how player experience is shaped; for example a digital game can induce frustration and aggression but still can be experienced as a positive and challenging activity.

Because the digital gaming field has been lacking a common vocabulary, player experience is studied in a fragmented way [14], which gives an incomplete and imprecise picture of what player experience actually is. IJsselsteijn, de Kort, & Poels [15] therefore developed the Game Experience Questionnaire (GEQ) which enables game researchers to empirically explore and test player experience of digital games in a quantitative and comprehensive way. The questionnaire was based on focus group investigations [14] and two subsequent large scale survey investigations among frequent gamers [15].

The GEQ includes player enjoyment-related scales of positive affect, competence, challenge and frustration (besides more involvement-oriented scales probing flow, immersion, and boredom). Positive affect basically probes the fun and enjoyment of gaming, or how good players feel. Competence is defined as the extent to which players feel strong and skilful in playing a game, and challenge probes whether players feel stimulated and put a lot of effort into playing. Frustration is a negatively valenced experience, measuring the degree of feeling tense and irritable.

Aggressive feelings, which potentially follow from in- or at-game frustration or from violent content in games, are not explicitly addressed in the GEQ, as these did not surface based on the empirical studies reported in [14] and [15]. However, since frustration can turn to aggression when a player's goals are thwarted, and since post-game aggression appears to surface regularly in the media and literature, the authors felt that in-game aggressive feelings might present an additional relevant construct when considering player enjoyment.

1.2 Aim of the Present Study

To date, situational characteristics, such as socio-spatial context have not received sufficient, or sufficiently thorough attention in player experience research. First, digital gaming often takes place in different social contexts. After all, one can play against a friend side by side, or one can play online against a complete stranger. Second, by treating player experience as a single dimension, the rich and varied set of experiences that shape player experience have also been disregarded.

We therefore present a study in which player enjoyment is empirically studied in a comprehensive way, and in which socio-spatial context is systematically varied. Employing the GEQ and an Aggression State Questionnaire, player enjoyment was investigated for three common play configurations with increasing levels of co-player presence. Additionally, we explored whether the relationship between objective co-player presence and player enjoyment was mediated by social presence, measured with the Social Presence in Gaming Questionnaire (SPGQ).

2   Method

2.1   Experimental Design

For exploring differences in player enjoyment between three common social play settings, a mixed groups design was employed. Co-Player Presence was manipulated as a within groups factor (virtual co-play vs. mediated co-play vs. co-located co-play). Familiarity (friends vs. strangers) and Performance (winners vs. losers) were treated as between groups factors. The latter factor was logically created post-hoc Player enjoyment was measured by self-reports and player performance was registered by the experimenter.

2.2   Participants

Eighty-six Dutch (post-) graduate students (27 females), aged between 16 and 34 (M_{age} = 22.4, SD_{age} = 3.5), played in pairs against each other; 26 pairs were friends and 16 were strangers from each other. However, since participants played in dyads, and dyadic data are non-independent, only half of the data was actually used for analysis (the data of all players '1'). Therefore the actual sample size was 42 participants (15 females; 26 friends). Participants were recruited from a participant database via email, or approached personally on the university campus. All participants had played digital games before; a substantial portion of them played them regularly.

2.3 Experimental Procedure and Manipulations

The experiment was conducted in a lab at the Eindhoven University of Technology, consisting of eight separate participant booths. Participants were led to believe that the purpose of the study concerned latency in online games, and were asked to fill in a consent form. During the experiment, they played the game WoodPong [16] on a 17" monitor display as described in [13]. Players wore headphones to hear the music and in-game sound effects. For each condition, participants were redirected to another booth: in the 'virtual' play configuration participants were told that they played against the computer (in separate rooms), although in fact they played against their partner (see below). In the 'mediated' setting they played online against each other (in separate booths), and in the 'co-located' setting they played against each other in the same booth, on the same console (see Figure 1).

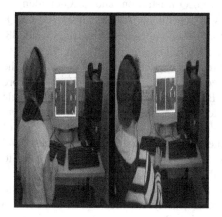 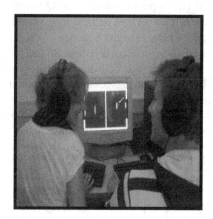

Fig. 1. (a) Setting in virtual and mediated co-playing. (b) Setting in co-located co-playing.

Based on the results of a pilot study [13], the decision was not to have participants play against the computer in the 'virtual' play configuration for two reasons. First, results showed that all players lost their game against the AI, which provided a confound in that study. Second, in case there would be an effect of co-player presence, it would be impossible to attribute this to either the social meanings and affordances of the setting, or alternatively, to the fact that computers play differently than humans. This basically implies that in the current study the virtual and the mediated co-presence conditions were identical, except for the fact that in the first condition players thought they were playing against the computer (see figure 1a). To strengthen the impression, a clearly visible cable was connected between the two computers in the mediated setting. However in the virtual setting, cables which connected both computers were hidden. The third setting remained the same as in the pilot study, both players played on the same computer, side by side (see figure 1b).

In each condition, three sets of WoodPong were played before filling in the questionnaire. The games were started by the experimenter via a wireless keyboard, and ended automatically after one of the participants had won six points. After three sets a winner was noted, and participants received an on-screen request to fill in their questionnaires individually, in separate rooms. The order of conditions was randomly assigned per couple. Lastly, participants were debriefed, paid and thanked for their participation. The experiment lasted 30 minutes; participants received a standard compensation of €5,-.

2.4 Measurements

After each condition participants completed a set of self-report measures in which they rated their player experiences during the game. This combined questionnaire[1] probed two categories of experiences: player enjoyment, and social presence. Player enjoyment was measured with four scales from the Game Experience Questionnaire [15] (GEQ-positive affect, GEQ-competence, GEQ-frustration, and GEQ-challenge). Reliabilities of the scales were satisfactory to excellent. Alpha values for GEQ-positive affect ranged between .74 and .84, for GEQ-competence between .86 and .88, for GEQ-frustration between .80 and .87, and for GEQ-challenge between .53 and 73.

Because it was felt that the aspect of aggression was insufficiently covered in the GEQ, a separate aggression scale was included in the questionnaire. Since the authore were not able to trace a suitable state scale, Buss and Perry's Trait Aggression Scale [17] was shortened, and converted into a state scale; e.g., "*I have trouble controlling my temper*" was converted into "*I had trouble controlling my temper*". It consists of four subscales. The anger scale measures the degree of loosing ones calmness, and reliabilities differed from .60 to .77. The verbal aggression scale measures the need to verbally express one's (dis-)agreement with a situation. Reliabilities were poor, ranging between .14 and .53. The physical aggression scale measures the need to physically express ones (dis)-agreement to others, its reliabilities varied from .38 to .80. Lastly, hostility measures players' impression that their co-players were more lucky and were laughing behind their back. Its reliabilities ranged from .07 to .71 (with a perhaps understandably very low score for the virtual player condition).

Two subscales from the Social Presence in Gaming Questionnaire [5] were administered to verify the manipulation of social presence in the three play configurations under study (as was also established in [13]); Cronbach's alpha varied between .66 and .79 for SPGQ-psychological involvement (SPGQ-PI), and between .85 and .91 for SPGQ-behavioral engagement (SPGQ-BE).

The combined questionnaire included 55 items. Participants could respond on 5-point unipolar scales, ranging from 1 (not at all) to 5 (extremely), to indicate the intensity of the described experience. Additionally, all in-game scores were logged to determine whether players had won or lost the game (post-hoc constructed factor).

---

[1] The questionnaire consisted also of scales measuring player involvement (e.g., flow, immersion, boredom, engagement). These data will be reported in a separate publication [19].

3   Results

Linear Mixed Model Analysis was performed on the self-report data for each scale with Co-Player Presence, Familiarity and Performance as fixed factors, and participant number as random factor.

3.1   Social Presence of the Co-player

Figure 2a presents the scores of the social presence indicators. Linear Mixed Model Analysis was performed on each component of the SPGQ with Co-Player Presence as a within groups factor, and Familiarity and Performance as between groups factors.

Results showed significant differences for Co-Player Presence on both social presence scales: SPGQ-BE ($F(2,77.8) = 9.31$; $p<.00$) and SPGQ-PI ($F(2,80.2) = 82.88$; $p<.001$). Virtual co-play was rated lowest on both social presence scales ($M_{BE} = 2.5$ (0.2); $M_{PI} = 1.2^2$ (0.1), co-located co-play scored highest on both ($M_{BE} = 3.1$ (0.2); $M_{PI} = 2.8$ (0.1)), and mediated co-play scored in between ($M_{BE} = 2.8$ (0.2); $M_{PI} = 1.7$ (0.1)). Contrast analyses showed that scores increased significantly with each subsequent category for both scales, although the difference for SPGQ-BE between virtual and mediated co-play was only marginally significant.

Furthermore, SPGQ-PI showed a significant main effect of Familiarity ($F(1,39.7) = 10.66$; $p<.01$) and a significant interaction effect between Familiarity and Co-Player Presence ($F(2,78.2) = 3.61$; $p<.04$). Friends ($M = 2.1$ (0.1)) experienced more psychological involvement than strangers ($M = 1.7$ (0.1)), and the increase for each subsequent category of Co-Player Presence was larger for friends than for strangers (see Figure 2b). Logically, the values were equal for the virtual condition.

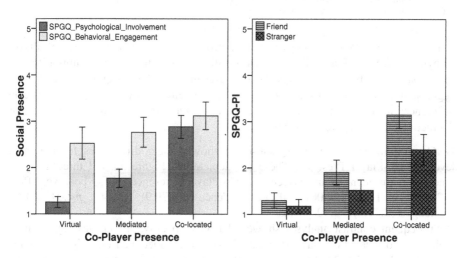

Fig. 2. (a) Social Presence scales measured by self-report as a function of Co-Player Presence. (b) SPGQ-PI scale measured by self-report as a function of Co-Player Presence and Familiarity (1 = not at all, 5 = extremely; SE indicated in graph).

---

[2] Standard errors indicated in brackets.

3.2 Player Enjoyment

Player Enjoyment was measured employing four GEQ scales - positive affect, competence, challenge, and frustration - and four state aggression scales - anger, verbal aggression, physical aggression, and hostility. Table 1 below shows the bivariate correlations between these components. A high correlation emerged between GEQ-positive affect and GEQ-competence, and moderate ones between the remaining GEQ scales. Moderate to high correlations also emerged between the state aggression scales.

Table 1. Pearson Correlations for Player Enjoyment components from participant's self-reports of all conditions

	GEQ-Pos.A	GEQ-Comp.	GEQ-Chal.	GEQ-Frust.	Anger	Verb. Aggr.	Phys. Aggr.	Host.
GEQ-Pos.A	1	.70**	.54**	-.35**	-.11	-.10	-.38	-.17
GEQ-Comp	.70**	1	.25**	-.38**	-.20*	-.18*	-.08	-.30**
GEQ-Chal.	.54**	.25**	1	.06	.13	.14	.13	.08
GEQ-Frust.	-.35**	-.38**	.06	1	.52**	.57**	.54**	.56**
Anger	-.11	-.20*	.13	.52**	1	.61**	.66**	.45**
Verb. Aggr.	-.10	-.18*	.14	.57**	.61**	1	.56**	.42**
Phys. Aggr.	-.04	-.08	.13	.54**	.66**	.56**	1	.48**
Host.	-.17	-.30**	.08	.56**	.45**	.42**	.48**	1

**. Correlation is significant at the 0.01 level (2-tailed).
*. Correlation is significant at the 0.05 level (2-tailed).

Linear Mixed Model Analyses were performed for each component of Player enjoyment with Co-Player Presence as a within groups factor, and Familiarity and Performance as between groups factors. Results for the GEQ scales and state aggression scales are discussed below. A schematic overview of significant differences for each scale of Co-Player Presence, Familiarity, Performance and their interaction effects is given in Table 2.

GEQ components. Three GEQ subscales showed clear differences for the three levels of Co-Player Presence. These are depicted in Figure 3a. All three analyses rendered significant main effects of Co-Player Presence (GEQ-positive affect $F(2,79.5) = 11.30$, $p<.001$; GEQ-competence $F(2,79.9) = 3.47$, $p<.04$; GEQ-challenge $F(2,79.3) = 4.40$, $p<.02$.

Subsequent contrast analyses showed that GEQ-positive affect was significantly higher for co-located co-play ($M = 3.5$ (0.1)) than for mediated ($M = 3.1$ (0.1)) and virtual co-play ($M = 2.9$ (0.1)). The contrast between mediated and virtual co-play was marginally significant. GEQ-Competence was significantly higher in co-located ($M = 3.0$ (0.1)) than virtual co-play ($M = 2.6$ (0.1)), the difference with mediated

Table 2. Schematic overview of the presence of significant differences for each scale in Co-Player Presence (CPP), Familiarity (Fam.), Performance (Perf.) and their interaction effects (CPP*Fam. and CPP*Perf.)

	GEQ-Pos.A	GEQ-Comp.	GEQ-Chal.	GEQ-Frust.	Anger	Verb. Aggr.	Phys. Aggr.	Host.
CPP	**	*	*	-	-	-	-	-
Fam.	-	-	-	-	-	(*)	-	*
Perf.	**	**	-	**	-	-	-	**
CPP*Fam.	-	-	-	-	-	**	-	-
CPP*Perf.	-	-	-	-	-	-	(*)	-

**. Significant at the 0.01 level
*. Significant at the 0.05 level
(*). Marginal significant.

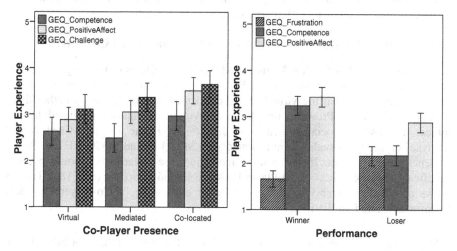

Fig. 3. (a) Player Experience as a function of Co-Player Presence, (b) Player Experience as a function of Performance (1 = not at all, 5 = extremely; SE indicated in graph)

co-play was marginally significant (M = 2.7 (0.1)). The same pattern emerged for GEQ-challenge (co-located co-play M = 3.6 (0.2); mediated M = 3.3 (0.2); virtual M = 3.1 (0.2)). GEQ-Frustration did not show significant differences for Co-Player Presence.

Performance showed significant effects on GEQ-positive affect, GEQ-competence, and GEQ-frustration (see Figure 3b). Winners (M = 3.5 (0.1) reported more positive affect than losers (M = 2.9 (0.1); $F(1,115.7)$ = 17.68; $p<.001$). The same picture emerged for competence: winners (M = 3.3 (0.1)) experienced more competence than losers (M = 2.2 (0.1); $F(1,115.7)$ = 17.68; $p<.001$). Conversely and logically, winners reported less frustration (M = 2.1 (0.1)) than losers (M = 1.6, SE = 0.1; F(1,103.1) = 14.97; p<.001).

State Aggression components. The same analyses were performed on the four state aggression scales (anger, verbal aggression, hostility and physical aggression). Notably, Co-Player Presence showed no significant main effects on any of the scales.

Verbal Aggression did show a significant interaction effect of Familiarity and Co-Player Presence ($F(2,77.1) = 5.29$; $p<.01$), which qualified the marginally significant main effect of Familiarity on the verbal aggression ($F(1,39.3) = 3.95$; $p<.06$). Friends ($M = 1.7$ (0.1)) reported more verbal aggression than strangers ($M = 1.3$ (0.2)), particularly for mediated and co-located co-play (which makes sense since the virtual co-play conditions are identical for strangers and friends: they both compete with the computer).

Hostility showed main effects of both Familiarity ($F(1,39.1) = 6.59$; $p<.02$) and Performance ($F(1,115.9) = 26.05$; $p<.001$). Among friends ($M = 1.7$ (0.1)) more hostility was reported than among strangers ($M = 1.3$ (0.1)). Furthermore, winners ($M = 1.2$ (0.1)) reported less hostility than losers ($M = 1.7$ (0.1)) did.

Lastly, for Physical Aggression a marginally significant interaction effect was found between Performance and Co-Player Presence ($F(2,83.7) = 2.76$; $p<.07$); winners reported more physical aggression in mediated and virtual co-play than in co-located co-play, whereas no differences were found for losers.

3.3 Mediation of Player Enjoyment by Social Presence of the Co-player

The results reported in Section 3.2 indicated significant effects of Co-Player Presence on three GEQ scales; the analyses in Section 3.1 had already indicated that social presence increased from the virtual to the co-located setting. To test whether these effects of Co-Player Presence on player enjoyment are indeed mediated by the subjective sense of social presence of the co-player, the Linear Mixed Model Analyses on the GEQ scales were repeated with SPGQ-PI and SPGQ-BE (i.e. Social Presence) as covariates. In the case of mediation, the covariate(s) should become significant, and the effects of Co-Player Presence should disappear (see [18]). Table 3 shows a schematic overview of the results for each scale of Co-Player Presence, Performance, and Familiarity.

Table 3. Schematic overview of effects of Co-Player Presence (CPP), Familiarity (Fam.), Performance (Perf.), and interaction terms (CPP*Fam. and CPP*Perf.) on GEQ scales, with SPGQ-Behavioral Engagement and SPGQ-Psychological Involvement are as covariates

	GEQ-Pos.A	GEQ-Comp.	GEQ-Chal.
CPP	-	-	-
Fam.	-	-	-
Perf.	**	**	-
CPP*Fam.	-	-	-
CPP*Perf.	-	-	-
SPGQ-BE	-	-	-
SPGQ-PI	**	(*)	*

**. Significant at the 0.01 level.
*. Significant at the 0.05 level
(*). Marginal significant.

The main effects in Co-Player Presence on GEQ-Positive Affect, GEQ-Competence and GEQ-Challenge all disappeared due to the inclusion of the social presence scales as covariates. In the mediation analysis for GEQ-Positive Affect, SPGQ-PI was highly significant ($F(1,111.1) = 8.34$; $p<.01$), for GEQ-Challenge it was significant ($F(1,107.8) = 4.47$; $p<.04$), and for GEQ-Competence it was marginally significant ($F(1,114.6) = 3.77$; $p<.06$). Main effects of Performance remained intact for GEQ-Positive Affect ($M_{Winner} = 3.5$ (0.1); $M_{Winner} = 2.9$ (0.1)) and GEQ-Competence ($M_{Winner} = 3.3$ (0.1); $M_{Winner} = 2.2$ (0.1).

These findings indicate that indeed the differences between the three settings of Co-Player Presence are fully accounted for by the subjective sense of social presence, in particular of the psychological involvement subscale.

4   Discussion

Digital gaming takes place in many different locations and different social contexts. Yet the role of co-player presence on player enjoyment has been overlooked in the majority of player experience studies to date. The current study systematically varied co-player presence according to three common two-player settings (virtual, mediated, and co-located) and investigated effects on player enjoyment. Effects of familiarity and winning or losing were also taken into account. Player enjoyment was treated as a multidimensional construct, consisting of fun (positive affect), competence, challenge, and frustration, and four subscales probing aggression as a state variable. Results indicate that, compared to playing against a virtual or mediated co-player, playing against a co-located other significantly adds to the fun, challenge, and perceived competence in the game. Winning also contributes to enjoyment and perceived competence. Perhaps surprisingly, winning was also positively related to frustration. Losing resulted in more reported hostility. Lastly, players reported more verbal aggression and hostility when competing with a friend than with a stranger.

In the current study, the virtual co-player setting was identical to the mediated setting, except for the players' (bogus) conviction they were competing with a non-human other. Players' subjective sense of the other players' presence increased progressively and significantly from virtual to mediated to co-located settings. Although the virtual and mediated co-play setting were in essence identical, players reported higher levels of social presence in mediated co-play. This result can only be attributed to the player's awareness of playing against a (non-)human. Differences between mediated and co-located co-play lay in the opportunity for richer social interaction between players during co-located play.

Player enjoyment increased from virtual and mediated to co-located co-play. More fun, perceived competence, and challenge were experienced when players were in the same room, than when they were apart. Yet no differences in frustration or aggression were reported. Moreover, mediation analyses demonstrated that these effects could be attributed to the subjective sense of social presence induced in the three settings. These outcomes suggest that players experience more player enjoyment with increasing affordances for communication. The social cues and opportunities for social interaction directly shape player enjoyment in social play. Although social presence differed between virtual and mediated co-play, contrast analyses showed no significant differences between these setting on player enjoyment scales, except for a trend on positive affect. This suggests that the difference between playing against a non-human co-player or human co-player – all remaining factors equal – who is not physically present is only marginal.

Familiarity also proved a relevant determinant of player enjoyment. Interestingly, more aggression (verbal aggression and hostility) was reported among friends than among strangers. This suggests that perhaps play among friends is more intense than among strangers. Future research should explore whether these feelings were sincerely negative, or rather should be interpreted as friendly banter.

Performance demonstrated effects on player enjoyment, in particular on positive affect, competence, frustration and hostility. Logically, winners experienced more enjoyment in playing than losers did.

4.1 Conclusions

Although the social relevance of digital gaming has been discussed and investigated in cultural and sociological readings, in particular for massively multi-player online playing games, social context has been largely neglected in terms of in-game player experience of other types of games. From the results of the current study, we conclude that social context is an important determinant of player enjoyment and should be incorporated in player experience models. Results indicate that, compared to playing against a virtual or mediated co-player, a co-located co-player significantly adds to the fun, challenge, and perceived competence in the game. The effect of social context was mediated by the level of social presence experienced, which is determined by affordances for communication & interaction, and the amount of social cues exchanged. These affordances directly shape player enjoyment in social play.

Acknowledgments. The authors thank Martin Boschman for assisting with the laboratory setup. Support from the Games@Large, FUGA, and PASION project is gratefully acknowledged.

References

1. Huizinga, J.: Homo Ludens: A Study of the Play Element in Culture. Beacon Press, Boston (1950)
2. Durkin, K., Aisbett, K.: Computer Games and Australians Today. Office of Film and Literature Classification, Sydney (1999)
3. Nielsen Interactive Entertainment: Video gamers in Europe – 2005. Research Report Prepared for the Interactive Software Federation of Europe (2005)
4. Tychsen, A., Smith, J.H., Hitchens, M., Tosca, S.: Communication in multi-player role playing games - the effect of medium. In: Göbel, S., Malkewitz, R., Iurgel, I. (eds.) TIDSE 2006. LNCS, vol. 4326, pp. 277–288. Springer, Heidelberg (2006)
5. de Kort, Y.A.W., IJsselsteijn, W.A., Poels, K.: Digital games as social presence technology: Development of the social presence questionnaire (SPGQ). In: Presence 2007 Conference, Barcelona, October 25-27 (2007)
6. Ravaja, N., Saari, T., Turpeinen, M., Laarni, J., Slaminen, M., Kivikangas, M.: Spatial presence and emotions during video game playing: Does it matter with whom you play? Presence: Teleoperators and Virtual Environments 15, 381–392 (2006)

7. Mandryk, R.L., Inkpen, K.M.: Physiological indicators for the evaluation of co-located collaborative play. In: CSCW 2004, Chicago, IL, USA, November 6-10, 2004 (2006)
8. Ermi, L., Mäyra, F.: Fundamental components of the gameplay experience: Analyzing immersion. In: de Castell, S., Jenson, J. (eds.) Changing Views: Worlds in Play. Selected papers of the 2005 DiGRA's Second International Conference (2005)
9. Sweetser, P., Wyeth, P.: GameFlow: A Model for Evaluating Player Enjoyment in Games. ACM Computers in Entertainment 3(3) Article 3A (2005)
10. Klimmt, C.: Dimensions and determinants of the enjoyment of playing digital games: a three-level model. In: Copier, M., Raessens, J. (eds.) Level up: Digital games research conference, Faculty of Arts, Utrecht University (2003)
11. de Kort, Y.A.W., IJsselsteijn, W.A., Gajadhar, B.J.: People, places and play: A research framework for digital game experience in a socio-spatial context. In: DiGRA 2007 Conference, Tokyo, September 24-28 (2007)
12. Biocca, F., Harms, C., Burgoon, J.K.: Criteria for a theory and measure of social presence. Presence: Teleoperators & Virtual Environments 12(5), 456–480 (2003)
13. Gajadhar, B.J., de Kort, Y.A.W., IJsselsteijn, W.A.: Influence of social setting on player experience of digital games. In: CHI 2008 Conference, Florence, April 5-10 (2008)
14. Poels, K., de Kort, Y.A.W., IJsselsteijn, W.A.: It is always a lot of fun! Exploring Dimensions of Digital Game Experience using Focus Group Methodology. In: Proceedings of Futureplay 2007, Toronto, Canada, pp. 83–89 (2007)
15. IJsselsteijn, W.A., de Kort, Y.A.W. & Poels, K.: The Game Experience Questionnaire: Development of a self-report measure to assess the psychological impact of digital games (2008) (in preparation)
16. Resinari, R.: WoodPong. DoubleR Software, PC (2007)
17. Buss, A.H., Perry, M.: The aggression questionnaire. Journal of Personality and Social Psychology 63, 452–459 (1992)
18. Baron, R.M., Kenny, D.A.: The moderator-mediator variable distinction in social psychological research: Conceptual, strategic and statistical considerations. Journal of Personality and Social Psychology 51, 1173–1182 (1986)
19. Gajadhar, B.J:, de Kort, Y.A.W., IJsselsteijn, W.A.: Rules of Engagement: Influence of social setting on player enjoyment in digital games (in preperation)

The Unlikeability of a Cuddly Toy Interface: An Experimental Study of Preschoolers' Likeability and Usability of a 3D Game Played with a Cuddly Toy Versus a Keyboard

Vero Vanden Abeele[1], Bieke Zaman[2], and Mariek Vanden Abeele[3]

[1] eMedia, Groep T Leuven Engineering School, Vesaliusstraat 13,
3000 Leuven, Belgium
vero@groept.be
[2] CUO, IBBT, Katholieke Universiteit Leuven, Parkstraat 45, bus 3605,
3000 Leuven, Belgium
bieke.zaman@soc.kuleuven.be
[3] MASSCOM, Katholieke Universiteit Leuven, Parkstraat 45, bus 3603,
3000 Leuven, Belgium
mariek.vandenabeele@soc.kuleuven.be

Abstract. We report on a comparative study of the likeability and usability of a cuddly toy interface versus a keyboard interface. We put 35 preschoolers to the test and asked them to play a 3D game via a keyboard and via a cuddly toy interface. Afterwards the usability (user-friendliness) and the likeability (joy-of-use) of both interfaces were assessed. Our results indicate that the cuddly toy interface was neither more likeable nor more usable than the keyboard interface. Based on additional qualitative data, we argument that the causes might be fatigue, a lack of meaningful use of gestures, and the occurrence of 'satisficing'.

Keywords: Tangible Embedded Interaction, Gestural Interaction, Children, Preschoolers, Likeability, Usability.

1 Introduction

Embodied interaction, tangible manipulation and physical mediation of digital data are the recent focus of many HCI researchers, carried out under the label of 'Tangible Embedded Interaction'(TEI) [1]. Donald Norman addresses this trend as physicality or *"the return to physical devices, where we control things by physical body movement, by turning, moving, and manipulating appropriate mechanical devices [2]"*. The common premise of these new interaction styles is the focus on perceptual-motor skills and physical affordances that new input/output devices offer. TEI is considered as more natural and to be preferred over a cognition driven approach, associated with personal computing paradigms [3, 4, 5]. Tangibles are linked to

P. Markopoulos et al. (Eds.): Fun and Games 2008, LNCS 5294, pp. 118–131, 2008.

affective interaction [6, 7]. TEI stimulates social interaction and sharing [8, 9]. What concerns interface designs for children, TEI is considered to enhance play and stimulate learning [10, 11, 12].

Consequently, in the last years, many creative TEI-projects have been carried out to augment children's play experience and learning. Many research articles on these TEI projects report on the 'positive effects' on the end user. These user studies provide interesting, inspiring and necessary qualitative information. However, as exploratory studies, they are characterized by observations with a limited number of participants, and the absence of comparative conditions. We agree with Xie et al. and Marshall et al. [13, 14, 15] that empirical evidence supporting the claims of TEI is scarce. Most conclusions are made on the basis of theoretical accounts [5, 8, 10] and small, informal user observations. Many research projects about tangible or embedded interfaces for children do not go further than describing participants' mostly enthusiastic experiences with tangibles. User research on TEI, certainly in combination with children, lacks experimental validation on whether it is really the 'tangible' or 'embedded' interaction that is causing the positive effects. To make reliable claims about the effects of tangible or embedded interaction, experimental research designs and methods are needed. In this paper, we report on an experimental study that assesses the influence of a cuddly toy interface on the usability and the likeability of a 3D game for preschoolers.

In this paper, we will first elaborate on our cuddly toy interface and the related research questions. Next, we describe the experimental design adapted to the needs of preschoolers. Then, we elaborate on the results. Finally, in the discussion we try to offer explanations with insights from the researchers' observations during the experiments.

2   A Cuddly Toy Interface

Fig. 1. A 3D game played with a cuddly toy interface

The subject of our study is 'Toewie', a 3D game for 3-5 years old children, to be played with a 'cuddly toy interface'. The main character in the game (figure 1) is the cuddly toy, which contains sensors (2 pressure sensors, 1 gyro sensor and 1 acceleration sensor) in the arms and body. When the child interacts with the cuddly toy, the sensors will recognize these movements, and translate them into on-screen action. Consequently, by manipulating the cuddly toy interface, the preschooler is able to jump forward, look around and interact with the game environment.

The game itself is a 3D game of an outdoor landscape in which birthday presents are located at several points. The goal is to collect all 7 presents and bring these to a friend located at the other end of the 3D world, only then can the birthday party start.

The main intention of Toewie is to familiarize a young audience with navigation and interaction in a 3D virtual environment, and simply to have fun in a 3D world.[1]

3   Research Questions

With traditional game controllers, moving around, turning, jumping over obstacles, picking up objects, etc. usually happens by a combination of arrow keys, joysticks, mice and several other buttons. For novice gamers, these are complex input mechanisms that need to be mastered and require some learning time. For preschoolers, this interaction is even more problematic, as their behavioral and cognitive skills are not yet developed enough to understand complex mappings [17]. Apart from the fine motor skills which are necessary to work with the mouse and/or other small buttons, preschoolers lack spatial perception to map the movement of the mouse or controller to the movement on the screen [18]. Similar to [19, 20], we wanted children to have intuitive controls for directing a protagonist in a 3D game, and we wanted to avoid that children need to learn complex mappings between buttons and on screen action [21]. Therefore we addressed enactive knowledge [22] or *"knowledge stored in the form of motor responses and acquired by the act of doing.* *[23]"* According to Bruner, this knowledge is innate and precedes iconic and symbolic knowledge. With our cuddly toy interface, we relied on enactive knowledge such as moving the cuddly toy up and down for hopping (sensed by the acceleration sensor), turning the cuddly toy for turning within the game (gyrosensor) and squeezing the arms for picking up objects (via air pressure sensors). Therefore, we expected our cuddly toy interface to be more user-friendly than a traditional keyboard interface for our preschoolers.

H1 The cuddly toy interface is more 'usable' than a keyboard interface

Besides being simple to learn and easy to interact with, we also wanted our game controller to be *likeable*. Therefore, our cuddly toy was carefully designed and developed as a soft, round, and colorful toy, stimulating visceral emotions [24] and inviting children to hug, fiddle and empathize with it. Furthermore, similar to Johnsons research on sympathetic interfaces [25], our cuddly toy was haptically engaging. In the Likeability framework for preschoolers, [26, 27], *'body & senses'* are listed as an important gratification, children enjoy touching objects and moving around themselves. Therefore, the cuddly toy was explicitly designed to let children feel the soft fabric and round shape and to stimulate movement of the preschoolers. Therefore we expected our cuddly toy interface to be more likeable than a traditional keyboard interface for our preschoolers.

H2 The cuddly toy interface is more likeable than a keyboard interface

---

[1] For more in-depth information about the technological details and the design rationale behind Toewie, we refer to [16].

4   Research Methodology

4.1   Participants

Thirty-five preschoolers from one elementary school participated in the experiment, nineteen girls and sixteen boys. The age ranged from 49 to 80 months old, with a mean age of 64.5 months (5.4 years). All children were in kindergarten and not yet literate. All children were tested in their natural environment, namely in the (old) kitchen of the kindergarten.

4.2   Research Design

Fig. 2. Research setup of the experiment

All children were asked to play the 3D game twice, once with the cuddly toy interface (experimental condition TEI) and once with the keyboard (experimental condition KB). Exactly the same 3D game was presented in both conditions. Both games were played on identical laptops, positioned next to each other (figure 2). The options were to navigate forward (visualized as hopping forward in the game), to turn around and to pick up objects. In the keyboard condition these options were mapped to the arrow keys (arrow up was moving forward, arrow left was turning to the left, arrow right was turning to the right) and spacebar (picking up objects). In the cuddly toy condition the options were moving the cuddly toy up and down as if it were hopping (hopping activated the acceleration sensor and was translated as moving forward) and turning (turning the cuddly toy activated the gyrosensor and was translated as turning). Squeezing in the arms/hands of the cuddly toy interface activated the pressure sensors and was used for picking up objects. To rule out order effects, we counterbalanced the conditions. 17 preschoolers first played with the cuddly toy interface, 18 preschoolers first played with the keyboard.

4.3   Procedure

In each condition a facilitator was sitting next to the child. The procedure started with a tutorial phase of 2 minutes, during which the preschooler was familiarized with the input device, be it KB or TEI. Pilot trials revealed that the game could be completed within ten minutes. Therefore, after the tutorial, the child was given a maximum of ten minutes to play the game.

When testing games with young children, Barendregt [18, p21] emphasizes the importance of undirected play: *"Giving tasks conflicts with the explorative nature of games and the need for intrinsically motivating goals."* Therefore, we did not give any tasks other than explaining the main goal of the game, which was done inside the game by the main character Toewie when the game started. Furthermore, Barendregt mentions problems with verbalizing with young children: *"[...] this may make them mention non-problems in order to please the facilitator.* " Consequently, we did not prompt children during play; in fact the facilitator tried to obtrude as little as possible and only provided help when this was explicitly asked for by the child.

The child entered the room, played the game until it was finished with one of both interfaces. If the child did not succeed in completing the game within the ten minutes time frame the game was ended. After a short break, the child then played the game with the remaining interface (again first the guided tutorial, then free play for a maximum of ten minutes). The two conditions were counterbalanced so that an equal amount of children played with the keyboard interface first as with the cuddly toy interface. All children played alone. We ensured that while one child played on one interface no other child was playing on the other interface.

After both conditions were finished, a list of likeability questions was administered.

4.4 Measures

Measuring usability and likeability with preschoolers requires an adaptation of traditional testing methods because of the cognitive, emotional and behavioral limitations [17, 18, 28, 29, 30]. One cannot simply administer a list of questions with this young age group.

Measuring Usability. The international standard, ISO 9241-11, provides guidance on usability and defines it as: *"The extent to which a product can be used by specified users to achieve specified goals with effectiveness, efficiency and satisfaction in a specified context of use." [31]* Quantitatively, usability is often measured by the time to complete the task and the number of errors made [32]. Similarly, we operationalized the efficiency by time necessary to complete the game (*time*), and effectiveness by the number of subtask successfully completed in the game (*tasks*) and whether the child succeeded in finishing the game (*success*). Since we did not direct play and did not provide clear tasks, we could not establish whether 'illogical actions' were to be considered exploration or errors. Therefore, it was not possible to log the number of errors.

Measuring Likeability. Likeability is a complex construct [27] and should be understood as 'the perception of a positive experience with a (digital) product'. For measuring likeability we relied on the 'This-or-That method' as proposed by Zaman & Abeele in [34]. This method consists of asking direct questions to the preschooler, and asking to make a choice between the two conditions. For discriminating between the two options the facilitator actively points to the two alternatives while prompting *"This one or that one? That one or this one?"* The child can consequently indicate the preferred game, simply by pointing. The 'This-or-That' method counteracts the tendency of children for social desirability, and minimizes cognitive load by offering only two alternatives.

We measured likeability with five questions: 1) Which game did you find most fun (*most fun*), 2) Which game would you want to receive as a gift (*wanted gift*), 3) which game would you like to take home with you (*take home*), 4) which game would you like to play again (*play again*) and 5) which game did you find the most stupid (*most stupid* – this question was reversed in the final likeability measure)? We triangulated these answers with *free play* at the end of the test: as a 'reward' for participating the child could choose one of the two interfaces and play the game again.

Qualitative Data. Besides quantitative measurements, also qualitative material was gathered. We video-recorded interaction styles and comments uttered by the preschooler when playing the game. Only after the complete test was finalized (playing the two conditions and answering the likeability questions) the facilitator would follow up on this qualitative information and ask the preschooler to explain a little more on exactly why one condition was chosen over one another according to a laddering method [34].

Other Characteristics. Besides age and gender, the kindergarten teachers also gave information about the existence of siblings and about preschoolers' computer experience. The ratings of computer experience were based on the frequency with which preschoolers were playing on the school's game computer.

5 Results

5.1 Usability Results

When looking at the mean completion *time* (in seconds) with the cuddly toy interface (TEI) versus the keyboard interface (KB), on average the preschoolers needed 36 seconds more to complete the game in the TEI condition (table 1). However, these differences are non-significant interface (t (34) =-1.29, p=.21). When comparing the number of *tasks* successfully completed in the game, we found that that in the TEI condition, preschoolers on average completed 6,31 tasks while in the KB condition on average 6,83 tasks were completed. Again these differences are non-significant (t (34) =1.54, p=.13). When children *success*fully completed all 7 tasks and delivered the presents to the friend, they finished the game (coded 0 for unsuccessful completion of the game, 1 for successful completion). 83% of the children (29 children) successfully delivered the presents in the KB condition as compared to 74% (26 children) in the TEI condition. Again these differences are non-significant (t (34) =-.90, p=.37).

Table 1. Means (M), standard deviation (SD) and comparisons of completion time (time), number of tasks (tasks) and successful completion of the game (success)

	M	SD	One Sample t-test (Test Value = 0)					
time KB	0:06:47	0:02:13		*Mean Diff*	*SD*	*t*	*df*	*Sig. (2-tailed)*
time TEI	0:07:23	0:02:09	time (KB – TEI)	-35,94	164,98	-1,29	34	,21
tasks KB	6,83	,75		*Mean Diff*	*SD*	*t*	*df*	*Sig. (2-tailed)*
tasks TEI	6,31	1,91	tasks (KB – TEI)	,60	2,30	1,54	34	,13
success KB	,83	,38		*Mean Diff*	*SD*	*t*	*df*	*Sig. (2-tailed)*
success TEI	,74	,44	succes (KB – TEI)	,09	,56	,90	34	,37

Table 2. Means (M), standard deviation (SD) and comparisons of completion time (time), number of tasks (tasks) and successful completion of the game (success) according to the order within the experiment

Order		M	SD	One Sample t-test (test value = 0)					
TEI 1st	time KB	0:06:48	0:02:29		Mean Diff	SD	t	df	Sig. (2-tailed)
	time TEI	0:08:07	0:02:07	time (KB – TEI)	-79,18	173,88	-1,88	16	,08
	tasks KB	6,88	,46		Mean Diff	SD	t	df	Sig. (2-tailed)
	tasks TEI	6,41	1,50	tasks (KB – TEI)	,76	1,89	1,67	16	,11
	success KB	,82	,39		Mean Diff	SD	t	df	Sig. (2-tailed)
	success TEI	,53	,51	succes (KB – TEI)	,29	,59	2,06	16	,06
KB 1st	time KB	0:06:46	0:02:01		Mean Diff	SD	t	df	Sig. (2-tailed)
	time TEI	0:06:41	0:02:00	time (KB – TEI)	4,89	149,49	,14	17	,89
	tasks KB	6,78	,94		Mean Diff	SD	t	df	Sig. (2-tailed)
	tasks TEI	6,22	2,26	tasks (KB – TEI)	,44	2,68	,70	17	,49
	success KB	,83	,38		Mean Diff	SD	t	df	Sig. (2-tailed)
	success TEI	,94	,24	succes (KB – TEI)	-,11	,47	-1,00	17	,33

When taking into account the order in which the preschoolers played the two interfaces, we see only minor changes (table 2). In the group of children who played the TEI first, completion time $(t(16) = -1.88, p=.08)$ and success rate $(t(16)=2.06, p=.06)$ become marginally significant. We conclude that our hypothesis concerning the usability *(H1)* cannot be supported. On the contrary, these results point to a trend that favours the keyboard over the cuddly toy interface.

5.2 Likeability Results

With regard to the likeability, we first constructed a scale consisting of the five likeability questions (with the 'most stupid' question reversed) and the free play question. This scale was tested for internal consistency and proved to be very reliable $(\alpha = .88)$.

Next, a mean likeability score was computed for each child, with mean scores closer to 1 indicating a preference for the cuddly toy interface (TEI) and mean scores closer to 2 indicate a preference for the keyboard interface (KB). As we had already noticed in the scores for each separate likeability question (see table 3), the average preference within the total sample was 1,60 $(SD=.39)$. In other words, counter to our experimental hypothesis *(H2)*, children on average found the keyboard interface more likeable than the cuddly toy interface.

To see whether this preference was statistically significant, a one-sample t-test was conducted in which we compared the average likeability score of our sample with a standard test value of 1,5 (i.e. a test-value of 1,5 corresponds with no significant difference in the likeability of both interfaces). The results of this t-test demonstrate that the preference for the keyboard interface cannot be supported statistically: there is no significant difference in the preference of the keyboard interface over the cuddly toy interface $(t (31) =1.435, p=.161)$. However, we can conclude that there is a trend towards the keyboard.

Table 3. Overview of answers to the 5 likeability questions and free play

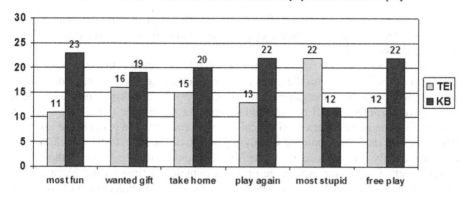

5.3 Correlation between Likeability and Usability

Next, we examined whether completion time (*time*) with both interfaces and the successful completion of the game (*success*) were related to the likeability score (*likeability*). A correlation analysis (see table 4) reveals that the likeability score is significantly related to whether the child was able to complete the video game successfully within the time frame or not ($r = -.444$, $p < .01$). Children who were unable to complete the game successfully with the cuddly toy interface ($M_{likeability} = 1.91$, $SD = .188$) preferred the keyboard interface significantly more than the children who completed the task successfully with the cuddly toy interface ($M_{likeability} = 1.52$, $SD = .387$)($t(28.791) = 3.901$, $p < .01$). If we repeat our one-sample t-test for the subgroup of children who were unsuccessful, we find a significant preference of the keyboard interface over the cuddly toy interface ($t(8) = 6.487$, $p < .000$).

In the subgroup of children who did manage to complete the game successfully while using the cuddly toy interface, there is no significant preference for one or the other interface ($t(25) = .304$, $p = .764$).

Table 4. Correlation matrix of usability measures, likability and other user characteristics (gender, age, presence of siblings and computer experience)

	gender	age	sibling	comp. exp.	time TEI	time KB	tasks TEI	tasks KB	succes TEI	succes KB	like- ability
gender	1	,125	,309*	-,149	,096	,071	-,349*	-,203	-,277	-,113	,093
age		1	-,049	,358ᵇ	-,197	-,456**	,114	,261	,079	,230	-,098
sibling			1	-,162	-,196	-,109	-,263.ᶜ	-,145	,116	,039	,295ᶜ
comp. exp.				1	-,380*	-,471*	,347	,290	,037	,234	,036
time TEI					1	,214	-,392*	,106	-,721**	-,161	,244
time KB						1	,036	-,449**	,001	-508**	-,119
tasks TEI							1	-,063	,346*	,051	-,043
tasks KB								1	-,072	,766**	-,154
success TEI									1	,079	-,444**
succes KB										1	-,107
likeability											1

*p < .05 level, **. p < .01, ᵃp=.071, ᵇp=.062, ᶜp=.085*

5.4 Other Moderator Effects

Because our sample of children differed on a great number of variables (e.g. gender, age, computer experience, siblings, etc.), we examined whether there might be any moderator effects.

A further look at the correlation table (table 3) shows that the successful completion of the game with the cuddly toy interface is significantly related with the time needed to complete the game (time) ($r=-.721$, $p<.01$) and this completion time is in turn significantly related to the child's computer experience ($r=-.380$, $p<.05$). In other words, the more experienced the child is with computers in general, the faster he will complete the game with the cuddly toy interface; and the faster the child is in using the cuddly toy interface, the higher the chances of success. Although there is no direct effect of computer experience or game completion time on the likeability of TEI, this chain of correlations might be an indication of an indirect effect of computer experience on the likeability of the cuddly toy interface.

Except for a successful game completion, only one other variable is marginally significant related to the likeability of both interfaces: whether the child has an older sibling or not ($r=.295$, p=.085. Bryant et al [17] report that gamers with older siblings model their gameplay according to the behavior of older siblings. In our research, children who had an older brother or sister ($M_{\text{likeability}} =1.72$, $SD=.387$) tended to prefer the keyboard interface more than eldest children ($M_{\text{likeability}} =1.55$, $SD=.355$) ($t(33)=-1.777$, p=.085). Might this result indicate that children with one or more older siblings regard the keyboard interface as less childish than the cuddly toy interface and therefore more likeable?

6 Discussion

Although the relationship between the usability and the likeability of a game is not straightforward (where usability is about removing obstacles, fun in games is about deliberately overcoming these obstacles [35]), our data show that usability and likeability correlate; the likeability score is significantly related to whether the child was able to complete the video game task successfully. This is in line with Jordan's hierarchy of player needs [36] and other models provided by game research groups [37,38] that suggest that playability and fun are related and even dependent on usability.

In trying to understand why our TEI was less usable and less likeable than the KB, we observed interaction styles and comments made by the children. From our qualitative data we interpret that the extra difficulty of the cuddly toy interface has four sources.

1) The biggest usability issue with our Cuddly Toy Interface concerned turning. Turning with our cuddly toy interface was challenging because we demanded of preschoolers to sequentially perform a turning movement and next a hopping movement while keeping the cuddly toy interface rotated. The combination of two sequential gestures was a challenge for some preschoolers and sometimes resulted in pure frustration. Should we have foreseen this usability flaw? We emphasize that when designing the Cuddly Toy Interface, this was done with help from a kindergarten teacher and preschoolers, who tried out the cuddly toy many times. Reports from users on the cuddly toy

interface were very enthusiast and positive. It seemed that turning with our cuddly toy interface tapped into their enactive knowledge, little explanation was necessary. It is only when comparing directly with the keyboard condition that we understood that turning with the TEI could and should be made even more user-friendly. Again this underlines the importance of empirical validation. With the keyboard interface, some of the preschoolers required a little more initial instruction. But once they understood the mappings (and this was surprisingly fast), for many preschoolers, pressing the arrow keys was preferred over manipulating the cuddle toy interface. As one boy remarked during the interview:*"I really like this one [hugs the cuddly toy interface], but for playing the game, I like this one [points to the keyboard] more."*

2) Navigating via the hopping movement required continuous body movement of our preschoolers. When designing the cuddly toy interface we presumed that body movement on its own would be received as a positive quality, basing ourselves on the Body & Senses gratification within the Extended Likeability Framework [26]. However, we observed that repetitious body movements quickly became dull. Many preschoolers expressed fatigue or at least were bored of making the hopping gesture.

3) Preschoolers also became bored with hopping because we did not make meaningful use of it. The acceleration and the gyrosensor allow for gestural interaction, which is in a sense 'continuous'. It is not 'discrete' as when pressing a button. For the preschoolers, it was not always clear why both a slow, delicate movement and a vehement frenzy movement both resulted in the same 'average' jump. In terms of the Interaction Frogger Framework [39], there was a non-unification of action and function on the dimension of dynamics and expression. The dynamics (*position, speed, acceleration and force)* and expression of the action provided by the preschooler were not recorded and there was no feedback in reaction. We hypothesize that e.g. if we translated frantic jumping with the Cuddly Toy Interface into frantic jumping within the game, this would have resulted in a greater like for the hopping movement. In other words, because we transformed a continuous gesture into a discrete response within the game, this gesture was not providing meaningful play [40] within the game.

4) Finally, from the observations during the experiment, we noticed a wide diversity in interaction styles with our TEI. Diversity in interaction styles is considered as a positive aspect of tangible interaction, in [7, 39] Wensveen et al. elaborate that *"freedom of interaction is based on the exploitation of a range of perceptual-motor skills by offering the user myriad ways to reach the product's functionality".* We anticipated a wide range in interaction styles, and our sensors were set to allow this.² At the beginning of the test, the facilitator demonstrated the 'standard use' of the TEI but once the child started playing, we did not intervene and let the child interact by his or her preferred way. Although we anticipated diversity, still the preschoolers surprised us, using the

---

² Although we allowed our sensors to detect a freedom of *action*, the game itself did not provide freedom of *interaction since it did not respond in a meaningful way to different interaction styles.* As such, this goes clearly against the guidelines that Wensveen offers for affective interaction in his Interaction Frogger Framework.

TEI in non-intended ways. Freedom of interaction in our case often resulted in suboptimal interaction strategies. Besides heavy and light bouncers (bouncing with the cuddly toy interface as we expected), we observed 'pushers' (pushing the TEI on the table); 'swipers' (swiping TEI over the table), 'tilters' (tipping TEI over), and 'throwers' (throwing TEI in the air).

The use of these suboptimal interaction styles does remind us of 'satisficing' as coined by Simon [41]. The term points towards the use of sub-optimal strategies for solving problems. It is a well-researched phenomenon within cognitive psychology and consequently within human-computer interaction: when dealing with problems, people do not look for the best solution but settle for good enough. We believe our preschoolers 'satisficed', they fell into a sub-optimal interaction style and stuck with it.

It is interesting to remark that 'satisficing' then not only applies cognitive tasks but also lends itself to behavioral tasks. This supports current views that cognitive and action systems richly interact [42] and in fact [43] pleads for an embodied, situated understanding of tangible interaction that avoids dualist notions of cognitive knowledge and bodily action.

7 Conclusion

In this paper we report on a comparative study of a cuddly toy interface versus a keyboard interface. We report on how, contrary to our hypotheses, the Cuddly Toy Interface was found to be less likeable and less usable than the keyboard interface. Drawing on our results, we offer the following design guidelines for physical/gestural interaction.

1. When implementing gestural interaction, be aware that simultaneous or sequential order of gestures are challenging and become usability traps, even if they are based on enactive knowledge.
2. Avoid long lasting repetitive movements as they might cause fatigue and bore players.
3. Provide meaningful gestural interaction. Based on the Interaction Frogger Framework [39] we emphasize that the expression and dynamics of gestures should be translated appropriately into in game action. If not the added value of gestural interaction is lost.
4. Finally, be aware of satisficing in interaction styles. Freedom of action can be a good thing but it can also lead to suboptimal interaction styles that complicate interaction.

Finally, we believe that our paper contributes to the field of research on Tangible Embedded Interaction by demonstrating the value of sound experimental validation of TEI. It is only then that we can move forward.

Acknowledgments. We like to thank Jelle Husson (Game developer and Digital artist) and Johannes Taelman (Creative Engineering Mind) for constructing the

Toewie game and cuddly toy interface and for their patience and assistance during tests. Also, we like to thank David Molenberghs (Digital Artist) and Jan (Plush Toy Designer). Finally, we like to thank the teachers and preschoolers of BSGO De appeltuin who participated in our experiment.

References

1. TEI. International Conference on Tangible and Embedded Interaction,
    http://tei-conf.org/
2. Norman, D.A.: The next UI breakthrough, part 2: physicality. Interactions 14(4), 46–47 (2007), http://doi.acm.org/10.1145/1273961.1273986
3. Fitzmaurice, G.W., Ishii, H., Buxton, W.B.: Laying the Foundations for Graspable User Interfaces. In: Proceedings of CHI 1995, pp. 442–449 (1995)
4. Ullmer, B., Ishii, H.: Emerging Frameworks for Tangible User Interfaces. In: Carroll, J.M. (ed.) Human-Computer Interaction in the New Millenium, pp. 579–601. Addison-Wesley, Reading (2001)
5. Dourish, P.: Social Computing. In: Dourish, P. (ed.) Where the Action is. MIT Press, Cambridge (2001)
6. Djajadiningrat, T., Wensveen, S., Frens, J., Overbeeke, K.: Tangible products: redressing the balance between appearance and action. Personal Ubiquitous Comput. 8(5), 294–309 (2004), http://dx.doi.org/10.1007/s00779-004-0293-8
7. Wensveen, S., Overbeeke, K., Djajadiningrat, T., Kyffin, S.: Freedom of fun, freedom of interaction. Iterations 11(5), 59–61 (2004),
    http://doi.acm.org/10.1145/1015530.1015559
8. Hornecker, E., Buur, J.: Getting a grip on tangible interaction: a framework on physical space and social interaction. In: Proc. of CHI 2006, pp. 437–446. ACM Press, New York (2006)
9. Hornecker, E., Marshall, P., Rogers, Y.: From entry to access: how shareability comes about. In: Proceedings of the 2007 Conference on Designing Pleasurable Products and interfaces DPPI 2007, Helsinki, Finland, August 22 - 25. ACM, New York (2007)
10. Antle, A.N.: The CTI framework: informing the design of tangible systems for children. In: Proceedings of the 1st international Conference on Tangible and Embedded interaction, pp. 195–202. ACM Press, New York (2007)
11. Price, S., Rogers, Y., Scaife, M., Stanton, D., Neale, H.: Using 'tangibles' to promote novel forms of playful learning. In: Proceedings of the Interacting with Computers, vol. 15(2), pp. 169–185. ACM Press, New York (2003)
12. O'Malley, C., Fraser, D.S.: Literature Review in Learning with Tangible Technologies. NESTA Futurelab (2004)
13. Xie, L., Antle, A.N., Motamedi, N.: Are tangibles more fun?: comparing children's enjoyment and engagement using physical, graphical and tangible user interfaces. In: Proceedings of the 2nd international Conference on Tangible and Embedded interaction TEI 2008, Bonn, Germany, February 18 - 20, pp. 191–198. ACM, New York (2008)
14. Marshall, P., Rogers, Y., Hornecker, E.: Are Tangible Interfaces Really Any Better Than Other Kinds of Interfaces? In: Position paper for CHI 2007 workshop 'Tangible User Interfaces in Context and Theory' (2007)
15. Marshall, P.: Do tangible interfaces enhance learning? In: Proceedings of the 1st international Conference on Tangible and Embedded interaction TEI 2007, Baton Rouge, Louisiana, February 15 - 17, pp. 163–170. ACM, New York (2007),
    http://doi.acm.org/10.1145/1226969.1227004

16. Abeele, V.V., Husson, J., Taelman, J.: Toewie: a 3D game for 3-5 years old children to be played with a Cuddly toy interface. IDC, Italy, Milano (2009) (under review)
17. Bryant, J.A., Akerman, A., Drell, J.: Wee Wii. Preschoolers and motion-based gameplay. In: ICA 2008, Montreal, Canada (2008)
18. Barendregt, W.: Evaluating fun and usability in computer games with childrenProefschrift aan de Technische Universiteit Eindhoven, Nederland (09-02-2006), http://alexandria.tue.nl/extra2/200513731.pdf
19. Mazalek, A., Nitsche, M.: Tangible interfaces for real-time 3D virtual environments. In: Proceedings of the international Conference on Advances in Computer Entertainment Technology, ACE 2007, Salzburg, Austria, June 13 - 15, vol. 203 (2007)
20. Paiva, A., Prada, R., Chaves, R., Vala, M., Bullock, A., Andersson, G., Höök, K.: Towards tangibility in gameplay: building a tangible affective interface for a computer game. In: Proceedings of the 5th international Conference on Multimodal interfaces ICMI 2003, Vancouver, British Columbia, Canada, November 05 - 07 (2003)
21. Norman, D.A.: Emotional design. Ubiquity 4(45), 1 (2004), http://doi.acm.org/10.1145/966012.966013
22. Bruner, J.: Processes of cognitive growth: Infancy. Clark University Press, Worcester (1968)
23. Enactive Network (12-07-2008), http://www.enactivenetwork.org
24. Norman, D.A.: The Design of Everyday Things. Basic Books (2002)
25. Johnson, M.P., Wilson, A., Blumberg, B., Kline, C., Bobick, A.: Sympathetic interfaces: using a plush toy to direct synthetic characters. In: Proceedings of the SIGCHI Conference on Human Factors in Computing Systems: the CHI Is the Limit CHI 1999 (1999)
26. Zaman, B., Abeele, V.V.: Towards a Likeability Framework that meets Child-Computer Interaction & Communication Sciences. In: Proceedings of IDC 2007, pp. 1–8 (2007)
27. Abeele, V.V., Zaman, B.: The Extended Likeability Framework: A Theoretical Framework for and a Practical Case of Designing Likeable Media Applications for Preschoolers. Advances in Human-Computer Interaction. Special Issue on Interactive Play and Learning for Children. Hindawi Publishing Corporation (forthcoming), http://www.hindawi.com
28. Hanna, L., Risden, K., Alexander, K.: Guidelines for usability testing with children. Interactions 4, 9–14 (1997)
29. Zaman, B.: Evaluating games with children. In: Proceedings of Interact 2005 Workshop on Child computer Interaction: Methodological Research (2005)
30. Read, J., MacFarlane, C.C.: Endurability, engagement and expectations: Measuring children's fun. In: Proceedings of IDC 2002, Eindhoven (2002)
31. International Organization for Standardization, ISO 9041 (1997), http://www.iso.org/iso/en/CatalogueDetailPage.CatalogueDetail?CSNUMBER=28786&scopelist=
32. Rubin, J.: Handbook of Usability Testing: How to Plan, Design, and Conduct Effective Test, 1st edn. Wiley, Chichester (1994)
33. Zaman, B., Abeele, V.V.: How to Measure the Likeability of Tangible Interaction with Preschoolers. In: Proceedings CHI Nederland, pp. 57–59. Infotec Nederland BV Woerden, Eindhoven (2007)
34. Zaman, B.: Introducing contextual laddering to evaluate the likeability of games with children (2007), http://www.springerlink.com/content/5136364 v28514567/

35. Pagulayan, R.J., Keeker, K., Wixon, D., Romero, R.L., Fuller, T.: User-centered design in games. In the Human-Computer interaction Handbook: Fundamentals, Evolving Technologies and Emerging Applications. In: Jacko, J.A., Sears, A. (eds.) Human Factors And Ergonomics, pp. 883–906. Lawrence Erlbaum Associates, Mahwah (2003)

36. Jordan, P.W.: Pleasure with Products: Human Factors for Body, Mind and Soul. In: Green, W., Jordan, P. (eds.) Human Factors in Product Design: Current Practise and Future Trends. Taylor & Francis, UK (1999)

37. Korhonen, H., Koivisto, E.M.: Playability heuristics for mobile games. In: Proceedings of the 8th Conference on Human-Computer interaction with Mobile Devices and Services MobileHCI 2006, Helsinki, Finland, September 12 - 15, vol. 159, pp. 9–16. ACM, New York (2006)

38. Järvinen, A., Heliö, S., Mäyrä, F.: Communication and Community in Digital Entertainment Services. Prestudy Research Report. Hypermedia Laboratory Net Series 2, p. 17 (2002), http://tampub.uta.fi/tup/951-44-5432-4.pdf

39. Wensveen, S.A., Djajadiningrat, J.P., Overbeeke, C.J.: Interaction frogger: a design framework to couple action and function through feedback and feedforward. In: Proceedings of the 5th Conference on Designing interactive Systems DIS 2004, Cambridge, MA, USA, August 01 - 04, pp. 177–184. ACM, New York (2004)

40. Salen, K., Zimmerman, E.: Rules of Play: Game Design Fundamentals. MIT Press, Cambridge (2003) (17-02-2007), http://www.nyls.edu/pdfs/zimmerman.pdf

41. Simon, H.A.: The Sciences of the Artificial, 2nd edn. MIT Press, Cambridge (1981)

42. Dale, R., Roche, J., Snyder, K., McCall, R.: Exploring Action Dynamics as an Index of Paired-Associate Learning. PLoS ONE 3(3), e1728 (2008)

43. Fernaeus, Y., Tholander, J., Jonsson, M.: Towards a new set of ideals: consequences of the practice turn in tangible interaction. In: Proceedings of the 2nd international Conference on Tangible and Embedded interaction TEI 2008, Bonn, Germany, February 18 - 20 (2008)

Think Aloud during fMRI: Neuronal Correlates of Subjective Experience in Video Games

Martin Klasen[1], Mikhail Zvyagintsev[1], René Weber[2], Krystyna A. Mathiak[1,3], and Klaus Mathiak[1,3]

[1] RWTH Aachen University Hospital, Aachen, Germany
mklasen@ukaachen.de
[2] University of California Santa Barbara, CA, USA
[3] Institute of Psychiatry, King's College London, London, UK

Abstract. Experience of computer games can be assessed indirectly by measuring physiological responses and relating the pattern to assumed emotional states or directly by introspection of the player. We combine both approaches by measuring brain activity with functional magnetic resonance imaging (fMRI) during Think Aloud (TA). TA assesses subjects' thoughts and feelings during the game play. The comments and playing behavior were recorded while the brain scans were performed, content of game and TA was analyzed, and related to the brain activation. The fMRI data illustrated that brain activation can be matched to behavioral and experiential content. One category (focus) was associated with increased visual activity and its displeasurable experience with preparatory motor activity. We argue that the combination of subjective introspective with neurophysiological data can 1) reveal meaningful neural mechanisms and 2) validate the introspective method.

1 Introduction

Interactive video game play is an exciting aspect of new mass media that has experienced considerable growth during the last years. The subjective experience of video games and its impact on a person's behavior have been subject of public debate as well as of scientific research. Recently, neuroimaging has been applied to study the neural correlates of behavior during video games [1]. However, a reliable method of measuring objective correlates of experience has not been established. In this article we present an integrative approach to determine objective measures of neuronal correlates based on qualitative reports of subjective experience: Brain activation was measured with functional Magnetic Resonance Imaging (fMRI) during playing and re-watching of a video game. The re-watching served to record verbalizations of thoughts and feelings with Think Aloud (TA) methodology [2]. Thereby objectively obtained brain states can be correlated with subjective and introspective data. This procedure gives insight into the neural correlates of complex functions such as subjective states in virtual interaction.

The TA method was developed from the much older introspection method [3]. Introspection is based on the assumption that a person is able to observe his or her

P. Markopoulos et al. (Eds.): Fun and Games 2008, LNCS 5294, pp. 132–138, 2008.

thoughts, feelings, and cognitive processes, like processes in the outside world. These skills can also be trained so that the subject can observe themselves in a systematic way and make their experience accessible to others by verbalization. The TA method asks a person to continuously verbalize his or her thoughts and feelings. In contrast to introspection, it minimizes subjective biases by not asking for interpretation by the subject but focusing on creating verbal protocols of a "stream of consciousness" that can be categorized objectively in a later step of data analysis.

In our design subjects first played a video game in an unrestricted fashion. In a second step they watched a video recording of the game just played and performed retrospective TA according to specified content categories. During both phases, the brain activation was measured with fMRI.

2 Methods

2.1 Subjects

Seventeen male German volunteers (age 18-33; mean: 24.4) were recruited with ads posted at the local university, via email, and in online newsgroups. Inclusion criteria were: age between 18 and 35 years, playing at least 5 hours weekly of First Person Shooter digital games, right-handedness, and German as a native language. No individual had any contraindications against MR investigations, acute or anamnesis of major neurological, psychiatric, or ophthalmologic disorders.

2.2 Experimental Paradigm

The subjects first completed standard MR safety questionnaires and consent forms. Then they practiced the game with the MR compatible controller (trackball and five mouse buttons) until they felt comfortable with the equipment (5-20 mins) and trained TA technique (see below for details) until a good performance was achieved. After completing the training, subjects played three game sessions, 12 minute each, followed by a 12 minute TA phase on the recently played session. The set of MR measurements ended with an 11 minutes anatomical scan for reference to a standardized neuroanatomical template. Excluding data loss due to incompliance or technical glitches, 42 complete playing sessions and 40 TA sessions were obtained from the 17 subjects.

Game session. The First Person Shooter (FPS) game "*Counter Strike: Source*" (CSS, Valve Corporation, Bellevue, Washington; 2004) was used in the study. In this game, two teams fight against each other as terrorists and special warrior action team (SWAT).

In order to get acquainted with the scanner, participants played the game inside the MR scanner for 10 minutes before the measurement. For the purpose of this study we selected the single player mode in which all game characters except for the player's avatar are generated by the computer. This setting allowed for the control that a players' performance was not influenced by other human players' skills or actions. A set of three different game maps was chosen, based on best applicability for the MR environment. MR compatible headphones and video goggles (Resonance Technology,

Inc., Los Angeles, CA) delivered the visual and auditory signals of the FPS game. Visual and auditory output of the video game was captured by the *Fraps software (Beepa® P/L)*.

Think Aloud. Before the measurement started the experimenter explained the technique of the TA in details in an adjacent room and gave examples for possible TA comments by performing TA on a short game video clip. Subjects also performed a 12 minutes test block outside the scanner. It consisted of a six minutes playing session followed by a TA phase on the previously played sequence. The experimenter ensured that the subject had understood the instructions and was able to complete the task.

The TA sessions took place directly after the game play inside the scanner. This technique has three main advantages: First, it does not interrupt or disturb the game play itself as it would be the case if the players performed TA simultaneously during the play; second, the player still has the immediate impression of the recently finished session and can perform the TA in the same setting as the game play which facilitates memory effects; and, third, fMRI can be measured during the TA session itself, giving insight into neural correlates of speech production, memory, and empathy. Participants were instructed to focus mainly on two aspects: the difficulty of the game (*How hard/easy was the game play in the respective situation?*) and the aspect of subjective game enjoyment (*How much did you enjoy the game play in the respective situation?*). Speech was recorded with an MR compatible optical microphone (Sennheiser Electronics, Wedemark, Germany). The signal was filtered online to reduce the EPI noise of the scanning sequences. The experimenter could listen to the speech in on-line mode and deliver visual prompts if necessary ("Please speak up!", "Please keep on talking!", and "Please focus on game enjoyment and game difficulty!").

Imaging Parameters. fMRI was conducted at 3 Tesla field strength (Gyroscan Achieva, Philips Health Care, Hamburg, Germany) by means of single-echo single-shot echo-planar imaging (EPI; flip angle: 77 degrees; echo time TE = 24 ms; 64×64 matrix size with 3.6×3.6×5 mm^3 resolution; 4 mm slice thickness plus 1 mm gap). Twenty-eight interleaved oblique-transverse slices obtained whole brain coverage with repetition time TR = 2.0 s (360 volumes per session).

After the functional scans, we conducted an anatomical scan (standard protocol; inversion time TI = 500 ms; echo time TE = 3.6 ms; flip angle = 8°; bandwidth: 15.63 kHz; field of view: 240x240 mm^2; slice thickness 1.5 mm; 3d partitions: 124) that we used for obtaining individual references.

3 Data Analysis

3.1 Game Content Analysis

Based on flow theoretical concepts [5], we developed an event-related content analytical coding scheme in an iterative, deductive-inductive process. The trained coders rated the virtual behavior of the subjects within specific virtual game environments. The recorded and digitized videos of the subjects' game play were analyzed and frame-by-frame categorized into one content categories and level, i.e.

high, medium or low. The codes were noted with 100-ms time resolution. The coding was performed by three independent coders and one supervisor who decided on discrepant coding based on a consent discussion. Each video was coded by two coders independently to avoid subjective interpretation biases. For testing inter-coder reliability we used Krippendorff's Alpha coefficient [6]. Intensive trainings yielded inter-coder reliabilities above 0.7. The game content analysis was based on the scheme developed by Weber, Ritterfeld, & Mathiak [1] and was validated by expert ratings. Five content dimensions connected to the concept of the Flow experience [5] could be encoded based on the observed behavior: 1. Balance between the player's ability and challenge of the game situation; 2. Concentration and focusing of the player; 3. Direct feedback of game success; 4. Control over the game activity; 5. Clear goal (actual task) versus lack of goal (no actual task).

3.2 Think Aloud Analysis

Like the game content coding, the evaluation of the TA recordings was performed by the same three independent coders and one supervisor. To cover positive and negative valence aspects of the game experience we postulated two aspects of the game enjoyment, the positive one being called "game enjoyment" and the negative one termed "game displeasure." The coders assigned all verbal utterances explicitly reporting the game enjoyment or displeasure to their respective categories. Difficulty ratings were assigned to the categories "easy," "medium," and "hard." For this purpose, each coder received about 20 h of intensive training on some additional TA sessions not used in the study. Like in the game content analysis, each TA session was coded by two coders independently to avoid subjective interpretation biases. Krippendorff's Alpha showed inter-coder reliabilities above 0.7. The codes were referred to the respective time points in the game recordings and fMRI data.

3.3 fMRI Data Analysis

The events as determined by the content analysis entered into a hybrid (event-related and block) design in the standard fMRI data analysis package SPM5. This approach proved to be very effective in previous experiments of virtual violence during game play. The model functions were folded by a generic filter to adapt to the hemodynamic response. Statistical parametric mapping was conducted following the standard SPM5 procedures with normalization into a template space for functional and anatomical data, smoothing with 12-mm full-width at half-maximum Gaussian kernel, as well as first and second level analysis based on the general linear model.

4 Results

In order to illustrate the feasibility and efficiency of this approach we present here first data that reflects a) the brain response during the selective game play events chosen based on b) the results of the game content analysis and c) the subjective interpretation of these events. Preliminary data confirm the feasibility of the TA method and also validate this method by revealing the correlation between the subjective interpretation, the brain activation and the game content.

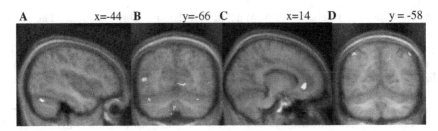

Fig. 1. Activation increasing (**A,B**) and decreasing (**C,D**) with focus. **A** Cerebellum and **B** the visual system reflect attention to objects and actions being focused whereas **C** ACC can be viewed as an interface area between emotion and cognition [7] and **D** the intraparietal sulcus may be associated with spatial attention. (Coordinates of slices reflect MNI system).

Brain activity and game content. The analysis of the game content furthermore reveals specific brain activation patterns during the game play sessions that are closely related to specific characteristics of game situations. As one example, game situations that were more demanding and asked for higher concentration and focusing were characterized by increasing activation clusters in the visual system and the cerebellum (Fig. 1 A, B). Higher concentration was also accompanied by a decreasing activation in the anterior cingulate cortex (ACC) and bilaterally in the intraparietal sulcus (IPS; Fig. 1 C, D).

Subjective experience of game events. Interactions between subjective measures and game content were calculated with the fMRI data as the dependent variable. For instance, those players reporting higher overall game displeasure exhibited a significantly stronger activation to more demanding situations in the right precentral gyrus (PCG) as compared to subjects reporting less game displeasure (Fig. 2).

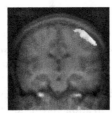
MNI y=-18

Fig. 2. Interaction of the subjectively experienced game displeasure and the flow dimension focus reveals a modulatory network at the right precentral gyrus. This structure reflects uniform networks for manual execution.

5 Discussion

We developed a method for determining neural correlates of subjective experience during semi-natural behavior in digital games. Combining the established technique of TA with a high-resolution content analysis led to the description of well-defined neural networks using functional MRI. First, significant activation clusters from the brain mapping procedure indicate that meaningful psychological models underly these neural correlates. Thus the findings present a neurophysiological observer-independent validation of the method and the underlying psychological processes. Second, we learn how the well investigated neural modules of simple functions as described by cognitive neuroscience are integrated during the performance of complex tasks. The networks led finally to a subjective evaluation of the game play.

Our data indicate that states of subjective experience are characterized by specific neuronal correlates and that TA and content analysis can help identifying the latter. We presented exemplary data on brain correlates of the association of subjective displeasure and focus during video game play. The enhanced activation in precentral cortex areas can be interpreted as perceptual-motor coordination and readiness for action. In other words, participants who respond with readiness for action in focus situation may not have enjoyed the game since they got 'tight' and 'tense.' As such the method offers the opportunity to disentangle neural subsystems which contribute to game experience. This will also provide us with an improved understanding of the neuroscience behind complex social interaction such as computer games.

Another important aspect of the presented data is the validation of subjective measures by neurological data. In our data, different subjective states could be characterized by different brain activation patterns. Therefore we argue that it represents an objective test on the reliability of introspective data, because otherwise no systematic effect would be revealed by statistical analysis. Concerning validity one still needs to systematically evaluate the underlying neurophysiology to determine whether the observed pattern can be attributed to the presumed subjective experience.

Outlook. The present findings suggest that the use of the TA method can detect neural correlates of subjective states even in a complex semi-natural task like a video game. Traditional fMRI experiments use simple stimuli like static pictures or tones that can easily be presented and controlled and facilitate data analysis. These stimuli are well suited for studying basic brain functions of attention, perception, emotion, or memory. However in video games these functions interact and are influenced by a complex multisensory environment. In order to understand the neural mechanisms under such complex conditions we need a method for creating and analyzing experiments that help us answer this question. The Think Aloud offers a way to assess thoughts and feelings of a person during complex and interactive tasks, and provides the basis for a structured, content-oriented data analysis.

Acknowledgements

This study was supported by the Deutsche Forschungsgemeinschaft (DFG, IRTG 1328) and the European Community (FUGA, NEST-PATH-028765). Klaus Mathiak is supported by an AstraZeneca foundation.

References

1. Weber, R., Ritterfeld, U., Mathiak, K.: Does Playing Violent Video Games Induce Aggression? Empirical Evidence of a Functional Magnetic Resonance Imaging Study. Media Psychology 8, 39–60 (2006)
2. van Someren, M.W., Barnard, Y., Sandberg, J.: The think aloud method - a practical approach to modelling cognitive processes. Academic Press, London (1994)

3. Titchener, E.B.: Systematic psychology: prolegomena. Macmillan, New York (1929)
4. Logothetis, N.K., Pfeuffer, J.: On the nature of the BOLD fMRI contrast mechanism. Magnetic Resonance Imaging 22(10), 1517–1531 (2004)
5. Csíkszentmihályi, M.: Beyond Boredom and Anxiety. Jossey-Bass, San Francisco (1975)
6. Krippendorff, K.: Content Analysis. An Introduction to Its Methodolog. Sage Publications, Thousand Oaks (2004)
7. Bush, G., Luu, P., Posner, M.I.: Cognitive and emotional influences in anterior cingulate cortex. Trends in Cognitive Sciences 4, 215–222 (2000)

Engagement and EMG in Serious Gaming: Experimenting with Sound and Dynamics in the Levee Patroller Training Game

Ellen Lisette Schuurink[1], Joske Houtkamp[2], and Alexander Toet[3]

[1] Faculty of Social Sciences, Universiteit Utrecht
E.L.Schuurink@uu.nl
[2] Center for Advanced Gaming and Simulation, Universiteit Utrecht
Joske.Houtkamp@cs.uu.nl
[3] Center for Advanced Gaming and Simulation, TNO
Lex.Toet@tno.nl

Abstract. We measured the effects of sound and visual dynamic elements on user experience of a serious game, with special interest in engagement and arousal. Engagement was measured through questionnaires and arousal through the SAM and electromyography (EMG). We adopted the EMG of the corrugator (frown muscle) and the zygomatic muscle (smile muscle) as indicators for arousal and valence. We hypothesized that sound and dynamic elements would increase engagement, while user characteristics would determine the amount of arousal. We find that the addition of dynamic elements to the game increases the user experience. Sound increases the ease of navigation, but does not determine user experience, probably due to the dominance of other game elements and user characteristics. The subjective evaluation is inconsistent with the physiological data on arousal. Hence, further research is required to elucidate the relation between arousal and engagement.

Keywords: Serious gaming, engagement, EMG, affective appraisal.

1 Introduction

Explicit and intense training is a prerequisite for first responders and security personnel to deal effectively with catastrophic events like fires, earthquakes, plane crashes and levee breaks. Serious gaming and virtual environments provide repeated practice opportunities with life-threatening emergencies or rare incidents in a safe and reproducible setting. Improved realism and effective after action review are among the benefits of computer-simulated scenarios. In the Netherlands many professionals, among whom firemen and levee patrollers, receive training through serious gaming [1]. Challenges in serious gaming are, among other things, realism and engagement.

The requirements for the appearance and game elements of virtual environments used for serious gaming differ from those used for commercial 3D games. In general serious games offer a more engaging (virtual) training environment than traditional training procedures. In a well designed serious game the realism, didactics and

P. Markopoulos et al. (Eds.): Fun and Games 2008, LNCS 5294, pp. 139–149, 2008.

engagement factors are in balance to accomplish the purpose of the serious game: to learn in an informal engaging setting [1].

Engagement is one of the elements that helps to smooth the learning progress and that makes gaming fun; a similar concept is the notion of playfulness [2]. Engagement refers to the (emotional) state in which continuation of the activity doesn't require any effort. Engagement is also necessary for optimal performance [9] and to induce a state of flow [3]. The dependent factors for engagement are the user characteristics and environmental factors. A similar categorization is made for the notion of presence [16].

The first factor, user characteristics, depends on individual aspects like personal experience. Users with limited or no experience with navigation in virtual environments probably have less spatial navigation capabilities, which may result in qualitatively different mental representations of the virtual environment, and thereby in a different evaluation of that environment [20]. Besides experience, culture and personality probably also determine the degree of engagement. Personality determines the willingness to play different kind of game genres [19]. In addition mental imagery is related to mood change [17] and correlated with facial expressiveness [18]. The demographics of the user are of specific interest for serious games, because the target group generally is relatively small and its members differ in personality and experience.

Engagement also depends on environmental factors. This includes the setting where the game is played and the game elements. The effectiveness of specific game elements to induce engagement varies between different digital media. In multimedia engagement will increase if the environment provides challenge, feedback, control and variety [2]. Dickey [4] explains how to design a game for instructional learning that engages users, and identifies the following criteria: focused goals, clear and compelling standards, protection from adverse consequences from initial failures, affirmation of performance, affiliation with others, novelty and variety, choice and authenticity. In a specific study of student engagement on simulations, Davies [5] identifies the complexity of the simulation, the learning environment as a whole, and overcoming the 'barrier' of navigational opacity as important factors, in addition to sufficient time to get engaged.

Mallon and Web [6] categorize two dimensions of engagement for narrative evaluation: structure and interaction. Structure embodies spatial containment and causal connections. The dimension for interaction has four propositions, namely skill-based interaction, relevance of dialogue and causality, illusion of intelligence and invisibility of the medium. In this context, illusion of intelligence refers to the response of the game to random actions and the memory of previous actions. The invisibility of the medium represents the intuitiveness and lack of intrusion.

Another factor that is concealed in the emotional response to design is the aesthetic value of the product: the usability may get a higher rating if the design looks appealing [7].

The game elements stated above are considered the main requirements for engagement. However, specific characteristics of the game environment such as sound and dynamic elements can also contribute to the experience of the game and thus to the engagement. Sound is known to determine perceived realism, to foster attention and recognition [23], to create a sense of place [24], to increase enjoyment, and to improve sense of presence, performance and memory [25] in virtual environments. However, sound can also have a negative influence on performance, and can sometimes be perceived as unpleasant [21] [26]. It has been shown that visual dynamic elements are important factors for the external, ecological and incremental validity of the environment [27].

In this study, the effects of sound and visual dynamic elements on engagement in the serious game Levee Patroller [1] were measured with questionnaires and through facial muscle tension. The electromyography (EMG) of the corrugator (frown muscle) and the zygomatic muscle (smile muscle) was adopted as an indicator for the experience of arousal and valence [18]. In addition to effects of sound and dynamic elements, we expected that user characteristics may determine the amount of arousal experienced during the game.

2 Method

2.1 Participants

Participants were 55 (27 male, 28 female) Dutch residents. The average age was 44.7 years with a standard deviation of 18.5 years. Five participants were excluded from the data analysis because of severe navigational problems.

2.2 Stimuli

For the purpose of this experiment a special version of Levee Patroller was created. Levee Patroller is a first-person serious game, developed by GeoDelft (now Deltares) and Delft University of Technology. It is used to train levee inspectors to timely recognize failure symptoms in an early stage and to properly communicate relevant findings to a central field office [1]. A smaller area of the original training program was selected that represented a polder landscape, containing three possible causes of levee failure, the so-called failure mechanisms. The failure mechanisms were missing stones, piping and breach. The differences between the conditions were the absence or presence of sounds and dynamic elements (see Table 1).

In the first and second conditions, some dynamic elements that were already in the game, were retained: raindrops, clouds, water surfaces, the failure mechanisms, and a meadow gate that opens on approach. The dynamic visual effects that were added in conditions 3 and 4 were: lightning, moving trees, more and stronger waves, seagulls, sheep, passing cars, a boat, a sinking dinghy and a street lamp pole that falls over in the storm. To conditions 2 and 4 sounds were added: a continuous soundtrack of rain, strong wind and thunder, and positioned sounds for the animals, and the events pertaining to the failure mechanisms.

Table 1. Conditions

Condition	Presence or absence
Condition 1	static, no sound
Condition 2	static, with sound
Condition 3	dynamic, no sound
Condition 4	dynamic, with sound

2.3   Questionnaires

User characteristics
The participants' age, gender and level of education were asked. In addition, the participants were questioned regarding their experience with computers in general, and experience with usage and development of 3D environments in particular. The fantasy proneness was rated through five questions, which were inspired by the creative experience questionnaire [12].

Engagement
An engagement questionnaire was derived from the two dimensions that Mallon and Webb [6] identified as important engagement factors. After a pilot experiment the propositions were adjusted to the context of Levee Patroller, namely: spatial characteristics, causality, interaction, control, communication and persuasion. Persuasion is the combination of illusion of intelligence and invisibility of the medium. Additional questions were added to measure involvement. These were inspired by the engagement factor of the ITC-SOPI, which refers to engagement as the psychological involvement and enjoyment of the content [8]. All questions were statements that could be agreed or disagreed upon, on a 5-point scale.

Emotional experience
The valence and arousal scale of the Self-Assessment Manikin (SAM) [10] was obtained before and directly after the game play. The SAM is an animated character with nine levels of pleasure, arousal and dominance. The question that accompanied the scale was: "how do you feel at this moment?" During the game the corrugator and the zygomatic muscle regions were monitored with Mobi and Kendall ECG electrodes (H124 SG). Electrode positions were chosen in accordance with the guidelines presented by Fridlund and Cacioppo [11]. Raw EMG data was off-line re-referenced to bipolar measures, rectified, and filtered with a low cutoff filter of 30 Hz, a high cutoff filter of 500 Hz, a 50-Hz notch filter, and a moving average filter integrating over 125 ms. Change values were defined as the activity relative to the baseline activity during the last second before stimulus onset.

Affective appraisal of the environment
The evaluation of the environment was obtained through the Russell and Pratt questionnaire [13]. The objectives were translated into Dutch and reviewed by a native speaker.

Weather experience
Rain and wind play a crucial role in the level of seriousness of failure mechanisms on a levee. This makes the experience of the weather conditions in Levee Patroller of special interest. Several questions were asked specifically on the presentation of the rain and wind, and whether the sound matched the visual presentation. A list of weather objectives, derived from Stewart [14], had to be rated on a scale of one to ten.

General experience
In serious gaming the level of fun partly determines the degree of success of the game. Fun, clearness of the assignment, and overall beauty of the game were rated on a 5-point scale. The most noticeable visual and audio items were evaluated with open questions.

Fig. 1. Screenshot of a dynamic condition

2.4 Procedure

On arrival at the lab, participants read and signed the informed consent and had a moment to relax. Next, the pre-test questionnaire for general information and the creative experience questions were presented. Then the SAM had to be rated for the first time. This was followed by an instruction of the game, explaining how to use keyboard and mouse for navigation and how to recognize and mark failure mechanisms. Participants briefly rehearsed the assignment to ensure that they correctly understood the task. The electrodes were placed and checked for signal. The assignment was repeated and special attention was paid to navigation. In case of the sound conditions (2 and 4) the participants were asked to put on the headphones. If they felt irritated by the sound volume they were allowed to move the headphones to the back of their head (which only a few did). The assignment was to find the three different failure mechanisms and to mark them. The second assignment was to draw a map of the inspected area. This was done after the game. The game lasted for 8.40 minutes and stopped automatically. When the game finished, the headphones were removed and the participants were asked to complete the second series of questionnaires in the following order: SAM, Russell and Pratt, Engagement, weather experience and general experience.

2.5 Software Specifics and Equipment

Levee Patroller was developed using the Unreal Engine 2 Runtime game engine 1. The experiments were performed on a Dell Dimension XPS-710 Dual Core computer, equipped with a Dell 19" monitor. A standard keyboard and mouse were used for navigation. For the conditions with sound, Sennheiser EH 150 headphones were provided.

2.6 Analysis and Statistics

A between subject design was employed with four conditions. ANOVA's were executed to compare the conditions. Correlations were computed with Pearson product-moment correlation coefficient. The difference of muscle tension before and during game play was examined by comparison of the median, obtained with a t-test.

3 Results

It is beyond the scope of this article to discuss all data resulting from the experiment. The main focus here will be on the engagement, which was obtained through the engagement questionnaire, SAM, the EMG data and the correlation of these results with user characteristics.

3.1 Engagement

The spatial characteristics and causality were rated with five questions. Two of these questions correlated with the performance in the game. The goal of the game was to find the three different failure mechanisms. Participants who were successful in the search task agreed less on the statement that the area was too large to find all failure mechanisms ($r= -0.499$, $p< 0.01$), and rated the failure mechanisms as more perceptible ($r= 0.714$, $p< 0.01$). No difference in spatial characteristics between the conditions was found. Answers to the questions about causality indicated no difference between conditions. An overall average of 3.96 for visual explicitness indicates that in all conditions the failure mechanisms were visually explicitly present. The addition of sound to one of the failure mechanisms did not help the participants in locating it. An average rating of 2.63 (st.dev. of 1.34) and no difference between the conditions indicate that sound was not noticed as an explicit clue.

The proposition of interaction showed some variation in user characteristics. The age of the participant correlated with the ease of navigation ($r= -0.307$, $p< 0.01$). Older participants found it harder to learn the navigation and had more trouble with orientation in the virtual environment ($r= -0.492$, $p< 0.01$). The amount of computer experience correlated with the amount of attention that was necessary to navigate ($r= -0.356$, $p< 0.01$), or put differently, more experienced participants needed less attention. The amount of experience with 3D environments correlated positively with the ease in orientation ($r= 0.340$, $p< 0.01$). For navigation (amount of attention paid to navigation) an effect of dynamic elements was found. Most attention was needed in the condition with dynamic elements without sound (condition 3), and the least in the condition with both dynamic elements and sound (condition 4), $F(1,24)= 2.24$, $p<0.05$.

Control was measured with only one question. Seventy-four percent of the participants agreed on the feeling of control in the environment. This question can however be interpreted in various ways. Compared to a movie, the game gives the player freedom and control of movement. However, the player actually had no real control over the environment: whatever action was undertaken the failure mechanisms would still expand, which is different for the original Levee Patroller game or other (training) games.

The only form of communication in the game was a message in the upper part of the screen that popped-up whenever the boundary of the play field was reached. When the player didn't notice this message it was pointed out by the experimenter. The dynamic condition showed the highest score of relevance for communication.

The questions for persuasion were constructed to measure indirectly (a) the perceived realism and (b) the level of realism needed for this game. The questions whether the virtual environment reminds the participant of a real situation, and if it is important that the environment is in accordance with reality, show a difference between the original condition (1) and the full condition (4), $F(1,23) = 2.93$, $p < 0.05$. Compared to the original condition, in the full condition more participants were reminded of a real situation and stated it was less necessary that the environment had to be as realistic as possible. This suggests that the full condition (4) was more persuasive.

For involvement a difference was found between the original condition (1) and the dynamic condition (3), $F(1,25) = 2.21$, $p < 0.05$. The dynamic conditions (3 and 4) had a higher evaluation of 0.5 points over the static conditions.

3.2 SAM

Averaged over all conditions, valence was rated higher after game play than before ($t(49) = -3.21$, $p < 0.01$; Figure 2). This is in concordance with the high rating of

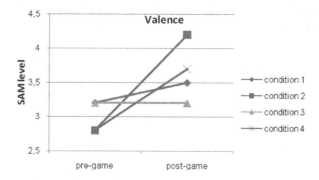

Fig. 2. Valence before and after game play

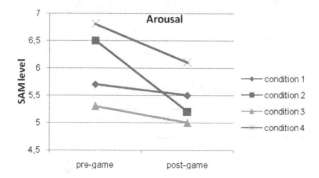

Fig. 3. Arousal before and after game play

pleasure experienced by playing the game, which had an overall average rating of 3.9 on a scale 1-5. Although the increase was highest in the sound conditions (2 & 4), however, no interaction effects were found due to large variations between participants. A decrease in the evaluation of arousal was found over the course of the experiment (t(49)= 3.32, p<0.01; Figure 3).

3.3 EMG

Figure 4 shows the facial muscle tension of a typical participant. The blue area (X) shows the tension of the zygomatic region and the green area (Y) the tension of the corrugator region. The red lines present the triggers which were marked for the actions that followed the discovery of the failure mechanisms. The muscle tension measured in the zygomatic region did not show action potentials shortly before or after these triggers. Interestingly, a gradational increase of zygomatic muscle tension was found over all participants. The median of the tension before the game differs significantly from the median during the game play (t(42)= 0.00, p< 0.01). No difference of increased tension was found between the conditions, Table 2.

The corrugator region showed clear action potentials during the game. These could not be matched to the triggers, but more likely represent "moments of reflection". Trouble with navigation and unclear focus, or the complexity of the assignment could contribute to the amount of increased tension in the corrugator region. No significant difference was found between the conditions, in which large individual differences were noticed (Table 3).

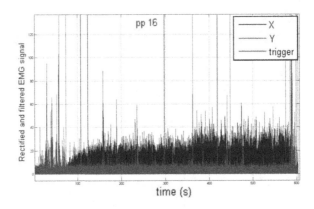

Fig. 4. Example of EMG data acquired during game play

Table 2. EMG zygomatic region

Condition	Average difference in median in μV	Percentage of change
1	5.51	64%
2	12.01	46%
3	4.73	69%
4	7.03	76%

Table 3. EMG corrugator region

Condition	Average frequency of action potentials	Std. dev.
1	13.9	11.2
2	11.9	8.9
3	16.5	14.1
4	8.0	9.7

4 Discussion

The subjective evaluation through the engagement questionnaire shows that sounds and dynamic elements only have a modest influence on some aspects of engagement, and that the influence of user characteristics is stronger. This suggests that sound and dynamic elements don't contribute much to the user engagement of this game, compared to other game design elements like challenge, discovery, feedback, and control as defined by several authors [26]. However, sound does support navigation in a richer dynamic environment. Since it is known that sound, which is perceived as an auditory background, affects performance in computer games [21], this finding suggest that the sound was perceived as a background stimulus in the condition with sound and dynamics, and as more obtrusive in the sound and static condition. The interaction effect of dynamics and sound is in consensus with Huang [27].

The higher rating for communication in the dynamic conditions indicates that the richer environment increases the participant's awareness of possible changes on the screen; although participants judge the environment in the dynamic conditions just as neutral as in the other conditions.

The effects of dynamics and sound show a significant influence on the affective appraisal of the environment. Sound increases the arousing and distressing qualities of the environment: sound in combination with dynamic elements seems to have a positive effect on the environment, in contrast with the sound only condition. The weather questionnaire shows an increase of validity for the combination of sound and dynamic elements (see [22] for a detailed evaluation of the affective appraisal).

The arousal measurement shows contradicting results, which is in consensus with Schneider, Lang, Shin and Bradley [15] who also found that the subjective evaluation of arousal did not match the physiological data. The subjective evaluation of arousal, acquired with the SAM, shows a decrease in intensity, whereas the facial muscle tension increased during the game. The laboratory setting and stress for the unknown may have given the participants a relatively high aroused feeling before the experiment started. The ease of the task (an overall average of 2.5 out of 3 subtasks were successfully completed) may have relaxed the participants in the course of the experiment. We did not register the excitement that was present during the task. This suggests that the second time the SAM was obtained, it did not measure the influence of the game on arousal, but instead measured the arousal after completing the game. The unexpected decrease of arousal in the subjective evaluation may partly be attributed to the setting. Levee Patroller is developed as a training instrument for levee patrollers and not for novices. In the experiment the participants received information about levee safety and instructions of the failure mechanisms. This is different from the training setting in which the discovery element is even higher. The participants had no experience with levee patrolling and therefore probably had a different feeling of urgency and seriousness than professional levee patrollers may have. An experiment with experts may provide an in depth view of the incremental validity of the game and the engagement.

The EMG data shows an increase of tension in the zygomatic region during game play. This is an indication that the participants were more aroused during game play. The corrugator region shows a frequency of tension that cannot be related to the triggers. The corrugator region seems to react to striking events in the environment which were not under control of the participant. In addition to a reaction on events, frustration due to navigational problems could cause the polarization. This cannot be related with the interaction questions of engagement questionnaire. The average of 9.2 polarizations over all participants indicates that the game elicited facial reactions. The influence of sound and dynamic elements on the facial muscle tension cannot be deduced from the data, due to large individual differences. A more controlled environment, for example a predefined route through the environment, may give more insight in the relation between physical reaction and environmental events.

Acknowledgments

This research has been supported by the GATE project, funded by the Netherlands Organization for Scientific Research (NWO) and the Netherlands ICT Research and Innovation Authority (ICT Regie). We are grateful to Deltares for providing us with the original model and performing the manipulations, and to the KNMI (Royal Netherlands Meteorological Institute) for advice on the representation of the weather circumstances.

References

1. Harteveld, C., Guimarães, R., Mayer, I., Bidarra, R.: Balancing pedagogy, game and reality components within a unique serious game for training levee inspection. In: Hui, K., et al. (eds.) Technologies for E-Learning and Digital Entertainment. Proceedings of the Second International Conference, Edutainment 2007, pp. 128–139. Springer, Heidelberg (2007)
2. Webster, J., Ho, H.: Audience engagement in multimedia presentations. The data base for Advances in Information Systems 28(2), 63–77 (1997)
3. Csikszentmihalyi, M.: Flow: The psychology of optimal experience. Harper & Row, New York (1990)
4. Dickey, M.D.: Engaging By Design: How Engagement Strategies in Popular Computer and Video Games Can Inform Instructional Design. Educational Technology Research and Development 53(2), 67–83 (2005)
5. Davies, C.H.J.: Student engagement with simulations: a case study. Computers & Education 39, 271–282 (2002)
6. Mallon, B., Webb, B.: Structure, causality, visibility and interaction: propositions for evaluating engagement in narrative multimedia. Int. J Human-Computer Studies 53, 269–287 (2000)
7. Norman, D.A.: Emotion & Attractive. Interaction 9(4), 36–42 (2002)
8. Lessiter, J., Freeman, J., Keogh, E., Davidoff, J.D.: A cross-media presence questionnaire: the ITC Sense of Presence Inventory. Presence: Teleoperators and Virtual Environments 10(3), 282–297 (2001)

9. Garris, R., Ahlers, R., Driskell, J.E.: Games, Motivation, and Learning: A Research and Practice Model. Stimulation Gaming 33(4), 441–467 (2002)

10. Lang, P.J.: Behavioral treatment and bio-behavioral assessment: computer applications. In: Sidowski, J.B., Johnson, J.H., Williams, T.A. (eds.) Technology in mental health care delivery systems, pp. 113–119. Ablex, Norwood (1980)

11. Fridlund, A.J., Cacioppo, J.T.: Guidelines for human electromyographic research. Psychophysiology 23(5), 567–589 (1986)

12. Merckelbach, H., Horselenberg, R., Murris, P.: The Creative Experiences Questionnaire (CEQ): a brief self-report measure of fantasy proneness. Personality and Individual Differences 31(6), 987–995 (2001)

13. Russell, J.A., Pratt, G.: A Description of the Affective Quality Attributed to Environments. Journal of Personality and Social Psychology 38(2), 311–322 (1980)

14. Stewart, A.E.: Linguistic dimensions of weather and climate perception. International Journal of Biometeorology 52(1), 57–67 (2007)

15. Schneider, E.F., Lang, A., Shin, M., Bradley, S.D.: Death with a story – How story impacts emotional, motivational, and physiological responses to first-shooter video games. Human communication Research 30(3), 361–375 (2004)

16. Baños, R.M., Botella, C., Alcañiz, M., Liaño, V., Guerrero., R.B.: Immersion and Emotion: Their impact on the sense of presence. Cyberpsychology & Behaviour 7(6) (2004)

17. Freeman, J., Lessiter, J., Keogh, E., Bond, F.W., Chapman, K.: Relaxation Island: virtual, and really relaxing. In: Presence 2004, pp. 67–72 (2004)

18. Lang, P.J., Greenwald, M.K., Bradley, M.M., Hamm, A.O.: Looking at pictures: Affective, facial, visceral, and behavioral reactions. Psychophysiology 30, 261–271 (1993)

19. Ravaja, N., Saari, T., Salminen, M., Laarni, J., Holopainen, J., Järvinen, A.: Emotional response Patterns and Sense of Presence during Video Games: Potential criteron variables for game design. In: NordiCHI 2004, pp. 339–247 (2004)

20. Cutmore, T.R.H., Hine, T.J., Kerry, K.J., Maberly, J., Langford, N.M., Hawgood, G.: Cognitive and gender factors influencing navigation ina virtual environment. Int. J. Human-Computer Studies 53, 223–249 (2000)

21. Wolfson, S., Case, G.: The effects of sound and colour on responses to computer game. Interacting with computers 13, 183–192 (2000)

22. Houtkamp, J.M., Schuurink, E.L., Toet, A.: Thunderstorms in my Computer: the Effect of Visual Dynamics and Sound in a 3D Environment (in preparation)

23. Rohrmaan, B., Bishop, I.: Subjective responses to computer simulations of urban environments. Journal of Environmental Psychology 22, 319–331 (2002)

24. Serafin, S.: Sound design to enhance presence in photorealistic virtual reality. In: Proceedigs of the 2004 International Conference on Auditory Display, pp. 1–4 (2004)

25. Larsson, P., Västfjäll, D., Kleiner, M.: Ecological acoustics and the multi-modal perception of rooms: real and unreal experiences of auditory-visual environments. In: Proceedings of the 2001 International Conference of Auditory Display, pp. 245–249 (2001)

26. Morinaga, M., Aono, S., Kuwano, S., Kato, T.: Psychological evaluation of waterside space using audio-visual information. Emperical Studies of the arts 21(2), 185–194 (2003)

27. Huang, S.-C.L.: An exploratory approach for using videos to represent dynamic environments. Landscape Research 29(2), 205–218 (2004)

28. Hetherington, J., Daniel, T.C., Brown, T.C.: Is motion more important than it sounds?: The medium of presentation in environmental research. Journal of environmental psychology 13, 283–291 (1993)

Log Who's Playing: Psychophysiological Game Analysis Made Easy through Event Logging

Lennart Nacke, Craig Lindley, and Sophie Stellmach

Blekinge Institute of Technology, Game and Media Arts Laboratory, Box 214,
374 24 Karlshamn, Sweden
{Lennart.Nacke,Craig.Lindley,Sophie.Stellmach}@bth.se

Abstract. Modern psychophysiological game research faces the problem that for understanding the computer game experience, it needs to analyze game events with high temporal resolution and within the game context. This is the only way to achieve greater understanding of gameplay and the player experience with the use of psychophysiological instrumentation. This paper presents a solution to recording in-game events with the frequency and accuracy of psychophysiological recording systems, by sending out event byte codes through a parallel port to the psychophysiological signal acquisition hardware. Thus, psychophysiological data can immediately be correlated with in-game data. By employing this system for psychophysiological game experiments, researchers will be able to analyze gameplay in greater detail in future studies.

Keywords: psychophysiology, digital games, interactive techniques, gameplay analysis, usability.

1 Introduction

The automatic logging of events to better understand user behavior within an interactive system has a long history in psychology and usability [1]. Historical automated logging solutions (e.g. Skinner's "operant conditioning chamber") kept track of animal interactions (e.g. pedals pressed by a rat) to study their behavior [2]. By analyzing the response rate logs, Skinner was able to create his theory of schedules of reinforcement. The idea of automated logging has survived until today. In recent human-computer interaction (HCI) history, behavioral observation logs are a common analysis tool. They also provide a basis for a detailed analysis of usability, fun [3] and game experience, which benefits greatly from employing classic usability metrics (e.g. time to complete a task, accuracy of input, user satisfaction) along with survey and observation measurements [4, 5].

Kim et al. [6] give a great overview of classic HCI instrumentations and discuss their shortcomings. They note that the amount of low-level event data recorded (e.g. number of keystrokes) is growing enormously with the complexity of modern systems. A possible solution for reducing data is to cluster them with contextual information, so that not all low-level data need to be reported. The system presented by Kim et al. combines the advantages from different research approaches, such as the

P. Markopoulos et al. (Eds.): Fun and Games 2008, LNCS 5294, pp. 150–157, 2008.

collection of user evaluation data, qualitative survey data and behavioral data [6]. These event-related data sets can also be accompanied by video recordings to provide contextual information.

The approach of combining different methodologies to provide a coherent view of the game experience is sound. However, we find that it could be greatly improved by adding one important facet of recent game experience research: human physiological responses (as an objective context for interpreting subjective survey data). The connection of system events with human behavioral responses is gaining importance as researchers want to analyze game events with high temporal resolution [7-9].

To overcome the limitations that self-report measures of emotional responses in games have, it is of great value to assess specific game events in more detail, since some game events may trigger different or contradictory emotional physiological responses [10]. In comparison to studies investigating only tonic measures, our objective was to create a system that allows reporting of phasic psychophysiological responses at game events.

Using such a system, it is then for example possible to report emotional valence and arousal elicited by a certain game event (at a time resolution limited only by the capacities of a game engine and the psychophysiological recording hardware). In addition to eliminating the time needed for scoring game events manually using video, another key advantage of an automated logging system is its accuracy. While manual scoring might introduce errors in the log, automated scoring of game events is almost fail-safe. Integrating game events and physiological responses with eye tracker recordings and survey data can provide an almost comprehensive overview of game experience.

Because of the desire to correlate game events and psychophysiological data, this work focuses on an integrated logging framework for psychophysiological systems (like the Biosemi ActiveTwo acquisition hardware). A comprehensive framework containing various possibilities for handling different psychophysiological measurements (e.g. Biosemi ActiveTwo and Tobii 1750 eye tracker) was created as part of an internship at the BTH Game and Media Arts Laboratory [11].

- In Section 2, we introduce the design concept behind the framework. As part of the design, we investigated the requirements underlying the framework.
- Next, we present the implementation of automated event logging in detail in Section 3. This includes a look at the transmission component and the event component. It also introduces the concept of a logging entity for graphical use within a level editor.
- We end with a discussion and an outlook using our software for psychophysiological game experiments in Section 4.

2   A Conceptual Design

Psychophysiological researchers are interested in questions about the relationship between mind and brain or the ability to control one's well-being with your thoughts [12]. It is the curiosity about how the relation of pure feelings and thinking manifests to bodily responses that drives the research field. Andreassi defines the field as exploring the "relations between psychological manipulations and resulting physiological responses, measured in the living organism, to promote understanding of the relation between mental and bodily processes" [13].

2.1 Requirements Analysis

To gather meaningful data for further analysis, psychophysiological researchers have to record precise markers during data acquisition to manually score the recordings for further analysis, which is a serious time investment. A logging system that operates at the run-time speed of a game engine and sends out game-related events with the same temporal resolution is greatly beneficial for researchers that want to study player experience in detail. The recording of such events with the help of the same hardware that is used to record biofeedback would enable a researcher to perform an instant correlation and analysis of game experience.

In digital games one has the possibility of interacting within a virtual environment and directly influences the occurring events. For a common understanding of the types of events that occur within an experimental gaming context, we differentiate the following events:

- *In-game events* (e.g. player picks up a reward)
- *Real-world events* (e.g. shouting at the computer in anger, moving nervously on the chair)

The definition of in-game events in the source code has the advantage of logging them automatically to a file. For the examination of real-world events other methods have to be used (e.g. sensors measuring physiological responses, positional sensors, accelerometers). In our case, events need to be automatically written to a file and to the psychophysiological recording hardware via a serial cable. The semantic clustering of game events is something that deserves more thorough investigation for future studies. Nevertheless, we considered the following example events most meaningful within a first-person shooter environment (e.g. *Half-Life 2*):

- Player fires a gun
- Player gets hurt
- Player dies

The event must be reported to the parallel port at game runtime and simultaneously to a log file. Information in the log files needs to contain an event description and the related timestamp. The ability to log data in two different ways allows researchers without a psychophysiological recording device (that collects trigger data from a parallel port) to receive automatic output from their experiments in form of log files. In addition, the log files come in handy for debugging the functionality of the port logging.

Each event, which is reported to the parallel port, has to be transmitted for a predefined minimal time amount. If the signal is not sent long enough, older psychophysiological hardware with a lower frequency resolution might not be able to correctly register the event. Therefore, we agreed on a minimum transmission time of 200 milliseconds.

3   Automated Game Event Logging

When planning the design of experimental game stimuli, we used the *Source SDK* that ships with the game *Half-Life 2* [14, 15]. Game development tools such as the Hammer editor and access to the source code made our preference for this solution. The fact that the *Source SDK* was used successfully in research contexts before [16, 17], including the development of serious games [18] also influenced our decision. Level designers should be able to easily integrate logging inside existing levels, so the logging system was designed as two modular components for *Half-Life 2*:

- – Transmission Component
- – Event Component

The transmission component is responsible for receiving signals and to communicate these to the parallel port and the log file. This is the base component on which the second module depends, because the event component will catch events anywhere in the code and report them to the transmission component.

3.1 Transmission Component

This module is a static C++ class, which has to be accessible from all other files in the project to enable the possibility for firing events from any given class. For the implementation of the port logging, functionality of the InpOut32 library for communicating with the parallel port was used [19]. The basic structure for this communication shall be presented, describing the main steps as executed in the source code:

1. *Load library file*
2. *Determine function's address*
3. *Send event code to port*
4. *Free library memory*

These steps are the basis for communicating with the parallel port and have been integrated within the transmission component to enable the writing of event codes to the parallel port. The process of logging to a regular text file is using an output stream. Text, represented as the datatype string or as an array of characters, is transmitted to the method *logMsg*.

3.2 Event Component

The event component is responsible for managing predefined events and reports them to the transmission component. However, different kinds of events exist, which have to be handled in their certain ways. First, we have in-game events that need to be distinguished before they are reported. Some events are applicable in a general manner, whereas others are just convenient for particular scenarios. Therefore, we should differentiate between common level-independent events (e.g. player is damaged or enemy is killed) and unique level-dependent events (e.g. player enters a certain area or encounters a certain *NPC*[1] type).

---

[1] Non-player character: *NPCs* in *Half-Life 2* can be either friendly or hostile.

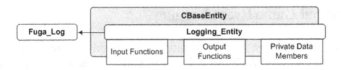

Fig. 1. Structural overview of the class *logging_entity* and its functions

In the specific case of *Half-Life 2*, the damage of a whole *NPC* class can be referred to as a general event. In contrast, the action by a particular *NPC* from this class can sincerely lead to a unique event. For the design of the event component this means that the ability to dynamically assign additional unique events within the level editing tool (Hammer Editor) would be desirable. Thus, one central entity called *logging_entity* was created, which provides the possibility to choose from a list of common events, but also to refer to this entity by other instances for defining unique events.

Figure 1 illustrates the general structure of the logging entity. It derives from the *CBaseEntity* class, which is, as the name suggests, the base class for all entities contained in the Source Engine. As shown there, the members of this class can be broken down in member variables, input functions and output functions.

Available events, which can be fired by the logging entity, are indicated by its output functions. In addition, when an event is fired (not only by this but also by other entities) the mentioned input functions can be explicitly called. This means that also events by other entities can trigger the *SetEventCode*[2] function as long as the logging entity has been given a name.

An example for calling the *SetEventCode* input function from another entity could be as follows. A level consists of different areas, which are sequentially playable. Every area has its distinct characteristics and it is desired to automatically log when the player moves on to a new area. A simple trigger can be created, which fires an *OnTrigger* output function (event), when the player passes through and sends a predefined event code to the logging class.

The work, however, is not done just by creating the class *logging_entity* as presented, because the output functions may be initialized, but they will not fire the desired output yet, because the exact spot in the source code, when the desired event takes place, still has to be determined. In a huge project as the *Source SDK* this becomes a complex and time-consuming task. But once the suitable point in the source code has been found, the approach for firing an event is always the same.

Due to the various events contained in the logging entity, working in several different source files is necessary. Thus, access to the logging entity has to be provided on a higher user level. All entities, which have been added to a certain level in the Hammer Editor, are listed in *gEntList*. If the logging entity is not found in this list, then nothing will happen and no error will occur. Otherwise, the event defined in the logging entity will be fired and, depending on the settings of the particular level, an input function will be called.

In order to find the entity in *gEntList*, the logging entity has to be given a specific debug name within the Hammer Editor (e.g. "FugaLog", see Figure 2). When adding

---

[2] *SetEventCode* is an input function contained in *logging_entity* for saving a given event code to the member variable *currentEventCode*. With the output function *SendToPort,* this value will then be sent to the parallel port.

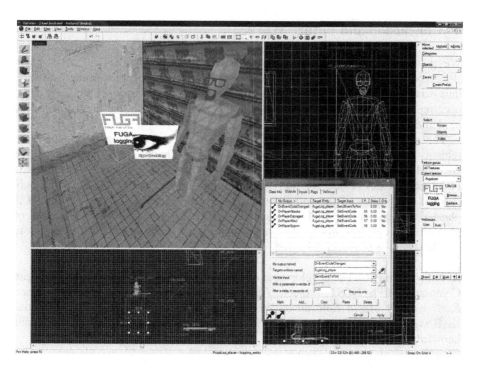

Fig. 2. Screenshot showing the logging entities and manually defined output codes inside the Hammer editing environment of the Source SDK [15]

other events the same procedure has to be followed. However, playtesting revealed that events concerning the player (e.g. "Player gets hurt") had to be distinguished from other events. Some events would, otherwise, not be logged. This had to do with the fact that closely related events would be sent simultaneously.

Designing the event component as an independent entity in the *Half-Life 2* level editor (Hammer) provides several helpful features for the user:

- *Existing event codes can easily be changed during level editing.* The user is able to adapt event codes within a well arranged menu within the Hammer Editor. Otherwise one would have to go through thousands of lines of code in order to find the specific spot where a certain event code would be sent. Something which is impossible for ordinary users.
- *It is possible to define event codes for unique events.* Events closely related to a certain scenario can easily be added by defining them within the Hammer Editor. In case of the occurrence of this event, it can refer to *logging_entity* and send a predefined event code.
- *Logging entity exceeds simple logging functionality.* The logging entity can be used for more than just logging events. Output functions defined in this entity can trigger other entities. For example, if the player is damaged, a health kit should be created. This can be done by calling the function "Spawn health kit" at the event "Player is damaged".

4 Conclusion and Future Work

We presented a system that writes game events to a text file and sends them simultaneously as a byte code to the port of psychophysiological recording hardware, thus making it possible to index phasic psychophysiological responses precisely at the occurrence of game events. We focused in this paper on describing the details of the implementation of this tool.

The application of the tool within empirical studies investigating game experience remains to be presented in future studies, which we have already conducted. The created logging framework presented in this study has also been used within the EU FP6 NEST FUGA project for studying the fun of gaming. Although, this paper only presents the portion of the software concerned with logging of general events, it is planned to extend the tool to visualize and cross-correlate several streams of physiological data, eye tracker data, and usability data. Thus, it will enable even more detailed analysis of player behavior.

Acknowledgments. The development of this software was supported by the European Community FP6 NEST project: *The Fun of Gaming: Measuring the Human Experience of Media Enjoyment*. We would like to thank Niklas Ravaja, Matias Kivikangas, Dennis Sasse, and Charlotte Sennersten for supporting us with their knowledge and valuable feedback.

References

1. Hilbert, D.M., Redmiles, D.F.: Extracting usability information from user interface events. ACM Computing Surveys 32, 384–421 (2000)
2. Skinner, B.F.: The Behavior of Organisms: An Experimental Analysis. D. Appleton-Century Company, incorporated (1938)
3. Wiberg, C.: A Measure of Fun: Extending the scope of web usability. Department of Informatics, vol. PhD. Umeå University, Umeå, Sweden (2003)
4. Nielsen, J.: Usability Engineering. Morgan Kaufmann, San Francisco (1993)
5. Bernhaupt, R., Eckschlager, M., Tscheligi, M.: Methods for evaluating games: how to measure usability and user experience in games? In: Proceedings of the international conference on Advances in computer entertainment technology, pp. 309–310 (2007)
6. Kim, J.H., Gunn, D.V., Schuh, E., Phillips, B., Pagulayan, R.J., Wixon, D.: Tracking real-time user experience (TRUE): a comprehensive instrumentation solution for complex systems. In: Proceedings of the twenty-sixth annual SIGCHI conference on Human factors in computing systems (CHI 2008). ACM, Florence, Italy (2008)
7. Ravaja, N., Turpeinen, M., Saari, T., Puttonen, S., Keltikangas-Jarvinen, L.: The Psychophysiology of James Bond: Phasic Emotional Responses to Violent Video Game Events. Emotion 8, 114–120 (2008)
8. Salminen, M., Ravaja, N.: Increased oscillatory theta activation evoked by violent digital game events. Neuroscience Letters 435, 69–72 (2008)
9. Kivikangas, J.M.: Psychophysiology of flow experience: An explorative study. Faculty of Behavioural Sciences, Department of Psychology, Vol. Master's Thesis. University of Helsinki, Helsinki, Finland (2006)

10. Ravaja, N., Saari, T., Salminen, M., Laarni, J., Kallinen, K.: Phasic Emotional Reactions to Video Game Events: A Psychophysiological Investigation. Media Psychology 8, 343–367 (2006)
11. Stellmach, S.: A psychophysiological logging system for a digital game modification. Department of Simulation and Graphics, Bachelor thesis. Otto-von-Guericke-University, Magdeburg (2007)
12. Cacioppo, J.T., Tassinary, L.G., Berntson, G.G.: Psychophysiological science. Handbook of psychophysiology, 3–26 (2000)
13. Andreassi, J.L.: Human Behavior and Physiological Response. Psychophysiology 4, 1–12 (2000)
14. Half-Life 2 (digital game). Valve Corporation (2004)
15. Valve Developer Community (2004), http://developer.valvesoftware.com
16. Arango, F., Chenghung, C., Esche, S.K., Chassapis, C.: A scenario for collaborative learning in virtual engineering laboratories. In: Frontiers in education conference - global engineering: knowledge without borders, opportunities without passports. FIE 2007. 37th annual (2007) F3G-7-F3G-12 (2007)
17. McQuiggan, S., Lee, S., Lester, J.: Predicting User Physiological Response for Interactive Environments: An Inductive Approach. In: Proceedings of the 2nd Artificial Intelligence for Interactive Digital Entertainment Conference, pp. 60–65 (2006)
18. Mac Namee, B., Rooney, P., Lindstrom, P., Ritchie, A., Boylan, F., Burke, G.: Serious Gordon: Using Serious Games To Teach Food Safety in the Kitchen. In: Proceedings of the 9th International Conference on Computer Games: AI, Animation, Mobile, Educational & Serious Games (CGAMES 2006) (2006)
19. Logix4U: http://logix4u.net/

Acting Your Age in Second Life

Darren J. Reed and Geraldine Fitzpatrick

Interact Lab,
University of Sussex,
Sussex,
BN1 9RH
d.reed@sussex.ac.uk

Abstract. This paper is concerned with age-identity in the virtual environment Second Life and explores some initial questions about how older people understand and utilise their understandings of physical age characteristics in creating an avatar. Through a hands-on seminar, 22 older people who had no experience of Second Life, created an avatar and adapted its appearance, after which they filled in a questionnaire on their experience The study approach is based on a behavioural model rooted in the sociological concept of performativity, to begin to talk about appearance, identity and behaviour in virtual environments. We detail and discuss questionnaire responses and individual interviews through a series of user profiles. By speaking to the 'performativity of age-identity' we draw out themes and issues involved in older people's use of character personalisation in virtual environments*.

Keywords: Second life, older users, age-identity, performativity, play.

1 Introduction

Increasingly computer games are being targeted at older users. So-called 'brain training' games for example are presented as fun ways to maintain mental activity. There are growing interests in adapting game consoles to encourage physical activities and even support recuperative measures after major illness (e.g. see [10]). The reason that this is remarkable is that computer games have typically been seen as a younger person's pursuit, and therefore pejoratively as a form of playful time-wasting. One way that such moves have been understood is to speak of 'serious games' (see for example [22]). The 're-branding' of mainstream computer gaming as worthwhile activity for older people brings with it a number of questions, not least being how age is framed and represented inside the game itself.

Social identity has been studied within sociology and psychology. Sherry Turkle famously looked at identity and the internet [21]. In social terms social identity is related to social role, and hence incorporates social expectations of appropriate behaviour and appearance. While classical authors such as Mead [14] asserted that each person undertakes a variety of roles for different interactional purposes, these are only partially a matter of choice and a product of deliberate adaptation. Griebel [9]

P. Markopoulos et al. (Eds.): Fun and Games 2008, LNCS 5294, pp. 158–169, 2008.

picks up on this issue of choice by looking at how 'real-world' personality trait impose themselves on 'simulated' identities in computer games such as the SIMS.

The primary question that motivates the research behind this paper is, given a choice about how they represent themselves in a virtual environment, what would older users choose? We explored this by running a Second Life workshop with 22 participants and conducting a post-workshop interview as well as collecting pictures of their avatars. We also followed two of the participants through subsequent hands-on interviews and were given access to extracts from a journal created by a third participant From analysis of these data we are able to highlight key issues and present short-hand representation, or user profiles, that might act as exemplars of older people's use of Second Life.

1.1 Second Life

Second Life is a three dimensional world, which is typically understood to be game-like. It is promoted as a creative collective endeavour limited only by imagination. There is increasing interest in the news media, and more serious interest from educational establishments with regard to online learning, recruitment of students and academic interactions [13][11]. Recently there has been a move to understand the interactional behaviours within the virtual environment itself [1].

Identity and online interaction has a long history. Rhiengold [20] and other spoke of the freedom to represent yourself and essentially be whoever, or what ever you wish. Touting the ability to be anonymous by shrouding yourself in alternative identities. Second life taps into this supposed freedom with the possibility of personalising the physical features of your online character, "The Second Life world is a place dedicated to your creativity. After all, an avatar is your persona in the virtual world. ... Despite offering almost infinite possibilities, the tool to personalize your avatar is very simple to use and allows you to change anything you like, from the tip of your nose to the tint of your skin" (www.secondlife.com/whatis/avatar.php).

A secondary question of the research is then whether these 'infinite possibilities' include matters of age, and specifically whether it is possible to look like an older person in Second Life.

2 Methodology

Twenty-two participants were recruited from University of York staff by offering an introduction seminar to Second Life. The ages of the participants started at around fifty, commonly accepted as the onset of 'old age' by such organisations as Age Concern in the UK, and each had no prior experience of the virtual environment.

A series of small group seminars, with four to six people in each group, were carried out that introduced Second Life through a presentation, a live walkthrough, and initial character creation. The presentation introduced the basic features of Second Life; the walkthrough visited four exemplar locations, the globe theatre, Sussex University campus, NASA space centre, and the NHS's polyclinic. Each has interesting features. The first is a replica of an historical building, the second a realistic copy of parts of a university campus, the third includes multiple features including a direct video link to the International Space Station, and the fourth is a representation of a health service concept from the UK government. Visitors are introduced to the polyclinic idea, a suggested form of healthcare provision that is situated between General Practitioners and hospitals that allows people to walk through a mock up building and feedback their impressions and opinions. On individual computers each participant then went through the process of registering and creating a login for Second Life. Once enrolled and logged in, each participant was then instructed to create an avatar that resembled him or her.

The registration process was not without problems, and in some instances existing avatars were used.

At the end of the hour and a half session, participants were asked to complete a brief questionnaire that pursued issues of age-representation in the created avatars and the participant's preferences for character personalisation. In addition each participant was asked to take a 'snapshot' (a facility within the software) of his or her avatar and email it to the researcher. In a couple of instances, due to technical issues in the session, these snapshots were sent at some later date, or not at all. With the snapshot, the participants could add additional comments.

Two participants undertook individual discussions with the researcher two weeks after the initial seminar. In these sessions, each participant interacted with their avatar in the presence of the researcher. Through prompts such as 'what can you see', and 'what would you like to do' participants were encouraged to 'think-out-loud' their actions, objectives and reactions. One of these participants created a journal-like document detailing her experiences of Second Life participation in the intervening period.

This methodology was chosen as a means to investigate those new to Second Life. The combination of questionnaire, interview and observation was a means to draw out rich insights.

2.1 Participant Questionnaire

Participants were asked how similar they felt the avatar that they had created was to them, they were also asked in a separate question whether their character looked younger, the same age, or older than them. They were also asked whether they would prefer to have a character that looked younger, the same age, or older than them. The results are presented in Table 1 below.

The average similarity rating was 5.1 (column one, where 1 means completely different and 10 means completely the same), meaning that the participants felt their avatar has some similarities and features that would identify them, but not so the person was immediately recognisable. It should be noted that there was a good deal of variance, with response scores ranging from 1 to 9. Participants were not in agreement as to how similar their characters were to themselves. The large majority of respondents felt that their character looked younger than them (column two). None of the participants wanted their character to look older than them and scores ranged between 3 and 5 (column three). The average preferred age rating being 4. Out of the total group 50% would prefer to look their own age, the remaining 50% would prefer to look slightly younger. Perhaps the most surprising results are those where there is a high similarity score given (1x9, 3x8) and yet in all but one of these cases, the person feels the created character looks younger. This would infer that some participants do not necessarily equate 'similarity' with apparent age.

Table 1. Questionnaire responses

"How similar is your second life character to you?" (1-10 where 1 is completely different, and 10 is completely the same)	"My character looks...younger than me/the same age as me/older than me" (please delete)	Given the choice , how old or young would you like your character to look? (between 1 and 10, where 5 is the same age as you, 10 is much older than you, and 1 being much younger than you)
6	younger than me	4.5
1	younger than me	5
9	younger than me	4
4	younger than me	5
5	younger than me	5
2.75	younger than me	3.5
2	younger than me	5
3	same age as me	5
8	younger than me	3
7	younger than me	4
8	same age as me	5
3	younger than me	5
5	younger than me	3
6	same age as me	5
8	younger than me	3
2	younger than me	3
5	younger than me	4
7.5	[no answer]	5

The created avatars ranged in style, with some having a deliberately older body shape. Some examples can be seen in the following table.

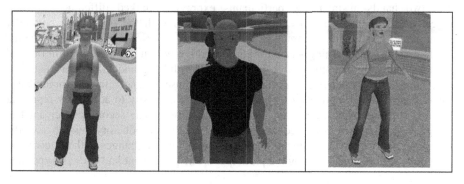

Fig. 1. Selected avatar snapshots

One interesting point is that the Second Life 'orientation island' (the initial training area) contains an 'ol lady' shape, that can be seen in the first of the snapshots in Figure 1 above. There isn't however an 'ol man' shape available. The second snapshot was a male participant's attempt to replicate baldness.

In another question participants were asked to list physical features that they would like to change or add to make their character look more like them. A selection of the answers is given in the following table.

Table 2. Answers to question relating additional features that would enable the creation of an avatar that resembled the participant

detailed shoes, broader moustache, pot belly
older faces, spectacles, different body shapes more hairstyles,
accessories (jewellery, bags, scarves).
more wrinkles, more control over hair
hair style and colour, body shape, clothes, wrinkles, face shape
hair, age, clothing
older, different clothes
longer shirt to cover belly
fatter, lose trendy clothes, less makeup,
a big white hat, silky skirt, shinny textured shoes, dotted handbag

A number of participants mentioned wrinkles as a characteristic they would like to add; others just said 'older' meaning they wanted to age the character in some unspecified way. There were suggestions to make the character less glamorous, such as being able to wear less makeup, and less 'trendy' clothes. One interesting one is the idea of a longer t-shirt to hide the character's belly. This comes up later when a different participant mentions the same issue in a follow-up interview.

Of course many of the aspects mentioned by participants can be changed. It is just that in the short period of time available these opportunities had not been seen.

2.2 Individual Hands-On Interviews and Additional Data

The two hands-on interview participants expressed marked difference in their objectives. The first was concerned to get to grips with the use of the computer programme. Movement, communication and personalization were initial concerns; but motivating this learning was the wish to find out how it might be used in the real world. Could it for example enable her to interact with her grandchildren in Australia? Could she persuade others to take part with her and use Second Life to communicate? These concerns and motivations were to lead to the necessity to accurately represent her real appearance in the avatar (see user profile two). The second participant had spent considerable time in Second Life between the introductory session and the follow up interview. Her character had gone through many changes in the intervening time due to strategic choices by the participant. The participant had even incorporated a new body shape that included anatomical features not present in the standard avatar. This participant had also created a simple journal-like text that expressed her experiences and feelings during the intervening week between introduction seminar and the individual interview (see user profile one).

A third participant who had been particularly memorable in the introductory sessions had been unable to successfully register during the session. Instead she followed the provided instructions in her own time at home. She sent a snapshot and accompanying message two weeks later (see user profile three).

2.3 User Profiles

To drawn out some of the rich detail of this additional and connect through to the questionnaire responses, we will take a more qualitative approach to the data collected in combination with the observations and experiences of the researcher in undertaking the seminar and research exercises. We will do this by talking to the three individuals in terms of rounded 'user profiles' which are similar to design personas in Human Computer Interaction (HCI (see [5]) but are based on real people and behaviour as opposed to fictional aggregates. While we don't have space to draw out the point, they might be seen as a form of 'verbatim theatre' or 'ethno-drama' [15]. All recognizable details however have been obscured to protect the privacy of the participants.

Profile one: The adventurer
Julie is a university professional. She was the most enthusiastic Second Life newcomer, spending many hours after the introduction session on SL. Her thirteen-year-old son was jealous of her newfound toy, saying that he felt that he should have been first to experience Second Life, rather than his mother. So taken by her initial experiences and the questions and concerns it raised, she wrote a brief description of the first few adventures in Second Life. The account starts,

> Our remit was to create a character that looked as near to ourselves as possible. I'm white, 5'7'', medium-length blonde hair, size 14, and age 50 next year. It quickly became clear that the avatar could be created with features that were much more appealing than those in first life (FL). So my avatar went through a series of quick changes to produce a taller, thinner, much younger, and more glamorous character than myself. One who could then be more provocative both in terms of her character by the way she acts and what she can wear and say. Thus she is now in her late twenties, with long hair that swishes when she walks and she usually wears micro skirts and low tops (sometimes see-through), high-heels, make-up and sparkly earrings – not like me at all.

She goes on to say that her character was 'deliberately more sexualised' and that this was a means to attract attention and interaction with other Second Life characters. Her primary goal being to "learn about SL: how to operate within it, what there is to explore; and what experiences are available.". In the intervening two weeks between introduction seminar and the follow on interview, Julie had spent around twelve hours online. In that time she had learned much about her character's appearance and her own feelings about the attention she was getting. She learned that "the fewer clothes she wears the more it attracts the male gaze". She found herself immediately 'covering up' or even logging out completely. She decided that her character looked too young, and so 'made her older (in her 20s or 30s), still much younger than her actual age.

> With this change, she and I have become bolder and with some coaxing from two male avatars, Flint and Joe, who were prepared to have long conversations with me, they helped me feel more comfortable about Crystal as she is. Now, Crystal is not afraid of approaching others to initiate conversations and with this confidence she has become empowered with the female gaze.

What is most interesting about this quote is the move to identify with the Second Life avatar as a separate character, speaking about the avatar as having emotions and being confident.

Profile two: The curious hairdresser

Sarah is a university administrator and involved in activities in support of older people. Her primary motivation was to use Second Life to communicate with her relatives in Australia, and to find a means to do this that would interest her grandchildren. Also she was keen to persuade her partner to use Second Life for the same purpose, and so wanted a level of understanding that would enable her to explain the benefits and basic features. During the registration and set up process, she found much of the interface confusing. During the initial set up of her avatar and in a follow-up individual session her primary concern was to make an acceptable avatar. An immediate concern was that somehow her avatar was wearing a short t-shirt which revealed its midriff, it was 'showing its belly'. Various parameters were changed to try to cover up the torso - lengthening the t-shirt, adding an additional coat. None seemed to cover her up. Next was a concern that the default character was wearing jeans. These were inappropriate, and attempts were made to change the style of trousers, as well as the texture of the jeans. Finally, there was the hair. Sarah wanted the hair to resemble her own style. Changing the colour to white was easy enough, but it simply wasn't the right shape. Second Life has numerous parameters that can be changed: the length, fullness, texture. Much time was spent trying out these parameters. Sarah found a tool that enabled the user to change the 'camera angle'. This enabled her to look at the hairstyle from multiple angles.

Persona Three: The Playful Grandma

Jane is a mature student studying Women's Studies. As she set up her character she looked for a playful name. Amused by the play on 'zimmer frame', a device to aid infirm older people to walk, she chose the name Zeta Zimmer. Unfortunately a computer fault meant that she had to choose another name, she settled on Baker Boom. She created a character with colourful clothes and spiked hair. She sent a snapshot of herself to the researcher with the following message.

Table 3. Jane's snapshot and message

	hi darren - i knew you'd want a postcard of baker's face, but i didn't know how. thanks for the tip. i may try to find my way around so i can become a goth rather than the girl next door! of course, with a first name like baker, i can change gender too. can't wait to show my grandchildren! regards jane

Jane was keen to work out the possibilities for her avatar. In the questionnaire she listed a number of features that she might want to change: "older faces, spectacles, different body shapes (over and above the changes that can be made to the basic 'young' shape), more hairstyles, accessories (jewellery, bags, scarves)." but after a couple of weeks of using Second Life on her own, she was still trying out more playful characterisations.

3 Discussion

In what was a small-scale initial investigation of older people creating an avatar for Second Life, there was a range of motivations and activities. We have begun to characterise these as user profiles in the previous section. What is clear is that just because a person is older than 50 doesn't mean that they have a common attitude and approach to this activity. Most agreed that their character looked younger than them. This can be explained in terms of the restrictions imposed on them by the computer system, which gave basic body shape choices and allowed for specific changes in various aspects such as face shape, body shape, skin colour and the like. Even though there were multiple parameters, they were still within particular boundaries that restricted the possibilities. In short, the user could not easily create an aged character. There are in fact ways to mimic ageing, by creating a larger belly and a white beard, for example. However in the limited time available, the users did not work this out. It is important to note that this possibility is not specifically geared to ageing and there isn't a parameter that simply ages the character. There is however an "ol-lady" shape, mentioned previously, that can be downloaded and imposed on the avatar. This shape sets height and hip width parameters to create a short 'hour-class' figure. Those that found this shape had no problem in using it, even though it made their character short and dumpy.

The variability of responses to the Second Life character creation facility has broader relevance. As has been shown in discursive gerontology and biographical approaches to ageing, chronology is not a predictor of individual motivation. As Kaufman puts it, "older people do not perceive meaning in ageing itself; rather, they perceive meaning in being themselves in old age" ([12], p. 6). The acceptance that age is merely one aspect of a person's identity is important. A person's identity is far richer than how old they are and draws on their history of experiences, their expectations, their relationships and many other factors. However, importantly, each person recognises a specific range of age-related expectations and characterisations and they are able to voice these expectations in terms of what they should say. Put simply, they know what an aged person should say about age-identity. We see some of these societal expectations expressed in the list of additional characteristics. Wrinkles, and a potbelly fit a generic, common sense estimation of age representation. If a person chose to express old age, they would do it in these ways. Put another way, each person is aware of what characteristics are needed to 'do' older person. This perspective enables them to think about doing or being an alternative age. By objectifying age characteristics, the user is free to choose between them. One way to conceptualise the possibility of this reflexive stance is to talk about the performativity of age, which is closely linked to a biographical understanding of ageing.

3.1 The Performativity of Age

A useful analytic frame is provided by the sociological concept of performativity, which is related to biographically understandings of ageing. Performativity is essentially the idea that a way a person behaves conveys their character and 'self'. Such performances draw on socially understood roles, behaviours and expectations about how these relate to one another. In many ways performativity relates to Goffman's 'dramaturgical' understanding of human psychology [8]. One difference is that performativity allows for 'transgression' and 'translation' of expected behaviours in the realisation of each new performance. Indeed Judith Butler [4] in talking about gender performativity claims that exact behavioural replication is impossible and each new iteration is imperfect. This idea also allows for deliberate 'transgressions' and hence introduces the idea of choice. In short a person may deliberately 'act their age', or not. This choice however, wholeheartedly relies on a system of established and expected behaviours.

Ann Bastings [2] has undertaken a study of age as a matter of performativity through an ethnography of 'senior theatre'. Different theatre groups approach common understandings of age in various ways; some celebrating ageing, while others deliberately upsetting commonly held conceptions. What makes these theatrical activities possible is the socially shared understanding of what age means and how it is recognised. A biographical and performative understanding of appearance similarly takes preconceived notions and makes them into a resource for understanding, expressing, and conveying the personal self and the unique experience of individuals. Reed [19] has recently combined performativity and age-identity in an examination of telephone based services that support isolated older individuals, to draw out some of the aspects in relation to technology use. In earlier work Monk and Reed [16] understood the same telecare service in terms of the flow of interaction in the telephone calls themselves and conceptualised these in terms of 'fun' and 'play'. The current work goes some way towards squaring the circle, bringing play – as performance – to other instances of communicative interaction.

3.2 Performativity and Play

Gregory Bateson [3] conceives of 'meta-communicative' cues that 'frame' behaviour beyond what is actually said or done; an example being the cue 'this is play' seen in the play fighting of animals. Erving Goffman extended this framing idea to include all social meaning. Frames become 'principles of organization which govern events – at least social ones – and our subjective involvement in them' ([7] pp.10-11). Another way to put this is to say that the Second Life character parameters 'afford' certain changes and not others. The term "affordance" is used in Human Computer HCI by Don Norman [17], drawing on J. J. Gibson [6], to describe design features of a device or object that enable particular behaviours through perceptual cues.

The activity of creating a character in second life could be understood in terms of communicative and meta-communicative behaviour. We can also conceptualise the personalisation process as a matter of "machinic framing and affordance". This would help us understand the distinctions between those who were intent on a clear and honest representation of themselves and those who were interested in taking on an alternative, more playful, identity, and their attempts to achieve this within this within the boundaries set by the computer software. Sarah was looking to instrumental objectives in understanding Second Life. Consequently she was keen to represent herself as closely as possible. This was not a playful motivation, and suggests a lack of playful framing through the incorporation of additional (i.e. imagined) physical attributes. Jane and Julie on the other hand were quite clearly looking to invest in the possibilities of Second Life to play with identity and representation, as well as expand what they could do in the virtual world as well as in real life. Jane saw her playfulness as being relevant to her relationship with her grandchildren, but also due to her academic interests was also keen to explore alternative gender and age identities in the virtual world. Julie was the most playful. Again she spoke of real world relationships, but also the possibility of developing new relationships online. She was strategic in her choices about avatar personalisation and framing, attempting to attract attention and hence interaction which might further her wish to explore the possibilities of Second Life. Also with Julie we see most clearly that playful role-playing lifts her from the everyday, perhaps enabling a more fluid social life online than off-line. What we see then are different framing activities based upon the 'real-world' motivations of the participants.

The Second Life interface allows for various parameters to be changed. While this is wide ranging and 'analogue' (in the sense that each parameter is changed by moving a slider), and hence the personalisation may result in a large number of combinations and visual outcomes, the parameters are still bounded in a number of ways. There is a decision about quite what parameters are included. The height of the avatar can be changed, but a stoop or curving spine cannot be added. A person may appear to get shorter as they age because of just such a physical change. As we have seen from the suggestions of participants, wrinkles cannot be added, yet there are numerous changes that can be made to the facial features, from skin tone to head shape.

One important feature of Second Life is the ability to create 'objects' that can adorn the character. It is quite possible for example to model a big white hat, jewellery and scarves. But these would require additional skills. It is also possible to create a new body shape, but only within the parameter confines of the basic character. In terms of framing, these might be seen to limit the range of actions premised upon participant motivation. The 'infinite possibilities' of Second Life quite clearly restrict the playful framing of avatars, and prevent 'age' (especially old age) from being a meta-communicative frame.

We should say that the performativity of age in Second life is a combination of human activity within the frame of possibilities the computer application provides. In Science and Technology studies, Andrew Pickering conceives of performativity in just this way. Asserting that technology use is a mater of human *and* machine agency [18], the eventual integration of technology is a product of a process of 'resistance' and 'accommodation' and the 'control' is variously in the hands of the human and the machine. Second Life participants, especially those new to the environment, must navigate these various forces to reach their desired objectives.

4 Conclusions

What can we take from these initial investigations of age identity in Second Life? We must bear in mind the small-scale character of the research, with a limited number of participants, all of who were recruited through a university message board. The age range of participants was nearer 50 and none were over retirement age. We should then proceed with caution. However what the study reveals is the variability of motivations and behaviours of users. This variability underpinned the attempts to create an appropriate avatar.

Playfulness, in terms of fantastical representation, are closely linked to real-world, and virtual world, concerns. Whether this is in terms of relationships with family members, or prospective contacts in the computer environment. One strong impression is that participants are highly knowledgeable about what constitutes an aged identity. Their chances to embrace or reject associated expectations are hindered only by time and the possibilities afforded by the Second Life software.

Acknowledgement. This work was funded by the EPSRC Human Centered Technology Research Group Platform Grant GR/T10053/01, http://gow.epsrc.ac.uk/ViewGrant.aspx?GrantRef=GR/T10053/01.

References

[1] Antonijevic, S.: From text to gesture online: A microethnographic analysis of nonverbal communication in the Second Life virtual environment. Information, Communication & Society 11(2), 221–238 (2008)

[2] Basting, A.D.: The stages of age: performing age in contemporary American culture. University of Michigan Press, Ann Arbor (1998)

[3] Bateson, G.: A Theory of Play and Fantasy. In: Bateson, G. (ed.) Steps To An Ecology of Mind. Ballantine Books, New York (1972)

[4] Butler, J.P.: Gender Trouble (Thinking Gender). Routledge (1990); Chamberlayne, P., Bornat, J., Wengraf, T.: The Turn to Biographical Methods in Social Science: The Comparative Issues and Examples (Social Research Today). Routledge (2000)

[5] Cooper, A.: The Inmates are Running the Asylum. Why Hi-tech products drive us crazy and how to restore the sanity. SAMS, Indianapolis (2004)

[6] Gibson, J.J.: The Theory of Affordances. In: Shaw, R., Bransford, J. (eds.) Perceiving, Acting and Knowing. Erlbaum, Hillsdale (1977)

[7] Goffman, E.: Frame Analysis. An Essay on the Organization of Experience. Northeastern University Press, Boston (1974)

[8] Goffman, E.: The Presentation of Self in Everyday Life. Penguin Books Ltd (1990)

[9] Griebel, T.: Self-Portrayal in a Simulated Life: Projecting Personality and Values in The Sims 2. Game Studies 6(1) (2006)

[10] Guardian online, Wii Strikes in older people's homes April 30 (2008) (accessed May 8, 2008),
http://www.guardian.co.uk/society/2008/apr/30/health.longter mcare

[11] Mori, I.: Student Expectations Study. Key findings from online research and discussion evenings held in June 2007 for the Joint Infomation Systems Committee (July 2007)

[12] Kaufman, S.R.: The Ageless Self, Sources of Meaning in Late Life. The University of Wisconsin Press, Madison (1986)

[13] Kirriemuir, J.: A July 2007 "snapshot" of UK Higher and Further Education Developments in Second Life. Report commissioned by Eduserv (2007)

[14] Mead, G.H.: Mind, Self and Society. Chicago University Press, Chicago (1934)

[15] Mienczakowski, J.: The Theater of Ethnography: The Reconstruction of Ethnograph Into Theater with Emancipatory Potential. Qualitative Inquiry 1(3), 360–375 (1995)

[16] Monk, A., Reed, D.J.: Telephone conferences for fun: experimentation in people's homes. In: HOIT 2007 (2007)

[17] Norman, D.: The Design of Everyday Things. Doubleday, New York (2002)

[18] Pickering, A.: The Mangle of Practice: Time, Agency and Science. Chicago University Press (1995)

[19] Reed, D.J.: The Performativity of a Volunteer based Telecare Service. In: Loader, B. (ed.) Third Age Welfare, Routledge (forthcoming)

[20] Rheingold, H.: The Virtual Community. Minerva, London (1995)

[21] Turkle, S.: Life on the Screen. Identity in the age of the internet. Weidenfel & Nicolson, London (1997)

[22] www.seriousgamesinstitute.co.uk

Developing an Adaptive Memory Game for Seniors

Elly Zwartkruis-Pelgrim and Boris de Ruyter

Philips Research Europe,
High Tech Campus 34, 5656 AE Eindhoven,
The Netherlands
{Elly.Zwartkruis-Pelgrim,Boris.de.Ruyter}@philips.com

Abstract. This paper describes the development of a game application for seniors to train their memory and learning abilities. From an initial co-discovery evaluation participants were found to prefer more cognitive challenge and expected more synergy between the games. Based on this feedback, a redesign was developed consisting of nine cognitive games, which were integrated in a higher-level maze game. In addition, each game was extended with five difficulty levels. The results of a two week field trial show that training positively affects performance, although this effect is mediated by subjective vitality. In addition, the amount of effort that participants put into playing the games contributed significantly to their experience of engagement, this in turn positively affected performance, which positively affected participants' motivation to play the games. Participants with a high community rank experienced more pressure than participants with a lower acquired rank.

Keywords: seniors, memory, cognitive decline, gaming, community, engagement, motivation.

1 Introduction

After World War II many Western countries saw an increase in their birth rate, a generation now called 'Baby Boomers'. This generation currently represents a significant proportion of the population and will result in a rapid growth of the elderly population in the coming years. These seniors are an interesting target group not only due to its size, but also with regard to their changing needs. For example, many seniors are confronted with transition phases, which often involve adjustments in their way of life, like finding a new way to spend the day, find a new purpose and challenge in life and rearranging ones social network. Common transition phases are retirement, becoming a grandparent and changes in physical and cognitive abilities.

In the course of our lives, our cognitive abilities are said to increase until our late thirties or early forties, then a period of stability until our mid-fifties or early sixties, followed by a gradual decline [1]. The onset and course of this decline is difficult to determine, since it is not directly related to age. In spite of the stage they are in, cognitive decline is often a major concern for seniors. Fortunately, studies have

P. Markopoulos et al. (Eds.): Fun and Games 2008, LNCS 5294, pp. 170–181, 2008.

shown that training can indeed significantly improve cognitive performance ([2] [3] [4] [5] [6] [7]). In fact, this also seems to be common sense knowledge among seniors, since they frequently mention keeping up their cognitive abilities as a motive to play games or puzzles (as was also found during our user tests).

In addition to focusing on supporting healthy aging for this target group for the coming years, it is important to approach them from a more lifestyle-oriented perspective. For that purpose a game application was developed to support seniors with training their cognitive abilities, which is above all fun to play.

1.1 Information-Universal Versus Information-Specific Theories

[6] sort the theories that have been applied to explain age-related declines in cognitive performance into two categories, namely information-universal versus information-specific theories.

The mechanism underlying cognitive aging in information-universal theories is independent of the type or structure of the information that is being processed. For example, the *general slowing theory* (or *global-speed theory*) states that the speed of executive cognitive operations decreases with aging, regardless of the type of task or the mental operations involved in the task ([8] [9]) which causes an increase in time to perform the task and an increase in the error rate. In contrast according to the information-specific theories, the type or structure of the memory units play an important role in the effects of cognitive aging. For example, the *specific gain/loss theory* argues that the pattern of spared and impaired cognitive functions in old age is related to concurrent age-related neurobiological changes in the brain. More specifically, the hippocampus and the frontal lobes and the cognitive functions that rely on these parts of the brain are most susceptible to the effects of aging.

There is growing evidence for process-specific age-related differences on top of a global trend, affecting all processing components ([10]). In their comparison of the predictive power of the global-speed theory and specific gain/loss theory, [10] used two sets of tasks, which propose different demands on cognitive processing. For the executive function tasks higher demands are made on cognitive processing and performing these tasks relies heavily on the frontal brain structures. A typical example of executive function tasks are response selection, in which a right-hand response is required after the appearance of stimuli on the left side of the screen. Non-executive function tasks make fewer demands on cognitive processing and constitute simple-reaction tasks, which requires a speeded response to any stimulus appearing anywhere on the display. Thus according to the global-speed theory, it can be expected that performance on both executive and non-executive tasks will decline in similar proportions as a result of aging, whereas according to the specific gain/loss theory, age-related cognitive decline will be more prominent in the performance for the executive tasks, since these rely more heavily on the brain structures that are most susceptible to aging. However, the analysis of their data suggests that both global processing speed and executive functioning account for the age related decline in the efficiency of cognitive processing. Young adults and seniors differed both on global processing speed as well as on executive functioning. This indicated that the demands on executive functioning affect the speed of responding over and above global-speed effects.

1.2 The Effects of Practice on Cognitive Decline

Cognitive intervention studies suggest that cognitive decline in old age, for many older adults, might be attributed to disuse rather than to the deterioration of the physiological or neural substrates of cognitive behavior [11]. Relatively preserved in old age is memory performance involving highly practiced skills and familiar information, including factual, semantic and autobiographical information. Relatively impaired in old age is memory performance that requires the formation of new connections, such as recall of new facts. For example, studies have shown that elderly typically experience a decline in word retrieval, but not in retrieval of word meaning ([12]).

However, practice might ward off cognitive decline. In their longitudinal study on the effects of cognitive training on cognitive decline, [4] found that of the participants for whom a significant decrement was documented over a 14-year period, roughly 40 percent returned after training to the level at which they had functioned when first studied. Furthermore, 60 percent of the men and 70 percent of the women showed significant training gain (that is, a training improvement of 1 standard error of measurement). A 7-year follow-up study further demonstrated that those subjects who showed significant decline at initial training retained a substantial advantage over untrained comparison groups [4]. [5] also found that cognitive training positively affected performance on memory training, reasoning training and speed-of-processing training, both immediately after the intervention as well as at a 2-year follow up (although the training impact decreased over time, but it remained significant). The largest effects were found for speed-of-processing training. Note that cognitive training will also be effective in enhancing the performance of young adults, so age differences tend to remain robust ([13]).

1.3 Explaining the Effects of Practice

[14] proposed the differential-preservation hypothesis versus the preserved-differentiation hypothesis to account for the effects of practice. According to the *differential-preservation hypothesis* cognitive performance in older age depends on the level of mental activity a person engages in. On the other hand, the *preserved-differentiation hypothesis* argues that cognitive performance in older age depends on the level of mental activity that a person engaged in during his younger years. See figure 1 for a graphical overview of these hypotheses.

[2] illustrates this distinction with the finding that bridge players tend to have higher levels of cognitive functioning than people who do not play bridge. The differential-preservation hypothesis would suggest that playing bridge builds mental muscle that prevents deterioration of mental ability, whereas the preserved-differentiation hypothesis would suggest that a minimum level of mental strength is needed for individuals of any age to be capable of playing bridge.

A cultural advantage might account for the differences in mental activity as depicted by the preserved-differentiation hypothesis. [15] found that the trend for cognitive decline in late adulthood applies equally to individuals with different socio-economic backgrounds, although people from culturally and socially advantaged backgrounds entered old age at a higher average level of functioning and retained this advantage. Similarly, comparisons between people with high and low levels of

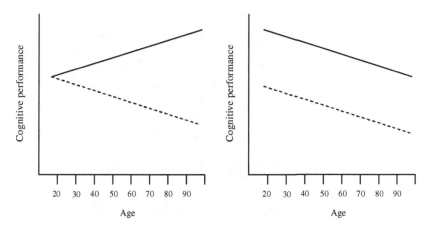

Fig. 1. *Cognitive performance* (accuracy and response time) at a given *age* as a function of *high mental activity* (*black line*) and *low mental activity* (*dotted line*). The left panel illustrates the differential-preservation hypothesis, while the right panel illustrates the preserved-differentiation hypothesis.

general intelligence have indicated that these people decline in similar rates, that is they decline with a similar amount of points. Hence a person with an original test score of 150 will be less affected by general decline, than a person with an initial test score of 70 ([16]).

From the literature reviewed here it can be concluded that although cognitive decline is part of normal aging, two main nuances are important to take into account in this respect, namely that it is not a matter of consistent overall decline and that cognitive training has a positive effect on cognitive functioning.

2 Developing the Prototype

2.1 Co-discovery Evaluation

Based on literature a first version of the game was tested in a lab setting by means of a co-discovery evaluation. At this point the game consisted of a set of six games focusing on memory and learning abilities, which were inspired by traditional laboratory tests to assess cognitive performance. Games included in this version were vigilance, passive working memory, active working memory, selective attention, pattern recognition and stimulus discrimination. In addition, participants were presented with various conceptual designs of score feedback, both for their individual performance history as well as their relative performance compared to peers.

Since the TV is the most accepted and familiar interactive device in the home environment, the prototype was implemented as an interactive application on a TV. Interaction with the prototype was done through a standard remote control with only numerical and arrow keys. No special function keys were used in order to not confuse the target users and to make the interaction as simple as possible.

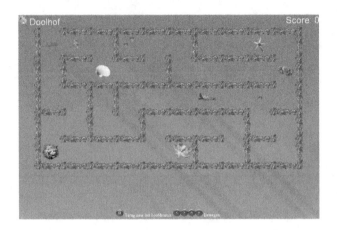

Fig. 2. The maze game consisting of nine sub-games

Fourteen senior participants (6 male and 8 female, all between the ages 56-79 with a mean age of 71) were invited in pairs to a home-like environment at Philips Research for a co-discovery evaluation of the prototype. During the co-discovery evaluation participants were asked to perform a number of tasks together. Using pairs of users enhances the value of their statements compared to single users thinking aloud ([17]). The seniors who were invited to participate in this test were asked to bring someone along he/she knows well to facilitate their willingness to reflect their personal opinion in an open and friendly atmosphere.

For most participants the interface was clear and they either immediately started playing the games by pressing the numbered buttons on the remote control or they pressed 'ok' to read the instructions. Participants liked the feedback on their selections (such as buttons switching to a darker color to represent being pressed), the interaction style with the remote control and the colorfulness of the application. Participants remarked that they thought these types of games would be beneficial for memory, although in their current form they thought they were too easy and short. The games required neither much concentration nor involvement, although this is what people would expect from activities to train memory. Participants noted that they liked to be challenged, whereas these games lacked difficulty levels and therefore were not sufficiently interesting.

2.2 Redesign of the Application

Based on the results of the lab test, a redesign of the games was developed. These modifications are now discussed. First, to make the games more challenging and engaging, they were integrated into one overall maze game (see figure 2). In addition, each individual game consisted of five difficulty levels, which would be adapted according to players' scores. The maze game consisted of nine sub-games, which are presented as icons throughout the maze. In addition to the existing games in the earlier version of the prototype, which were extended to make them more challenging, the games target detection, iconic memory, episodic memory and spatial memory were added as sub-games (vigilance was left out). The theme of the application was a sea setting, since it was evaluated as the most attractive theme during the co-discovery evaluation. A player is represented by a diver that can be operated by manipulating the arrows on the remote control. Each time a player runs into an obstacle or icon, the corresponding sub-game is initiated. The goal of this maze game is to find the exit and collect as many points as possible on the way by playing the sub-games.

In addition to these nine games, players have the option to view their scores, both in relation to their own personal history as well as in relation to their peers' scores.

3   Testing the Application in the Field

Although an evaluation in a controlled environment such as a laboratory provides valuable information, we acknowledge the value of studying the use of our prototype in real life settings. While we cannot control the context and prescribe the actual usage of the prototype in field settings, it will provide complementary insights into the evaluation of the application's usage.

The field trial was carried out to test whether the redesign of the game application suited the needs of the target user. Participants who subscribed to the experiment were asked to invite their peers to play along with them. In total 17 participants signed up for the field test, of which two discontinued their participation before the end of the experiment and for one participant installation was not possible due to technical complications in the Internet subscription. Hence, in total 14 participants completed the study (11 male and 3 female), all between the ages 46-78 with a mean age of 65, all living independently. However, the results of one participant could not be used for further analysis because he did not play all of the games in the maze and also did not fill in the questionnaire or diary.

Participants subscribed with peers, resulting in six communities (three communities with one player, one community with three players and two communities with four players).

Participants were asked to play the games on their own account during a two week period. They could contact the researchers when required, but they were not contacted to avoid additional external stimulation.

Several specific research questions were addressed in this part of the study relating to cognitive performance, interaction design and social stimulation, namely:

1. Does cognitive performance change over time?
2. Does cognitive performance differ for different people?
3. How can engagement be employed in the design to make the games more intrinsically motivating?
4. How does the feedback of scores affect motivation to play?
5. How does adaptivity of gaming level make the games more challenging?
6. Does a community stimulate people to play the games?

These questions were answered by using various methods, namely logging participants' playing behavior (frequency, timing and performance), a diary maintained by the participants, a questionnaire and an interview. The diary included day to day questions on participants' experiences. In addition to the diary, participants were sent a questionnaire towards the end of the field test, which they were asked to complete after the fourteen days of the trial. This questionnaire consisted of the following components:

- Questions relating to the socio-economic status of participants,
- Subjective vitality questionnaire ([18]). This questionnaire measures people's self-assessed feeling of being alert and having energy,
- The intrinsic motivation inventory ([19]). The Intrinsic Motivation Inventory (IMI) assesses participants' interest/enjoyment (which is considered to be the self-report measure of intrinsic motivation), perceived competence, effort, value/usefulness, felt pressure and tension, and perceived choice, thus yielding six subscale scores,
- The presence questionnaire ([20]). Presence is defined as the subjective experience of being in one place or environment, even when one is physically situated in another. In this presence questionnaire the questions are categorized in different factors, namely involvement/control, natural interaction, resolution and interface quality. Questions relating to auditory and haptic information were left out since these do not apply to the game application,
- Engagement questionnaire ([21]). The engagement questionnaire was included to measure game playability and interaction design. Subjects are asked to what extent they experience certain game aspects during the use of the application regarding three themes, namely engagement, control and richness.

Dutch translations of these questionnaires were used, since our participants were all Dutch. The field trial was concluded with an interview to discuss in more detail aspects like interaction, feedback, appearance, adaptivity, score representation, community overview and future use. The goal of the interview was to uncover motives and reasons behind people's opinions and to inquire suggestions for improvement.

3.1 Results of the Field Trial

The results in relation to the change in cognitive performance over time are limited due to the relatively short field trial. However, some inferences can be made when looking at the data from the frequent players in the sample. Statistical analysis showed a significant effect of playing frequency on the reaction time for stimulus discrimination ($F=4.59$; $p=0.032$) and a close to significant effect on percentage correct scoring on episodic memory ($F=3.56$; $p=0.060$) (playing frequency, percentage correct scores and reaction times were divided into five equally sized categories). Furthermore, some games seem to show an improvement in performance patterns for frequent players. More specifically, the games attention, pattern recognition, spatial memory, target detection and iconic memory consistently show an increase in the amount of correct responses, a decrease in the response time or both (for example see figure 3). However, it should be taken into account that the games might be more appealing to the frequent players and that this positively affects their performance.

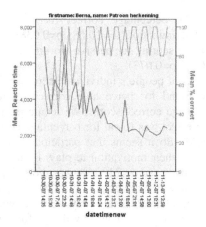

Fig. 3. Cognitive performance (*mean reaction time indicated by the blue line and mean percentage correct response indicated by the green line*) per trial (*date and time*) on the game pattern recognition for player 'Berna'

To test the effect of vitality on performance a one-way ANOVA was used. The analysis generated one significant effect, for percentage correct on passive working memory (F=9.72; p= 0.044), and two nearly significant effects, percentage correct for pattern recognition (F=6.64; p=0.073) and reaction time for spatial memory (F=5.54; p=0.093). Hence, vitality positively affects performance for the passive working memory game and seems to affect performance on the games pattern recognition and spatial memory. Vitality also affected participant's intrinsic motivation to play the games (F=10.78; p=0.038). That is, participants who felt healthier were also more motivated to play the games. No other effects of vitality were found on the intrinsic motivation variables.

In addition, a one-way ANOVA showed an almost significant effect of vitality on playing frequency (F=7.26, p=0.065) (playing frequency was divided into five equally sized categories), indicating that subjects who felt healthier might have been more frequent players.

Several aspects were implemented in the application to enhance engagement, namely natural interaction, involvement/control, richness, interest/enjoyment, perceived competence, effort/importance and perceived choice. The effects of these variables on engagement were tested by means of a one-way ANOVA. Only a significant effect was found for effort/importance (F=9.46; p=0.045). That is, putting effort into and trying hard on the activity enhances people's feeling of engagement. In addition, the effect of engagement on intrinsic motivation was tested, also by means of an ANOVA, but this did not generate a significant effect. The effect of effort/importance on intrinsic motivation was also not significant.

Another approach is to see whether engagement affects people's playing behavior. That is, does engagement stimulate people to play the games and does it stimulate people's performance. The answer to the first part of the question was no, since the effect of engagement on playing frequency did not yield a significant result. Regarding the second part of the question the answer might be yes. That is, engagement positively affected the reaction time for passive working memory

(F=9.03; p=0.048) and the percentage correct for pattern recognition (F=8.97; p=0.049) and stimulus discrimination (F=10.68; p=0.038), while it also seemed to affect the percentage correct scoring for passive working memory (F=6.37; p=0.078) and iconic memory (F=6.69; p=0.073).

With regard to the effect of people's individual scores on their motivation to play, significant effects were found for percentage correct scoring on spatial memory (F=5.28; p=0.022), percentage correct scoring on iconic memory (F=5.58; p=0.019) and a close to significant effect was found for percentage correct scoring on episodic memory (F=3.13; p=0.080). So it seems that participant's achievements on at least some of the games enhance their motivation to play. From the interviews it became clear that for some people their personal history was more important, while for others the community comparison was more important. Participants who found their own personal history more important stated that they were not competitive and that they did not really care about or were stimulated by the performance of others. Also the community overview would not reflect their development over time and hence for them it would not give a reliable result. Participants, who found the community overview more important than their personal history, stated that they were very motivated by the performance of others and thought the competitive aspect of the application was fun. These participants also mentioned that they played extra when they noticed that others were getting better. However, some people mentioned that they were also demotivated by the community view when they had already acquired a top score, since playing would put them at risk of losing their top position.

One-way ANOVA revealed that neither the rank that was achieved in the community nor the size of the community affected the playing frequency. A close to significant effect was found for the size of the community on engagement (F=3.21; p=0.084). Hence, it seems that people who were part of a bigger community also experienced more engagement when they were playing the games. An effect was also found for community rank on perceived pressure/tension (F=6.26; p=0.014). Hence, the higher the rank that people achieved in the community the more pressure/tension they felt when they were playing the games. In addition, pressure/tension affected participants' scores regarding the reaction time on stimulus discrimination (F=6.85; p=0.017).

No significant effects were found for the levels that were acquired in the individual games on challenge. Also no significant effects were found for the levels that were acquired in the individual games on intrinsic motivation and engagement. Hence, it seems that gaming level does not affect the challenge that participants experience, nor the intrinsic motivation to play the games and the feeling of engagement. During the interviews participants mentioned that they noticed the adaptivity in the games and most of them appreciated this because it made the games more fun and challenging and it showed progress. They also noted that is was rather unclear how their scores affected the increase in levels. The participants who did not like the adaptivity thought it made the games more difficult, which did not add to their enjoyment.

4   Conclusions and Discussion

From the literature study and the lab evaluation it became clear that elderly have an apparent need to keep their cognitive abilities fit and that they are actively looking for ways to do this. This study also confirmed that cognitive training by means of our game application seems to enhance cognitive performance. Since no differences were found between the active components in memory and the passive components, it is difficult to relate these findings to either the information-universal or information-specific theories of cognitive decline.

The question remains on how this improvement in cognitive performance translates to daily activities. In their study on the effects of cognitive training on cognitive abilities and performance on Activities of Daily Life (ADL) and Instrumental Activities of Daily Life (I-ADL), [5] found no significant effects of such training on everyday functioning. However, they concluded that this was due to the lack of functional impairment at baseline. Since the everyday abilities remained intact over a 2-year period, improved cognitive function could not improve these abilities. Also during our interviews participants noted that their game performance this did not translate to their daily activities.

Regarding the differences in performance between participants it was found that for some games there seemed to be a difference in performance patterns for people who perceived themselves as very vital and people who perceived themselves as less vital. Vitality also appeared to affect participant's intrinsic motivation to play the games. People who felt less vital were less motivated to play the games than people who felt very vital. This is reasonable and some participants mentioned that they skipped playing for several days because they were not feeling well.

Another aspect that affected people's performance was the feeling of engagement. The more engagement participants experienced, the better their performance on some of the games. Engagement in turn was influenced by the amount of effort people had put into the activity of playing the games.

For some games it was found that people's achievements, as reflected by their personal scores, affected their motivation to play the games. This is in line with Cognitive Evaluation Theory (CET), which states that social-contextual events (such as feedback and rewards) that conduce toward feelings of competence during action can enhance intrinsic motivation for that action ([22]). However, these feelings of competence will not enhance intrinsic motivation unless accompanied by a sense of autonomy, which is an internal perceived locus of causality. Since people had been playing the games individually this is indeed the case.

Statistically, the community overview did not appear to affect people's playing behavior, although it was mentioned during the interviews that when participants noticed they were lagging behind in the community view that this triggered them to play the games. From the analysis it was further found that the community rank that was achieved indeed affected the experienced pressure/tension when people were playing the games. Hence, although a direct effect between community rank or size and playing frequency could not be demonstrated, people do feel a certain pressure when they have achieved a high rank within their community to maintain this position.

Another aspect that is important for intrinsic motivation is challenge. It could not be statistically demonstrated that the level structure as implemented in the application indeed enhanced the challenge experienced by the games, but participants explicitly mentioned during the interviews that this adaptivity made the games more fun and challenging. Perhaps with a larger sample this finding could have been statistically supported as well.

With regard to the methods that were used to evaluate the prototypes it can be concluded that during the interviews in the lab test the seniors were very open in describing their personal situations and opinions. Little additional encouragement from the interviewer was required, since participants often encouraged each other to elaborate on their own experiences. The diary that the participants were asked to complete during the field trial appeared to work well since all participants noted down their experiences in the diaries, some of whom extended this with printed records of their scores, and additional notes. People also wrote down the reasons if they had not been playing on a particular day. All in all, participants were very committed to adhere to the researchers' requests, regarding the use of the application, filling in the diary and questionnaire and during the reflection of their experiences during the interviews.

Acknowledgments. The authors would like to thank Merlijn Sevenster, Harm Buisman, Alexander Sinitsyn and Johan Janssen for their contribution to this study and the development of the prototype, and all participants who participated in our studies.

References

1. Schaie, K.W.: Intellectual development in adulthood. In: Birren, J.E., Schaie, K.W. (eds.) Handbook of the Psychology of Aging, 3rd edn., pp. 291–309. Academic Press, San Diego (1990)
2. Salthouse, T.A.: Mental exercise and mental aging: evaluating the validity of the "use it or lose it" hypothesis. Perspectives on Psychological Science 1, 68–87 (2006)
3. Salthouse, T.A., Somberg, B.L.: Skilled performance: effects of adult age and experience on elementary processes. Journal of Experimental Psychology: General 111, 176–207 (1982)
4. Willis, S.L., Schaie, K.W.: Cognitive training in the normal elderly. In: Forette, F., Chisten, Y., Boller, F. (eds.) Plasticite cerebrale et stimulation cognitive, pp. 91–113. Foundation Nationale de Gerontologie, Paris (1994)
5. Ball, K., Berch, D.B., Helmers, K.F., Jobe, J.B., Leveck, M.D., Marsiske, M., Morris, J.N., Rebok, G.W., Smith, D.M., Tennstedt, S.L., Unverzagt, F.W., Willis, S.L.: Effects of cognitive training interventions with older adults: a randomized controlled trial. JAMA, The Journal of the American Medical Association 288, 2271–2281 (2002)
6. Burke, D.M., MacKay, D.G.: Memory, language and aging. Philosophical Transactions of the Royal Society: Biological Sciences 352, 1845–1856 (1997)
7. Kausler, D.H.: Learning and memory in normal aging. Academic Press, San Diego (1994)
8. Birren, J.E.: Age changes in speed of behavior: its central nature and physiological correlates. In: Welford, A.T., Birren, J.E. (eds.) Behaviour, aging and the nervous system, pp. 191–216. Charles C. Thomas, Springfield (1965)
9. Salthouse, T.A.: The processing-speed theory of adult age differences in cognition. Psychological Review 103, 403–428 (1996)
10. Span, M.M., Ridderinkhof, K.R., van der Molen, M.W.: Age-related changes in the efficiency of cognitive processing across the life span. Acta Psychologica. 117, 155–183 (2004)

11. Schaie, K.W.: Cognitive aging. In: Pew, R.W., van Hemel, S.B. (eds.) Technology for adaptive aging, pp. 43–63. The National Academies Press, Washington D.C (2004)
12. Burke, D.M., Shafto, M.A.: Aging and language production. Current Directions in Psychological Science 13, 21–24 (2004)
13. Baltes, P.B., Kliegl, R.: Further testing of limits of cognitive plasticity: Negative age differences in a mnemonic skill are robust. Developmental Psychology 28, 121–125 (1992)
14. Salthouse, T.A., Babcock, R.L., Skovronek, E., Mitchell, D.R.R., Palmon, R.: Age and experience effects in spatial visualization. Developmental Psychology 26, 128–136 (1990)
15. Mayer, K.U., Baltes, P.B.: Die Berliner Altersstudie. Akademie Verlag, Berlin (1996)
16. Rabbitt, P.: Cognitive changes across the lifespan. In: Johnson, M.L. (ed.) Age and aging, pp. 190–199. Cambridge University Press, Cambridge (2005)
17. Hackman, G.S., Biers, D.W.: Team usability testing: Are two heads better than one? In: Proceedings of the 36th Annual Meeting of the Human Factors Society, pp. 1205–1209. Human Factors Society, Santa Monica (1992)
18. Ryan, R.M., Frederick, C.M.: On energy, personality and health: Subjective vitality as a dynamic reflection of well-being. Journal of Personality 65, 529–565 (1997)
19. Ryan, R.M.: Control and information in the intrapersonal sphere: An extension of cognitive evaluation theory. Journal of Personality and Social Psychology 43, 450–461 (1982)
20. Witmer, B.G., Singer, M.J.: Measuring presence in virtual environments: A presence questionnaire. Presence 7, 225–240 (1998)
21. Rozendaal, M.C., Keyson, D.V., de Ridder, H.: Product behavior and appearance effects on experienced engagement during experiential and goal-directed tasks. In: Conference Proceedings of Designing Pleasurable Products and Interfaces, pp. 181–193. ACM, New York (2007)
22. Ryan, R.M., Deci, E.L.: Self-determination theory and the facilitation of intrinsic motivation, social development, and well-being. American Psychologist 55, 68–78 (2000)

A Tangible Tabletop Game Supporting Therapy of Children with Cerebral Palsy

Ying Li[1], Willem Fontijn[2], and Panos Markopoulos[1]

[1] USI Program, Eindhoven University of Technology,
Den Dolech 2, 5612 AZ Eindhoven
yingli5566@gmail.com, P.Markopoulos@tue.nl
[2] Philips Research Laboratories,
Prof. Holstlaan 4, High Tech Campus, 5656 AA Eindhoven
willem.fontijn@philips.com

Abstract. This paper presents the design of a table-top game supporting the treatment of children with Cerebral Palsy. The game was developed through a participatory design process involving therapists and children from the target user group. The game is implemented on top of a platform that supports the implementation of tangible user interfaces using sensing technology. We argue that physical interaction, motivated and constrained by the design of tangible interfaces, offers enormous potential for occupational and physical therapy where patients need to practice specific and repetitive movements.

Keywords: Tangible interfaces, table-top, children, cerebral palsy, therapy, serious games.

1 Introduction

In recent years, research in interactive table-top surfaces has shifted beyond its original scope of office applications explored in the early days of this field (see for example [6]), to explore the potential of supporting leisure and gaming activities (see for example, [2]). The potential of table-top interactive surfaces for supporting entertainment is enormous; they combine the advantages and flexibility of traditional screen displays with the physical and social implications of allowing people around the surface to have shared access and to interact through interactive artefacts presented as virtual or physical entities on the tabletop. This paper discusses an exploration into how table-top interactive surfaces can support therapy of children with Cerebral Palsy. This investigation is part of a broad assessment of the scope of potential applications of these technologies and specifically the opportunities they offer to support therapeutic applications.

The research reported builds on top of the technology platform ESP, a hardware and software system designed to facilitate the creation of applications that are based on tangible interaction. This platform provides a high level programming interface allowing designers, without programming skills, to specify the interaction with the

P. Markopoulos et al. (Eds.): Fun and Games 2008, LNCS 5294, pp. 182–193, 2008.

tangible artefacts, while making transparent to them the operation of hardware sensors used for input (wireless sensors and tabletop positioning technology), and output device drivers e.g., e.g., for audio output, LED lights, etc.

The ESP technology has been used before to implement games for children, e.g., [4] and [7]. The emphasis of this paper is on interaction design aiming to assess its suitability for the domain of therapy and to explore related opportunities for the development and deployment of tangible interfaces combined with interactive table-top surfaces.

The remainder of this paper describes first the target user group and more specifically how Cerebral Palsy is currently treated. Then the participatory design process through which the therapeutic game was developed is described, concluding with the evaluation of the game with children. Finally, reflections on the lessons learnt from this study are discussed and links are drawn to related research.

2 Children and Cerebral Palsy

The term Cerebral Palsy refers to any one of a number of neurological disorders that appear in infancy or early childhood and affect body movements and coordination permanently, though they do not worsen over time [3]. These disorders are caused by abnormalities in parts of the brain that control muscle movements.

Besides surgery and medication, physical therapy and occupational therapy are the main forms of treatment for children with Cerebral Palsy. Cerebral Palsy can not be cured, but such therapy can improve a child's abilities and self-confidence.

The problems that affected children have can be summarized as follows [5]:

- Muscle tightness or spasms because of which patients take abnormal postures.
- Poorly coordinated movements.
- Involuntary movement which is not under control of the brain.
- Difficulty with gross motor skills such as walking, running and stabilizing.
- Difficulty with fine motor skills such as writing, grasping/releasing objects and two hands coordination for task like cutting a paper.
- Difficulty in perception, especially in depth.

3 Current Therapy Practice for Children

The design effort focused on assisting fine motor skill training for children with Cerebral Palsy. Fine motor skills are instrumental for daily living activities such as dressing and eating. The design process started with an analysis of current therapy approaches for children with Cerebral Palsy. Figure 1 illustrates some movements that affected children typically need to train.

Contextual interviews and observations of therapy sessions were carried out in two therapy centers in our region to find out how therapists go about training children currently, how children experience these sessions and which problems they encounter that interactive technology could help tackle.

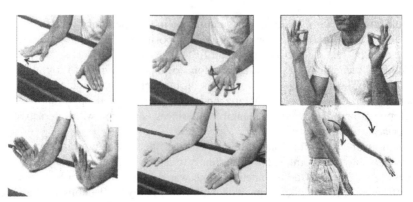

Fig. 1. Functions that children with Cerebral Palsy need to train; Source: [1]. Top Row from left to right: Finger abduction (curling and straightening), Finger Extension, Pincer Grasp. Bottom row from left to right: Extension of wrist, Supination, Extension of Elbow.

Therapists use various toys in playful training sessions that they carry out one-on-one, often in a small room. Training is very personalized. Examples of exercises are:

- For finger extension training, the children are asked to "wear" finger-puppets on their fingers (children have to extend and move their fingers to play) or they are asked to make stamp-prints of their hands on a paper. During the observation, "wearing" toys did not appear very appealing to the children however they seemed to enjoy thoroughly the stamping exercise.
- For pincer grasp training, therapists ask children to do some beading tasks, to slide coins into a box, or to move paper-clips from one side of a card to the other.
- To practice elbow extension children are asked to crouch on a small pulley and crawl around pushing their hands and arms against the ground. Other exercises include drawing on a blackboard, a fishing game and a puzzle game.
- For wrist extension a special rubber object was used that the therapist presses against the table surface to make it stick by suction. The children are asked to pull it off.
- To practice supination. card playing exercises are used, or opening water bottles, screwing/unscrewing screws, etc.

Some example of exercises with the occupational therapists are shown in figure 2.

Problems were noted during the contextual interviews regarding current training methods, focusing on the effectiveness of the method and how children experience it.

- Compensation: Children seem to always find a way to compensate for the movement they have problems with and need to practice e.g. by using their 'good' hands or arms. The therapist often needs to intervene to prevent them from doing so. Children resist this; this resistance often slows down therapy, reduces its effectiveness and is detrimental to the motivation.
- Lack of cognitive challenge: Many training tasks are repetitive and do not help children to appreciate the reason for carrying them out. Especially when they can do the tasks in an easier way than the therapist requests they resist redoing them,

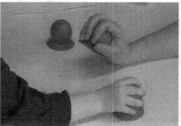

Fig. 2. Images from the video record of a therapy session featuring exercises currently given by occupational therapists to exercise elbow extension (left), wrist extension (middle) and supination (right)

losing interest and concentration. However, when these physical training tasks were embedded in puzzles or block building activities children showed more interest.

- Motivation and potential regression. After years of training many children, e.g., above 8 years old, lose motivation, and regard the sessions as work, not play. Children at that age often leave therapy centers to join mainstream education thus running the risk of regression. Therapists estimate that 20% of these children return to the therapy center for training after one or two years; this time round they are motivated again because they wish to be as independent as other children.
- Lack of reinforcement away from the therapy center. Therapists cannot force and have little means to stimulate children to use the affected hands and arms at home, so the total time spent exercising is very limited.
- As training is very personalized, children do not train in groups, so they miss chances for social interaction and the motivation and reinforcement associated with social interaction can not be utilized. A nice example of a therapy centre trying to tackle this is the Pirate Group at the St. Maartens clinic in Nijmegen, where a pirate theme structures role play and motivates the use of physical props, for which children have to reach, grasp, release, etc.

4 Design of a Tangible Training Game

The game design proceeded in an iterative fashion. The main aim of the design was to create a fun game for children that would motivate them to practice specific skills. First three different game concepts were designed, to support practicing supination, wrist extension and elbow extension in various combinations.

Given the focus on table-top interactive applications and the use of ESP described earlier, all design concepts involved, in some way or other, manipulating tangible interactive objects, while getting audio feedback and observing feedback from the computer on an horizontal array of led lights, (see figure 3).

The design concepts were visualized using video prototypes to show the physical interaction involved and the movements children were expected to carry out. These prototypes were reviewed by therapists; their feedback was generally positive regarding the playful activities anticipated for the children. They thought that audio and visual feedback would be enjoyed by children, thus motivating them for training, and that the system could, in principle, offer feedback as to the correct execution of

Fig. 3. Shots from the initial design concepts presented to therapists as video prototypes

the exercises. Furthermore, they appreciated the possibility of modifying exercises throughout the game. Therapists offered several corrections regarding the movements designed for the children. It is clear that it is almost impossible for interaction designers to plan the right movements without specialized knowledge: motions foreseen by the design were too difficult. If children could carry out the exercises they would not need training any more; also the designer could not foresee the ways in which children would compensate for the skills they were supposed to train.

A brainstorm session was held in which a therapist took part. The original game concepts were changed or refined correcting the flaws found. Therapists thought that the games as they evolved were likely to improve training for the children, but the most pressing question at that point was whether children would enjoy playing the games and whether they would be motivated to exercise with them as intended. At this stage, most of the game was visualized in the form of video prototypes.

An evaluation session was held. Four children of different ages with Cerebral Palsy took part along with five non affected children. It was anticipated that the comparison would expose how affected children compensate for their problem and to compare their performance on the game. Five test tasks were given. None of them involved the ESP technology as the final game would, but each task involved some of the arm-hand functions that needed to be trained.

Example test tasks were as follows:

- Catching a moving ball. The facilitator uses a stick to roll a steel ball around on a table. Catching the moving ball is very challenging, involving wrist and elbow extension as well as supination (figure 4.a.)
- Hitting the ball back with a block. The child holds a wooden block with two hands and has to hit back an approaching rolling ball (a tangible version of the famous pong game, see figure 4.b).
- Children have to solve a color puzzle that requires them to roll a wooden block over a table surface in various directions. The correct sequence of moves is determined by the pattern of colours presented on the table surface (figure 4.c).
- Children manipulate a wooden block to roll over matching colours on a paper with coloured squares, along a trajectory specified by the therapist (such that wrist extension would be practiced) This test was done with a small sized cube but also with a larger one weighing 1kg, with an edge of 7cm (Figure 4.d).
- Children manipulate a colour hammer to match the colour of objects spread around the table by the therapist (Figures 4.e and 4.f).

(a) Catching the Ball

(b) Batting the Ball

(c) Trajectory Game with Small Cube

(d) Large Cube Manipulation

(e) Colour Hammer Game

(e) Colour Hammer Game

Fig. 4. Images from sesions with children and therapists for the appraisal of the low tech game

Children understood and enjoyed the games. Observation of children taking part in these play sessions with the designer showed that the ball picking and catching tasks were too difficult for affected children. The puzzles involving colors were hard for both groups to understand; the therapists commented that this difficulty was caused by the lack of feedback in this non-technological simulation of the game. Affected children were indeed seen practicing the required movements but they also compensated very often; this was a serious concern for the therapists who indicated the need to further refine the physical interaction. Note that the concern regarding compensation is only partly warranted. If during the game the desired movement is made often enough, it matters less that compensation also takes place often.

Final game concept and prototype
The final game was implemented using the ESP platform. The playing surface that resembles an electronic chess board was chosen to implement the games. The squares on the board can be lit in different colors using LED lights. The final prototype combines aspects of the game concepts discussed into three sub-games: the colored hammer, the colored block and the rotating colored block. These are described briefly below.

Colored hammer game
As shown in Figure 5(a), the hammer has an octagon-shaped head; the square faces of the hammer head are colored. Tiles on the checkerboard light up during the game in different colors. The player has to hit the colored squares with the face of the hammer with the matching color before it extinguishes. This requires players to perform supination, and elbow extension.

Fig. 5. (a) The colored hammer game. (b) Solid colored block game.

Colored Block Game
Children manipulate a colored cube with a side of 10 cm, which is twice as much as the side of the squares on the checkerboard; see figure 5(b). The squares on the

Fig. 6. Rotating colored block game

checkerboard light up in different colors (groups of 4 adjacent squares have matching colors). Children must place the cube on the face with the color matching the color of the tiles on the board to extinguish or 'delete' the group of squares. The games ends when all groups are deleted.

Rotating Colored Block
This game is an extension of the solid colored block game. In this case the color pattern shown on the board is more complicated (only pairs of adjacent tiles have the same color) and children have to rotate the parts of the block to match colors on the face of the cube to a 2 by 2 group of adjacent tiles on the checkerboard (see figure 6).

5   Evaluation of the Game

On site testing and observation was adopted as the main method to evaluate the game. After each test, interviews were conducted with the therapists with questions focusing on the training qualities of the game and the motivation and fun of children compared to current training methods.

Participants

Child	Gender & age	Type of CP	Severity	Affected part of body
1	M, 6 years old	Quadriplegia	very severe	4 limbs
2	M, 4 years old	Quadriplegia	relatively severe	4 limbs
3	M, 7 years old	Hemiplegia	mild to light	Left hand
4	M, 11 years old	Hemiplegia	mild to severe	Right hand
5	M, 11 years old	Quadriplegia	relatively severe	4 limbs
6	F, 6 years old	Hemiplegia	very light	Right hand
7	M, 9 years old	Hemiplegia	Mild	Left hand

5.1   Experimental Setting and Procedure

Play testing was carried out at the same two therapy centers, where also the observations had taken place at an earlier stage in the project. The evaluation was set up as part of individual therapy session. Participants took part individually under the supervision of a therapist.

A height-adjustable table was used for supporting the gameboard. This was useful not only because of the different sizes of the children but also to allow wheelchairs to fit under the table surface. This enabled the children's arms to be in full contact with the board.

Each test session lasted about 20 minutes. The three sub-games were tested in the sequence: color hammer, color solid block and color rotating block (from lower to higher complexity).

Fig. 7. Spontaneous extensions of the elbow of the affected arm motivated by the game

Therapists explained and demonstrated how to play the game. Then children played independently without instruction or help during the game. The observation of the children's performance, focused on accuracy, errors, desired movements and compensation. The therapy session was recorded on video for later analysis.

5.2   Results

All participants said they enjoyed playing the game, though their preferences regarding the three sub-games varied with age. The youngest children (4 to 6) enjoyed the hammer game most. Older children found it too easy and in general preferred the rotating block game most because of the cognitive challenge it provides.

Therapists were happy to observe children engage in the desired movements spontaneously, something that they said was not common in their standard therapy sessions. For example, one child performed a spontaneously extreme extension of the elbow, something this child does only when requested by the therapist (Figure 7). Other desired movements like extension of fingers, finger abduction were also seen quite often when playing the games (Figure 8).

There is also room for improvement. Other important movements, like extension of wrist and supination were observed only rarely during the evaluation. Also, several desirable movements were often observed in tandem with unwanted movements, e.g., a combination of supination (wanted) and wrist flexion (unwanted movement) was seen quite a lot (see figure 9).

Fig. 8. Finger extension and thumb abduction seen during testing

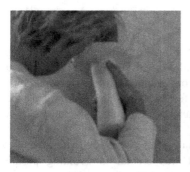 

Fig. 9. The combination of supination ans wrist flexion

The therapists found the games promising as a therapy aid since children did perform desired movements and they enjoyed it. However, to reach a conclusion with confidence regarding the effectiveness of the designed games and whether they are still fun for children after a few therapy sessions, a long term evaluation is needed involving a larger population.

All children extended their fingers in an extreme way to manipulate the block since it is relatively big compared to their hand sizes. Especially when playing the rotating block, the finger extension was better supported since they needed to rotate one part while holding it.

In general the evaluation showed that:

− *The game play is very energy consuming for the children with Cerebral Palsy. The* physical signs collected from observation, such as heavy breathing, taking clothes off, showed that children put a lot of physical effort into playing the game. The therapists also noticed this and remarked that this shows that the game is fulfilling its training purpose.

− *The game does encourage the children with Cerebral Palsy to make desired movements.* This was encountered in various forms, e.g., one child who has strong resistance in using the affected hand, started to use it spontaneously while rotating the block after sever failures in doing that by compensation.

− *Depth perception could influence the way children play the game.* During the test, we found that during the block game, most children first try to delete one color in different locations and then manipulate the block to see which side they will use for the next step. However, one child who has problems with depth perception played differently. He manipulated the block more and deleted the colors in no particular order. Therapists attributed this to him having difficulty to obtain an overview of the color pattern shown on the board.

− *All children used their affected hands to play the games.* The therapists did not specify that the children had to use their affected hand, but they have all been receiving therapy for a long time and they know they have to use the affected hand to play in the therapy room. Especially children with Hemiplegia, who have good hands as well, started to play the game with affected hand quite spontaneously.

Smaller interface usability issues were identified as well, e.g., ensuring that the colors on the board and the hammer match better.

6 Conclusion

This paper describes a design study that explored how tabletop games using tangible interaction can support therapy of children with Cerebral Palsy. Starting from contextual interviews and observations, opportunities for design intervention were identified, namely to provide motivating feedback to children following therapy and for designing the required physical interaction so that movements specified by therapists are practiced as part of a game.

A tangible interactive table-top game was developed iteratively with the participation of therapists, whose input was crucial in avoiding pitfalls and in designing the appropriate physical interaction. Indeed one of the requirements they expressed during the participatory design sessions was the ability to specify or adapt movements that would be used as elements of the game.

The game was evaluated, as a part of their therapy, with children suffering from Cerebral Palsy. All in all, the evaluation revealed both positive and negative aspects of the designed game; the game was experienced as fun and motivating which resulted in an increased duration and stimulation of hands and arms training. The game supports exercise for children with Cerebral Palsy, and was successful in evoking and training some of the most important movements that children with Cerebral Palsy need to train, e.g., elbow and finger extension, and thumb abduction were quite well supported. The extension of wrist and supination, were stimulated as well but less frequently.

The current designs do not completely address the problem of compensation movements, with children avoiding the movements trained by using other hands or skills that are not or are less impaired.

The generally positive evaluation of this game demonstrates the potential of tangible interactive technology for supporting therapy. The experience of designing this game is an example of how participatory design including children and therapists can help design the physical aspects of interaction in areas extending beyond the traditional domain of interaction design. Supporting therapists to specify the movements needed to play the game should be an interesting way to capitalize on the possibilities offered by tangible interactive technology.

Given the highly individual nature of the limitations of the children the treatment is inevitably highly personalized. It is therefore seen as very valuable by the therapists that can define individual exercises on the platform themselves using the high level programming interface of ESP.

Acknowledgements

The authors would like to thank Janneke Verhaegh, Sebastian van der Horst, Tom Koene and Robert van Herk for their collaboration. We are also very grateful to the therapists of Sint Maartenskliniek hospital, Anke Verhaegh and Pauline Aarts, Helga van der Linden and Phiep Nieuwenhuis from Blixembosch Revalidatie Centrum, Henk Seelen and Annick Timmermans from Stichting Revalidatie Limburg (SRL).

Special thanks also to the children pf the Sint Maartenskliniek hospital Nijmehen, Blixembosch Revalidatie Centrum Eindhoven, and the Chinese bridge language school Eindhoven, for their participation in the studies described.

References

[1] Boumans, M.T.A., van Ooy, A.: Elsevier/ De Tijdstroom, Maarssen (1999)
[2] Brederode, B., Markopoulos, P., Gielen, M., Vermeeren, A., de Ridder, H.: Powerball: the design of a novel mixed-reality game for children with mixed abilities. In: Proceedings IDC 2005, pp. 32–39. ACM, New York (2005)
[3] Ekstorm, A.L., Johansson, E., Granat, T., Brogren Carlberg, E.: Functional therapy for children with Cerebral Palsy: an ecological approach. Developmental Medicine & Child Neurology 47, 613–619 (2005)
[4] Fontijn., W.F.J., Mendel, P.: StoryToy the Interactive Storytelling Toy. In: Proceeding PerGames 2005, pp. 37–42 (2005)
[5] Ontario Federation of Cerebral Palsy. Downloaded on (9 May, 2008),
    http://www.ofcp.on.ca/aboutcp.html
[6] Ullmer, B., Ishii, H.: The metaDESK: Models and Prototypes for Tangible User Interfaces. In: Proceedings UIST 1997, pp. 223–232. ACM Press, New York (1997)
[7] Verhaegh, J., Fontijn, W., Hoonhout, J.: Tagtiles: optimal challenge in educational electronics. In: Proceedings TEI 2007, pp. 187–190 (2007)

A Music Educational Entertainment Environment for Preschoolers

Lisette Jansen[1], Betsy van Dijk[1], and José Retra[2]

[1] Human Media Interaction, University of Twente, P.O. Box 217, 7500 AE Enschede,
The Netherlands
a.e.jansen@alumnus.utwente.nl, e.m.a.g.vandijk@ewi.utwente.nl
[2] School of Education & Lifelong Learning University of Exeter, Heavitree Road,
Exeter, EX1 2LU, UK
j.retra@exeter.ac.uk

Abstract. This paper describes the design and evaluation of an interactive computer environment that envisions to contribute to young children's musical learning. The intent is to stimulate the child's inherent musical abilities by engaging the child in active musical interaction with the environment. The design of the environment is inspired by an existing preschool music education method and uses knowledge from several research areas. In this paper the design choices are motivated. The paper also describes the prototype that has been developed of the interactive environment and the results of a Wizard of Oz experiment.

Keywords: interaction design, multimodal interaction, tangible interaction, children, music education.

1 Introduction

All children are born with musical abilities [1], [7], [12]. These inborn musical abilities need to be preserved and developed in the early years [1], [7], [12]. To achieve this, it is important that the children are active participants in their musical interactions [7]. Considering that musical skills can give children a lot of joy during their lives and at the same time appear to support the general development [16], stimulating children's inherent musical abilities is an important underpinning of this research project.

In this project, an interactive music environment for two and three-year-old children was designed, with the intent to stimulate the children's inherent musical abilities through interaction with the environment. The aim is to make the child an active participant in musical interactions between the child and the environment. The environment presents its musical output in a way that aims to evoke movements and sounds from the child. Examples of musical responses are: moving to the music and singing or making body sounds like clapping the hands or clapping on the body. In turn, the environment adapts its output to the child's responses.

The requirements for the environment are derived from literature in the areas of early childhood learning, child-computer interaction, and early childhood music

P. Markopoulos et al. (Eds.): Fun and Games 2008, LNCS 5294, pp. 194–202, 2008.

education. The activities offered by the environment are derived from an acknowledged Dutch preschool music education method and interaction styles have been chosen that are eligible for a natural musical interaction between the child and the environment. The next section describes the requirements and design choices.

2 Background

The musical activities and form of interaction offered by the environment have to be tailored to the abilities and learning needs of the target age group. As the motor and vocal abilities of the children in this target group vary, the interactive environment will have to suit the minimal abilities of the youngest children but it will have to be challenging enough for older children as well.

2.1 Five Main Requirements

In the literature about children's needs in educational interactive technology and early childhood music education, five important requirements were found: play and exploration, fun and enjoyment, control, multiple forms of interaction, and interaction with adults. These were the main requirements of the environment.

1. **Play and Exploration.** Children's play is fundamental for their learning, for by playing they have the chance to experiment and explore the world [4], [15].
2. **Fun and Enjoyment.** Fun and enjoyment appear to be children's most important motivations for whether or not they want to interact with an interactive product [9], [12]. Furthermore, it enhances learning [11].
3. **Control.** Children want to feel in control of the technology they use [2]. Furthermore, being in control of their own learning is crucial for children to learn effectively [15].
4. **Multiple Forms of Interaction.** Children like technologies that offer different forms of interaction, and in which they have a choice in the way they interact with it [2]. Furthermore, for young children, music is a multimodal experience [16].
5. **Interaction with Adults.** Adults play an important role in the development of children's musical abilities, by taking children's music making seriously and setting the examples [16].

2.2 Interaction Stimulating Musical Abilities

Practical experience from the officially acknowledged Dutch Preschool Music Education method, also known as "Music on the lap" (MoL), has been used to choose the activities offered by the environment. The activities in the MoL lessons consist of a song accompanied by movements, frequently supported by a musical instrument or a toy, and they are tailored to the abilities of the children [13], [14].

While MoL covers the age group of four months to four years, for the study the age group of two and three-year-olds was chosen to be the target user group for the environment. Before children begin attending primary school (at the age of four in the Netherlands) they may spend more time playing at home, which gives them more opportunities to benefit from a music educational computer environment at home. The minimum age of two years was chosen because most two-year-olds are able to understand that their own behavior influences the reactions of the environment, which is crucial for effective interaction. Furthermore, compared to younger children, two-year-olds have an increased ability to sing parts of familiar songs and to make large movements (as they can generally walk), both of which makes computer detection easier.

The five above-mentioned requirements find their equivalent in MoL, and are incorporated in the method in different ways. Play and exploration is found in activities that incorporate guided experimentation time. MoL is process driven, and fun and enjoyment in the offered activities is important to motivate the children to join in [13]. In all activities the children have the choice to participate or not [14], which gives them control over the situation and their own learning. Movement is the most used form of interaction in the lessons. Other forms are singing, observing and playing with tangibles. The forms of interaction that the children use also depend on the phase of joining in the activity. Langelaar [10] distinguishes three subsequent phases in which young children join musical activities led by others. These are: first observing, then imitating the movements, and finally singing along.

The participating adults in MoL, teacher and parents, serve as role models. They set the example for the children by singing and moving in the offered activities. The aim is for the children to imitate the musical behavior of the adults and eventually internalize this behavior. The interaction between child and adult in MoL has been chosen to be the example for the interaction between the child and the environment.

Three musical learning aims from the MoL method were chosen for the interactive music environment, in agreement with their usage in the lessons:

1. Sense of beat and timing. The environment values direct (on the beat) as well as delayed (after the beat) musical movement responses [14].
2. Sense of dynamics. The environment offers songs that have different variations on a normal, low and high volume, with lyrics and movements that properly support the volume of the song.
3. Learning to associate timbre with the corresponding musical instrument. The environment gives the children the opportunity to listen to the instruments that are being played.

Because the activities are repeated many times and because appropriate short songs are used, children can step into the offered activities when they want to and they have ample opportunities to understand the activities.

2.3 Interaction Styles

Considering that the target age group cannot read yet, textual in- and output were not appropriate. Therefore the interaction between the child and the computer was chosen to take place without the traditional mouse and keyboard input and textual output, but with forms of interaction that are natural for children. The use of natural forms of interaction enables the children to quickly learn the basics of the interaction and to feel in control of the environment. This supports the children's enjoyment of the environment and hence promotes effective learning. As multiple forms of interaction are motivating for children, three ways of interaction were chosen for the environment: responding to the music by movement and singing, and playing with tangible objects. As has been treated in sections 2.1 and 2.2 these interaction styles are appropriate for natural musical interaction between the child and the environment.

These interaction styles need appropriate technology: motion tracking is necessary to follow the child's movements and to see whether the child moves in time to the music; sound detection should detect the child's singing; and tough sensors and RIFD technology enables the child to control the environment by playing with tangible objects. In this paper the choice of the proper detection methods will not be discussed. The different input modalities will be integrated in the input device that will be described in next section.

A virtual cartoon-like kangaroo called Panze was designed to resemble the role models that the adults provide in the MoL lessons. Panze is an embodied pedagogical agent. Embodied agents are virtual characters, which are often used to make human-computer interaction more natural. Pedagogical agents are getting more attention, as was illustrated by the special issue about pedagogical agents from the Educational Technology magazine [3]. For the target group this was also considered to be appropriate. The appearance and the name of Panze have been chosen by children in the target age group.

3 The Environment

To accomplish motivation to interact with the environment and enhanced learning, the environment was designed to be fun and enjoyable. It is discovery-oriented, which means that by playing with the environment, the users can discover its functionality. The system thus provides the user with an enjoyable interactive environment in which the user will learn about music by exploring and playing. The intention is that the system is used in a home environment by one child at a time, without any help from adults or peers.

The key-character of the environment is the pedagogical agent Panze. She offers the children activities that resemble the activities in the MoL lessons. The aim is that the child will imitate the musical behavior of the role model and will eventually internalize this behavior.

The environment consists of an input device connected to a television set. The television set shows Panze. The input device with motion tracking, sound detection, touch sensors and RFID technology tracks the child's actions. The input device

Fig. 1. Tangible CDs and instruments visible on the screen

also has the form of a kangaroo (the input kangaroo) with a large pouch in which tangible CDs and instruments can be inserted. With these tangibles, the child can control the environment: it can choose an activity and musical instruments as accompaniment. The chosen CDs and instruments are visible in the background image on the screen (see Figure 1). Touching the input kangaroo turns on the system. The system turns off automatically when it detects no reactions from the child for a few minutes.

When a tangible CD is inserted, Panze sings a song and makes movements to the music. The first time the chosen song is played, Panze makes simple movements, like clapping or stamping in time to the music. Until the child reacts or ejects the tangible CD, the activity is repeated. Like in the MoL lessons, the Panze environment provides for all three phases of joining in musical interaction: the child can choose to observe, move or sing during any activity. When the child joins in the singing or the movements, it will be rewarded by visual and sound effects. Panze will then start to make variations in the dynamics, lyrics and movements of the song to give the child new challenges. These activities are meant to develop the children's sense of beat and timing, and sense of dynamics, the first two music developmental aims. For the third aim, learning to associate timbre with the corresponding musical instrument, the children are given the opportunity to choose and listen to different musical instruments. These are played by virtual characters that accompany Panze when she sings.

4 Method

The concept of the Panze environment was tested to see whether the concept worked for children in the target age group. The children were observed to see how they reacted to Panze and how they handled the different forms of interaction and to check whether they indeed enjoyed the environment. The utility and learnability of the environment were tested as well. An improvement in the children's musical abilities was not expected in this short test. Before the larger scale WOz test, a small pilot test was conducted with two children in their home situation to test the setup.

A simple prototype of the Panze environment was used in a Wizard of Oz (WoZ) experiment. From [8] it appeared that the WoZ method is suitable to evaluate systems that use motion tracking as an input modality and that it can reveal valuable information about how children interact with a system. The main experiment was conducted in a preschool setting with 11 children (7 boys, 4 girls) all in the target age group. The parents of the children had previously given their written consent for the children's participation. Two preschools in the same building were involved. The environment was set up in a shared playing room between the two preschools. The application ran on a laptop with an extra wireless keyboard, extra loudspeakers and an extra screen attached to show Panze. The input kangaroo, the extra screen and the tangibles were placed on a low table, so the children could see and reach them well. In front of the table there was enough space for the children to move freely. The input kangaroo stood left to the screen, the tangibles were laid in front of the screen. Two video cameras were used to record the children's responses. The limited prototype application contained three activities and three instruments. The tangibles were made of foam and the input kangaroo was covered with fabric and paper. The prototype application used no real detection by the system. Instead, the experimenter acted as the 'wizard', who watched the children's actions and operated the prototype accordingly, using the wireless keyboard. The actions that evoked a reaction of the system were imitating Panze's movements (one type of movement per verse), singing along parts of the lyrics and inserting or ejecting tangibles. Moving along with Panze in time to the music evoked different reactions than moving not in time to the music. At all tests the experimenter was positioned at an appropriate distance from the children to observe them well. During the tests two observers looked at the responses of the children regarding the input kangaroo, the tangibles, the visual and audio rewards and the movements.

To find out how the children experience the technology, they should be observed closely while using the product [5]. According to Hanna et al. [6] it is difficult for children younger than six years to express in words what they do or don't like and also the often-used survey methods have inherent problems that make them not the best methods to use with children [12]. Therefore for testing with children aged two and three years, it was conceived that only observation of the children while using the system would be appropriate.

Each test took a maximum of ten minutes from the moment the program was started. With most of the tests, the main teacher of the children was present. Initially the tests were conducted with one child at a time and little explanation was given, for it was hoped that the child would experiment and discover how the application worked itself. This setting was changed later on as will be described in next section.

5 Results

In the pilot test, both children discovered the functionality of the tangibles by themselves. Both children moved to the music as was intended and were having fun (see Figure 2).

In the experiment in the preschool setting, all children but one directly stroked Panze when the experimenter told them to do so. The stroking varied between the children from just touching, stroking, kissing or pushing on the feet. Initially the only explanation that was given was: "This is Panze. Do you want to play with Panze? Go stroke Panze, and see what happens..." After three tests the amount of explanation that was given was increased because the children

Fig. 2. Participant of the pilot test

experimented very little and hardly reacted to what Panze told them. They seemed not to understand it. Extra explanation that was given was that Panze is a kangaroo and that she has a pouch. The CDs and instruments were shown and named and the children were asked to put the instruments and CDs in the pouch. If they understood this, they were asked to stroke Panze, and the program was started.

Many children appeared to be nervous during the test. For this reason, from the sixth test on, the tests were conducted with two children collaborating. This helped the children to feel more at ease and made them more focused on the environment and less on the experimenter and observers.

When Panze appeared on the screen and sang the welcome song, most children looked at Panze or at Panze and the input kangaroo and a few of them laughed. Two children were busy with the input kangaroo. None of the children grabbed the tangibles at the moment Panze first indicated this. Only one child started to experiment before Panze said so. All other children needed extra encouragement or instruction from one of the present adults to get started. The different amount of explanations the children got before the test made no difference. Most children seemed not to understand immediately what to do but eventually, with or without help, all children started to experiment with inserting CDs and instruments in the pouch of the input kangaroo. Many children had a high tempo of putting the tangibles in and out of the pouch and some children played with the tangibles themselves. The children were experimenting very fast and did not wait long to see or hear the effects of their actions. Some children laughed when the first activity started.

During the different activities, half of the children showed musical responses, be it shy and sometimes hardly visible. Only a few of them occasionally imitated Panze's movements. Also unpredicted musical reactions were seen. Many responding children made their own movements like swaying their bodies, moving with the hips and the knees, ticking with the tangibles and moving or stamping a foot. One child did not move to the music, but only held her hands together in a clapping position without really clapping. Another child made silent mouth movements, partly matching the lyrics. As these non-anticipated responses evoked no rewards from the application, the children did not discover the possibilities for interaction by movement and singing. None of the children reached a next variation of the activities.

As not many children imitated Panze, only few rewards appeared during the tests. The visual awards evoked no reactions from the children. Only one child managed to get sound effects and she clearly reacted by looking at the screen and to the teacher and sometimes she stopped moving.

6 Discussion

Fun and enjoyment indeed appeared to be related to motivation to interact with the Panze environment. Children who enjoyed themselves experimented a lot with the tangibles, while children who did not seem to enjoy themselves did only little experimenting.

The children's need to feel in control of the environment became apparent when they became more uncomfortable when they did not know what to do. This also revealed that the learnability of the environment needs improvement. They enjoyed experimenting once they understood that they could influence the environment. The children's pace of playing with the tangibles implicated that they enjoyed the play and exploration and that the tangibles are an appropriate form of interaction for the target age group. It also appeared that quick feedback on the user's actions is very important.

Furthermore, as the children did not react to visual-only effects and did not play with the tangibles and watch the screen at the same time, all feedback needs to be audible.

The children were willing to stroke the input kangaroo, which suggests that the touch sensor is also appropriate. As the children did not discover the possibility of interaction by movement and singing, these forms of interaction could not be evaluated. However, as many of the children visibly moved to the music, movement seems indeed a natural response to music, suitable to be used for interaction. Regarding the unpredicted spontaneous responses that the children gave to the music, the environment should provide detection and rewards or encouragements for a broader range of responses than was the case in this first concept.

The children's reactions to the agent Panze were positive. This is important, because a positive attitude towards Panze enhances motivation and engagement of the users. However, the children did not imitate Panze, or act according to her spoken encouragements. Reason might be that the children did not feel at ease because the experimental setting was far from ideal: preschool environment instead of home environment; many unknown adults observing the child, which was visible for the child. Both the character and the nature of the encouragements of Panze need to be improved.

7 Further Research

For further development of the Panze environment, the chosen input modalities have to be worked out and a functional prototype should be made and evaluated. The tangibles need to be embedded with RFID and appropriate software for sound and singing detection needs to be found or developed. Further research needs to be done to find an attractive and appropriate way to detect two and three-year-old's movements to music. Probably several options need to be combined for a sufficient detection of children's movements to the music.

In future research attention needs to be given to the style and frequency of Panze's instructions and encouragements. When the desired interaction between the child and the Panze environment has been reached, longitudinal tests will be needed to asses how the interaction between the child and the environment changes over multiple opportunities to play with the environment. Longitudinal tests are also needed to assess the learning effects of the environment and to test whether the Panze environment meets it's aim of supporting children to develop their musical abilities. Future testing should be done in home environments and with only one child at a time, for this is where and how the system is intended to be used.

References

1. Chen-Hafteck, L.: Music and movement from zero to three: A window to children's musicality. In: ECME conference The Musical Worlds of Children, Barcelona, Spain, pp. 1–13 (2004)
2. Druin, A., Bederson, B., Boltman, A., Miura, A., Knotts-Callahan, D., Platt, M.: Children as Our Technology Design Partners. In: Druin, A. (ed.) The design of children's technology, pp. 51–72. Morgan Kaufmann Publishers, San Francisco (1999)

3. Baylor, A.L.: Introduction to Special Issue on Pedagogical Agents. Educational Technology 47(1) (2007)
4. Gopnik, A., Meltzoff, A., Kuhl, P.: How babies think. Phoenix, London (2001)
5. Hanna, L., Risden, K., Alexander, K.J.: Guidelines for Usability Testing with Children. Interactions 4(5), 9–14 (1997)
6. Hanna, L., Risden, K., Czerwinski, M., Alexander, K.J.: The Role of Usability Research in Designing Children's Computer Products. In: Druin, A. (ed.) The design of children's technology, pp. 3–26. Morgan Kaufmann Publishers, San Francisco (1999)
7. Hodges, D.A.: Musicality from Birth to Five, http://www.music-research.org/ Publications/V01N1_musicality.html
8. Höysniemi, J., Hämäläinen, P., Turkki, L.: Wizard of Oz Prototyping of Computer Vision Based Action Games for Children. In: Proceedings of Interaction Design and Children 2004 (IDC 2004), pp. 27–34. College Park, Maryland (2004)
9. Inkpen, K.: Three Important Research Agendas for Educational Multimedia: Learning, Children and Gender. In: Proceedings of Educational MultiMedia, pp. 521–526. AB, Calgary (1997)
10. Langelaar, A.: Peuter en muziek. Muziek in de peuterspeelzaal. [Preschooler and music. Music in preschool]. Bosch & Keuning nv, Baarn (1980)
11. Pound, L., Harrison, C.: Supporting musical development in the early years. Open University Press, Buckingham (2003)
12. Read, J.C., MacFarlane, S.: Using the Fun Toolkit and Other Survey Methods to Gather Opinions in Child Computer Interaction. In: Proceedings of the 5th conference of Interaction Design and Children, pp. 81–88. Tampere, Finland (2006)
13. Retra, J.M.: Musical Movement Responses in Early Childhood Music Education Practice in The Netherlands. In: 2nd Conference European Network for Music Educators and Researchers of Young Children (MERYC), pp. 45–50. University of Exeter, UK (2005)
14. Retra, J.M.: Aspects of Musical Movement Representation in Dutch Early Childhood Music Education. In: Proceedings of the 9th International Conference on Music Perception and Cognition (ICMPC 9), pp. 1251–1256. Bologna (2006)
15. Siraj-Blatchford, J., Whitebread, D.: Supporting ICT in the early years. Open University Press, Berkshire (2003)
16. Young, S.: Music with the under-fours. RoutledgeFalmer, London (2003)

Author Index

Lecture Notes in Computer Science

Sublibrary 2: Programming and Software Engineering

For information about Vols. 1– 4640
please contact your bookseller or Springer

Vol. 5016: M. Bernardo, P. Degano, G. Zavattaro (Eds.), Formal Methods for Computational Systems Biology. X, 538 pages. 2008.

Vol. 5014: J. Cuellar, T. Maibaum, K. Sere (Eds.), FM 2008: Formal Methods. XIII, 436 pages. 2008.

Vol. 5007: Q. Wang, D. Pfahl, D.M. Raffo (Eds.), Making Globally Distributed Software Development a Success Story. XIV, 422 pages. 2008.

Vol. 5002: H. Giese (Ed.), Models in Software Engineering. X, 322 pages. 2008.

Vol. 4989: J. Garrigue, M.V. Hermenegildo (Eds.), Functional and Logic Programming. XI, 337 pages. 2008.

Vol. 4970: M. Nagl, W. Marquardt (Eds.), Collaborative and Distributed Chemical Engineering. XII, 851 pages. 2008.

Vol. 4966: B. Beckert, R. Hähnle (Eds.), Tests and Proofs. X, 193 pages. 2008.

Vol. 4954: C. Pautasso, É. Tanter (Eds.), Software Composition. X, 263 pages. 2008.

Vol. 4951: M. Luck, L. Padgham (Eds.), Agent-Oriented Software Engineering VIII. XIV, 225 pages. 2008.

Vol. 4949: R.M. Hierons, J.P. Bowen, M. Harman (Eds.), Formal Methods and Testing. XIII, 367 pages. 2008.

Vol. 4937: M. Dumas, R. Heckel (Eds.), Web Services and Formal Methods. IX, 169 pages. 2008.

Vol. 4922: M. Broy, I.H. Krüger, M. Meisinger (Eds.), Model-Driven Development of Reliable Automotive Services. XVIII, 183 pages. 2008.

Vol. 4916: S. Leue, P. Merino (Eds.), Formal Methods for Industrial Critical Systems. X, 251 pages. 2008.

Vol. 4909: I. Eusgeld, F.C. Freiling, R. Reussner (Eds.), Dependability Metrics. XI, 305 pages. 2008.

Vol. 4906: M. Cebulla (Ed.), Object-Oriented Technology. VIII, 204 pages. 2008.

Vol. 4902: P. Hudak, D.S. Warren (Eds.), Practical Aspects of Declarative Languages. X, 333 pages. 2007.

Vol. 4899: K. Yorav (Ed.), Hardware and Software: Verification and Testing. XII, 267 pages. 2008.

Vol. 4895: J.J. Cuadrado-Gallego, R. Braungarten, R.R. Dumke, A. Abran (Eds.), Software Process and Product Measurement. X, 203 pages. 2008.

Vol. 4888: F. Kordon, O. Sokolsky (Eds.), Composition of Embedded Systems. XII, 221 pages. 2007.

Vol. 4880: S. Overhage, C. Szyperski, R. Reussner, J.A. Stafford (Eds.), Software Architectures, Components, and Applications. X, 249 pages. 2008.

Vol. 4849: M. Winckler, H. Johnson, P. Palanque (Eds.), Task Models and Diagrams for User Interface Design. XIII, 299 pages. 2007.

Vol. 4839: O. Sokolsky, S. Taşıran (Eds.), Runtime Verification. VI, 215 pages. 2007.

Vol. 4834: R. Cerqueira, R.H. Campbell (Eds.), Middleware 2007. XIII, 451 pages. 2007.

Vol. 4829: M. Lumpe, W. Vanderperren (Eds.), Software Composition. VIII, 281 pages. 2007.

Vol. 4824: A. Paschke, Y. Biletskiy (Eds.), Advances in Rule Interchange and Applications. XIII, 243 pages. 2007.

Vol. 4821: J. Bennedsen, M.E. Caspersen, M. Kölling (Eds.), Reflections on the Teaching of Programming. X, 261 pages. 2008.

Vol. 4807: Z. Shao (Ed.), Programming Languages and Systems. XI, 431 pages. 2007.

Vol. 4799: A. Holzinger (Ed.), HCI and Usability for Medicine and Health Care. XVI, 458 pages. 2007.

Vol. 4789: M. Butler, M.G. Hinchey, M.M. Larrondo-Petrie (Eds.), Formal Methods and Software Engineering. VIII, 387 pages. 2007.

Vol. 4767: F. Arbab, M. Sirjani (Eds.), International Symposium on Fundamentals of Software Engineering. XIII, 450 pages. 2007.

Vol. 4765: A. Moreira, J. Grundy (Eds.), Early Aspects: Current Challenges and Future Directions. X, 199 pages. 2007.

Vol. 4764: P. Abrahamsson, N. Baddoo, T. Margaria, R. Messnarz (Eds.), Software Process Improvement. XI, 225 pages. 2007.

Vol. 4762: K.S. Namjoshi, T. Yoneda, T. Higashino, Y. Okamura (Eds.), Automated Technology for Verification and Analysis. XIV, 566 pages. 2007.

Vol. 4758: F. Oquendo (Ed.), Software Architecture. XVI, 340 pages. 2007.

Vol. 4757: F. Cappello, T. Herault, J. Dongarra (Eds.), Recent Advances in Parallel Virtual Machine and Message Passing Interface. XVI, 396 pages. 2007.

Vol. 4753: E. Duval, R. Klamma, M. Wolpers (Eds.), Creating New Learning Experiences on a Global Scale. XII, 518 pages. 2007.

Vol. 4749: B.J. Krämer, K.-J. Lin, P. Narasimhan (Eds.), Service-Oriented Computing – ICSOC 2007. XIX, 629 pages. 2007.

Vol. 4748: K. Wolter (Ed.), Formal Methods and Stochastic Models for Performance Evaluation. X, 301 pages. 2007.

Vol. 4741: C. Bessière (Ed.), Principles and Practice of Constraint Programming – CP 2007. XV, 890 pages. 2007.

Vol. 4735: G. Engels, B. Opdyke, D.C. Schmidt, F. Weil (Eds.), Model Driven Engineering Languages and Systems. XV, 698 pages. 2007.

Vol. 4716: B. Meyer, M. Joseph (Eds.), Software Engineering Approaches for Offshore and Outsourced Development. X, 201 pages. 2007.

Vol. 4709: F.S. de Boer, M.M. Bonsangue, S. Graf, W.-P. de Roever (Eds.), Formal Methods for Components and Objects. VIII, 297 pages. 2007.

Vol. 4680: F. Saglietti, N. Oster (Eds.), Computer Safety, Reliability, and Security. XV, 548 pages. 2007.

Vol. 4670: V. Dahl, I. Niemelä (Eds.), Logic Programming. XII, 470 pages. 2007.

Vol. 4652: D. Georgakopoulos, N. Ritter, B. Benatallah, C. Zirpins, G. Feuerlicht, M. Schoenherr, H.R. Motahari-Nezhad (Eds.), Service-Oriented Computing ICSOC 2006. XVI, 201 pages. 2007.